Internet QoS

Architectures and Mechanisms for Quality of Service

The Morgan Kaufmann Series in Networking

Series Editor, David Clark, M.I.T.

Internet QoS

Architectures and Mechanisms for Quality of Service

Zheng Wang

Bell Labs, Lucent Technology

MORGAN KAUFMANN PUBLISHERS

AN IMPRINT OF ACADEMIC PRESS

A Harcourt Science and Technology Company

SAN FRANCISCO   SAN DIEGO   NEW YORK   BOSTON
LONDON   SYDNEY   TOKYO

Senior Editor	Jennifer Mann
Publishing Services Manager	Scott Norton
Assistant Publishing Services Manager	Edward Wade
Associate Production Editor	Marnie Boyd
Assistant Acquisitions Editor	Karyn Johnson
Cover Design	Ross Carron Design
Text Design	Side By Side Studios, Mark Ong
Composition	Nancy Logan
Technical Illustration	Dartmouth Publishing, Inc.
Copyeditor	Karen Taschek
Proofreader	Ken DellaPenta
Indexer	Ty Koontz
Printer	Courier Corporation

Designations used by companies to distinguish their products are often claimed as trademarks or registered trademarks. In all instances where Morgan Kaufmann Publishers is aware of a claim, the product names appear in initial capital or all capital letters. Readers, however, should contact the appropriate companies for more complete information regarding trademarks and registration.

ACADEMIC PRESS
A Harcourt Science and Technology Company
525 B Street, Suite 1900, San Diego, CA 92101-4495, USA
http://www.academicpress.com

Academic Press
Harcourt Place, 32 Jamestown Road, London, NW1 7BY, United Kingdom
http://www.academicpress.com

Morgan Kaufmann Publishers
340 Pine Street, Sixth Floor, San Francisco, CA 94104-3205, USA
http://www.mkp.com

Library of Congress Cataloging-in-Publication Data

Wang, Zheng.
   Internet QoS : architectures and mechanisms for Quality of Service /
   Zheng Wang.
     p. cm.
   ISBN 1-55860-608-4
   1. Internet--Evaluation. 2. Telecommunication--Traffic--Management.
I. Title.
TK5105.875.I57 W373 2001
004.67--dc21   00-067265

This book is printed on acid-free paper.

Contents

Preface

The Internet has become an indispensable part of our life and work. Although most people probably only became acquainted with the Internet over the last few years, some have already started to wonder what life would be like without it! The Internet has made possible new applications and ways of communications we never thought possible. Email, e-commerce, digital video streaming, and Internet telephony are only the beginning of a profound revolution.

Although the Internet now runs faster and is increasing in size, its basic architecture remains unchanged from its early days. The Internet still operates as a datagram network, where each packet is delivered individually through the network. Delivery time of packets is not guaranteed, and packets may even be dropped because of congestion inside the network. This unpredictability does not mesh well with new applications such as Internet telephony or digital video conferencing, which cannot tolerate delay jitter or loss of data in transmission.

To overcome these problems, the Internet Engineering Task Force (IETF) has developed new technologies and standards to provide resource assurance and service differentiation in the Internet, under the umbrella term quality of service (QoS). This book presents four technologies that have emerged as core building blocks for supporting QoS on the Internet. Integrated Services and Differentiated Services are two technologies that address the issue of reserving and allocating resources to various types of flows in a network. Multiprotocol Label Switching (MPLS) and traffic engineering help to improve network performance; specifically, the way traffic flows are routed inside backbone networks.

This book goes beyond the basic concepts and protocol details that we can find in the protocol specifications. It explains how these new technologies came about and what problems they address. Throughout the book, practical examples are used to illustrate how QoS mechanisms and algorithms can be applied in real networks. The strengths and weaknesses of the technologies and the rationales behind the various approaches are also examined. In the discussions, I have tried to be objective and unbiased. Readers may, however, draw their own conclusions based on the different views and arguments presented.

Each chapter is self-contained so that readers may start with any of the chapters, but Chapter 1 should be read first since it provides a summary of the four technologies and discuss the logical connections between them. In the closing section of the book, I offer my personal perspective on how QoS may play out in the future.

This book is primarily aimed at technical professionals in the networking field: software and hardware engineers, system architects, and network designers. Each chapter has an extensive discussion of the concepts and overall architectures of the technologies. Some of the sections on QoS mechanisms and algorithms include highly technical details intended for more advanced readers involved in QoS implementation.

Organization of the Book

This book is organized into the following chapters:

1. A high-level look at QoS issues
2. Integrated Services
3. Differentiated Services
4. Multiprotocol Label Switching
5. Internet traffic engineering

The first chapter looks at the big picture of Internet QoS. In this chapter I provide a historical perspective on the evolution of Internet service models and describe the overall thread between the four new technologies covered in this book. For each technology I summarize the main issues and the proposed solutions and explain the rationales behind them.

Chapter 2 describes Integrated Services, the first QoS architecture proposed by the Internet community to provide resource guarantees to applications. I first examine the requirements of real-time applications that have been the driver for the development of Integrated Services and then present the overall architecture and new service models for Integrated Services. Chapter 2 also covers RSVP, the resource reservation protocol for supporting Integrated Services. To implement Integrated Services, routers must perform flow identification and advanced packet scheduling. Two sections of this chapter are devoted to the mechanisms and algorithms for identifying reserved flows and for scheduling packets to support delay and bandwidth guarantees.

Chapter 3 presents Differentiated Services, a QoS architecture for providing service differentiation through a small number of forwarding classes. In this chapter I first discuss the concepts and overall architecture of Differentiated Services and explain the key differences between Differentiated Services and Integrated Services. I then move on to the standard for encoding forwarding classes in the packet header and how traffic flows are classified and conditioned at the edge of a Differentiated Services network. The Differentiated Services architecture requires mechanisms for packet classification and token bucket traffic policing at the edge of the networks. These mechanisms are discussed and illustrated with practical examples.

Chapter 4 covers Multiprotocol Label Switching (MPLS), an Internet standard based on label switching. This chapter begins with a discussion of the factors behind the rise of label switching and the key benefits that MPLS brings to IP networks. I then describe the evolution of label switching and present an overview of four label-switching proposals that led to the current MPLS architecture. The concepts and architecture of MPLS are discussed in detail, and three label distribution protocols for MPLS, LDP, CR-LDP, and RSVP-TE are compared.

Chapter 5 deals with the issue of Internet traffic engineering. Traffic engineering provides a set of indispensable tools for service providers to manage resource utilization in backbone networks. In this chapter I first illustrate why current IP routing is not adequate for performance management and present an overview of traffic-engineering objectives and solutions. I then provide a detailed description of the building blocks in a traffic-engineering system, including topology, state discovery, and constraint-based routing. Approaches for traffic engineering based on full-mesh overlaying and shortest-path optimization are discussed in depth. Finally I present several hashing-based schemes for multipath load sharing to support efficient traffic engineering.

The further reading sections at the end of several chapters list what are called RFCs (Request for Comments). These RFCs are standard documents maintained by the IETF. Some RFCs, called Standards Tracks, are official Internet standards, whereas others are merely informational, or experimental.

RFCs are online at *www.ietf.org/rfc.html*.

Internet Drafts are work-in-progress documents by the working groups of the IETF. They are subject to changes and readers should check the Web site for the latest version and status.

Internet Drafts are on-line at *www.ietf.org/ID.html*.

Acknowledgments

I would like to express my gratitude to the people who have reviewed all or parts of the book. Steven Donegan, Shivkumar Kalyanaraman, Qingming Ma, Mike Minnich, and Scott Poretski reviewed all the chapters, and Fred Baker and Monique Morrow reviewed some. Dave Clark, the Morgan Kaufmann networking series editor, and Bruce Davie read the final manuscript. Al Aho (Bell Labs) made numerous suggestions on my initial book proposal, which led to the current form. He also enthusiastically provided me with many of his tips on book writing. The following people also reviewed my book proposal: John Brassil, Ross Callon, Andrew Campbell, Jon Crowcroft, Bob Natale, Lisa Phifer, and Luis Zapata. I would like to thank them all for their useful comments and suggestions, which have greatly enhanced the quality of the book.

Much of the input to this book came from my work at Bell Labs and my collaboration with colleagues. I would like to express appreciation to my management at Bell Labs, Lucent Technologies for their support and encouragement. My thanks to Vijay Kumar (Bell Labs) for giving me the opportunity to work on PacketStar and other IP router projects and to many of my colleagues (too many to list here) on the project, from whom I have learned a great deal. Some materials in this book come from my joint work with Joe Cao and Yufei Wang—I thank them for their contributions and collaboration.

The staff at Morgan Kaufmann Publishers have been wonderful. My thanks to Jennifer Mann and Karyn Johnson for their encouragement, patience, and excellent support during this long process. They also made numerous useful comments and suggestions on the manuscript.

Finally, I would never have been able to finish writing this book without the support and understanding of my family. Many thanks to my wife, Wei, for her support and patience and to my children, Dylan and Netta, for giving Daddy time to work on the book.

1

The Big Picture

The current Internet has its roots in the ARPANET, an experimental data network funded by the U.S. Defense Advanced Research Projects Agency (DARPA) in the early 1960s. An important goal was to build a robust network that could survive active military attacks such as bombing. To achieve this, the ARPANET was built on the *datagram model*, where each individual packet is forwarded independently to its destination. The datagram network has the strength of simplicity and the ability to adapt automatically to changes in network topology.

For many years the Internet was primarily used by scientists for networking research and for exchanging information among themselves. Remote access, file transfer, and email were among the most popular applications, and for these applications the datagram model works well. The World Wide Web, however, has fundamentally changed the Internet. It is now the world's largest public network. New applications, such as video conferencing, Web searching, electronic media, discussion boards, and Internet telephony, are coming out at an unprecedented speed. E-commerce is revolutionizing the way we do business. As we enter the twenty-first century, the Internet is destined to become the ubiquitous global communication infra-structure.

The phenomenal success of the Internet has brought us fresh new challenges. Many of the new applications have very different require-ments from those for which the Internet was originally designed. One issue is *performance assurance.* The datagram model, on which the Internet is based, has few resource management capabilities inside the network and so cannot provide any resource guarantees to users—you get what you get! When you try to reach a Web site or to make an Internet phone call, some parts of the network may be so busy that your packets cannot get through at all. Most real-time applications, such as video conferencing, also require some minimal level of resources to operate effectively. As the Internet becomes indispens-able in our life and work, the lack of predictable performance is cer-tainly an issue we have to address.

Another issue is *service differentiation.* Because the Internet treats all packets the same way, it can offer only a single level of service. The applications, however, have diverse requirements. Interactive applica-tions such as Internet telephony are sensitive to latency and packet losses. When the latency or the loss rate exceeds certain levels, these applications become literally unusable. In contrast, a file transfer can tolerate a fair amount of delay and losses without much degradation of perceived performance. Customer requirements also vary, depend-ing on what the Internet is used for. For example, organizations that use the Internet for bank transactions or for control of industrial equipment are probably willing to pay more to receive preferential treatment for their traffic. For many service providers, providing mul-tiple levels of services to meet different customer requirements is vital for the success of their business.

The capability to provide resource assurance and service differenti-ation in a network is often referred to as *quality of service* (QoS). Resource assurance is critical for many new Internet applications to flourish and prosper. The Internet will become a truly multiservice network only when service differentiation can be supported. Imple-menting these QoS capabilities in the Internet has been one of the toughest challenges in its evolution, touching on almost all aspects of Internet technologies and requiring changes to the basic architecture of the Internet. For more than a decade the Internet community has made continuous efforts to address the issue and developed a number of new technologies for enhancing the Internet with QoS capabilities.

This book focuses on four technologies that have emerged in the last few years as the core building blocks for enabling QoS in the Internet. The architectures and mechanisms developed in these technologies address two key QoS issues in the Internet: resource allocation and performance optimization. Integrated Services and Differentiated Services are two resource allocation architectures for the Internet. The new service models proposed in them make possible resource assurances and service differentiation for traffic flows and users. Multiprotocol Label Switching (MPLS) and traffic engineering, on the other hand, give service providers a set of management tools for bandwidth provisioning and performance optimization; without them, it would be difficult to support QoS on a large scale and at reasonable cost.

The four technologies will be discussed in depth in the next four chapters. Before we get down to the details, however, it is useful to look at the big picture. In this first chapter of the book we present a high-level description of the problems in the current Internet, the rationales behind these new technologies, and the approaches used in them to address QoS issues.

1.1 Resource Allocation

Fundamentally, many problems we see in the Internet all come down to the issue of *resource allocation*—packets get dropped or delayed because the resources in the network cannot meet all the traffic demands. A network, in its simplest form, consists of shared resources such as bandwidth and buffers, serving traffic from competing users. A network that supports QoS needs to take an active role in the resource allocation process and decides who should get the resources and how much.

The current Internet does not support any forms of active resource allocation. The network treats all individual packets exactly the same way and serves the packets on a first-come, first-serve (FCFS) basis. There is no admission control either—users can inject packets into the network as fast as possible.

The Internet currently relies on the TCP protocol in the hosts to detect congestion in the network and reduce the transmission rates accordingly. TCP uses a window-based scheme for congestion control. The window corresponds to the amount of data in transit between the sender and the receiver. If a TCP source detects a lost packet, it slows the transmission rate by reducing the window size by half and then increasing it gradually in case more bandwidth is available in the network.

TCP-based resource allocation requires all applications to use the same congestion control scheme. Although such cooperation is achievable within a small group, in a network as large as the Internet, it can be easily abused. For example, some people have tried to gain more than their fair share of the bandwidth by modifying the TCP stack or by opening multiple TCP connections between the sender and receiver. Furthermore, many UDP-based applications do not support TCP-like congestion control, and real-time applications typically cannot cope with large fluctuations in the transmission rate.

The service that the current Internet provides is often referred to as *best effort*. Best-effort service represents the simplest type of service that a network can offer; it does not provide any form of resource assurance to traffic flows. When a link is congested, packets are simply pushed out as the queue overflows. Since the network treats all packets equally, any flows could get hit by the congestion.

Although best-effort service is adequate for some applications that can tolerate large delay variation and packet losses, such as file transfer and email, it clearly does not satisfy the needs of many new applications and their users. New architectures for resource allocation that support resource assurance and different levels of services are essential for the Internet to evolve into a multiservice network.

Over the last decade the Internet community came up with Integrated Services and Differentiated Services, two new architectures for resource allocation in the Internet. The two architectures introduced a number of new concepts and primitives that are important to QoS support in the Internet:

○ Frameworks for resource allocation that support resource assurance and service differentiation
○ New service models for the Internet in addition to the existing best-effort service

○ Language for describing resource assurance and resource requirements
○ Mechanisms for enforcing resource allocation

Integrated Services and Differentiated Services represent two different solutions. Integrated Services provide resource assurance through
resource reservation for individual application flows, whereas Differentiated Services use a combination of edge policing, provisioning,
and traffic prioritization.

1.1.1 Integrated Services

Although the problems with the best-effort model have long been recognized, the real push for enhanced service architectures came in the
early 1990s after some large-scale video conferencing experiments
over the Internet. Real-time applications such as video conferencing
are sensitive to the timeliness of data and so do not work well in the
Internet, where the latency is typically unpredictable. The stringent
delay and jitter requirements of these applications require a new type
of service that can provide some level of resource assurance to the
applications.

In early 1990 the Internet Engineering Task Force (IETF) started
the Integrated Services working group to standardize a new resource
allocation architecture and new service models. At that time the
World Wide Web, as we know it today, did not yet exist, and multimedia conferencing was seen by many people as a potential killer
application for the Internet. Thus the requirements of the real-time
applications had major impacts on the architecture of Integrated
Services.

The Integrated Services architecture is based on *per-flow resource
reservation*. To receive resource assurance, an application must make a
reservation before it can transmit traffic onto the network. Resource
reservation involves several steps. First, the application must characterize its traffic source and the resource requirements. The network
then uses a routing protocol to find a path based on the requested
resources. Next a reservation protocol is used to install the reservation
state along that path. At each hop admission control checks whether
sufficient resources are available to accept the new reservation. Once
the reservation is established, the application can start to send traffic
over the path for which it has exclusive use of the resources. Resource

reservation is enforced by packet classification and scheduling mechanisms in the network elements, such as routers.

The Integrated Services working group proposed two new service models that a user can select: the *guaranteed service* and the *controlled load service models*. The guaranteed service model provides deterministic worst-case delay bound through strict admission control and fair queuing scheduling. This service was designed for applications that require absolute guarantees on delay. The other service model, the controlled load service, provides a less firm guarantee—a service that is close to a lightly loaded best-effort network. The Resource Reservation Setup Protocol (RSVP) was also standardized for signaling an application's requirements to the network and for setting up resource reservation along the path.

The Integrated Services model was the first attempt to enhance the Internet with QoS capabilities. The research and development efforts provided valuable insights into the complex issues of supporting QoS in the Internet. The resource allocation architecture, new service models, and RSVP protocol were standardized in the late 1990s.

But deployment of the Integrated Services architecture in the service provider's backbones has been rather slow for a number of reasons. For one, the Integrated Services architecture focused primarily on long-lasting and delay-sensitive applications. The World Wide Web, however, significantly changed the Internet landscape. Web-based applications now dominate the Internet, and much of Web traffic is short-lived transactions. Although per-flow reservation makes sense for long-lasting sessions, such as video conferencing, it is not appropriate for Web traffic. The overheads for setting up a reservation for each session are simply too high. Concerns also arose about the scalability of the mechanisms for supporting Integrated Services. To support per-flow reservation, each node in a network has to implement per-flow classification and scheduling. These mechanisms may not be able to cope with a very large number of flows at high speeds.

Resource reservation requires the support of accounting and settlement between different service providers. Since those who request reservation have to pay for the services, any reservations must be authorized, authenticated, and accounted. Such supporting infrastructures simply do not exist in the Internet. When multiple service providers are involved in a reservation, they have to agree on the charges for carrying traffic from other service providers' customers and settle these charges among them. Most network service providers are currently connected through bilateral peering agreements. To extend these bilateral agreements to an Internet-wide settlement agreement is difficult given the large number of players.

The Integrated Services architecture may become a viable framework for resource allocation in corporate networks. Corporate networks are typically limited in size and operated by a single administrative domain. Therefore many of the scaling and settlement issues we discussed above vanish. Integrated Services can support guaranteed bandwidth for IP telephony, video conferencing over corporate intranets. RSVP can also be used for resources allocation and admission control for traffic going out to wide-area networks.

The ideas, concepts, and mechanisms developed in Integrated Services also found their ways into later work on QoS. For example, controlled load service has influenced the development of Differentiated Services, and similar resource reservation capability has been incorporated into MPLS for bandwidth guarantees over traffic trunks in the backbones.

1.1.2 Differentiated Services

The Differentiated Services architecture was developed as an alternative resource allocation scheme for service providers' networks. By mid-1997 service providers felt that Integrated Services were not ready for large-scale deployment, and at the same time the need for an enhanced service model had become more urgent. The Internet community started to look for a simpler and more scalable approach to offer a *better than best-effort* service.

After a great deal of discussion, the IETF formed a new working group to develop a framework and standards for allocating different levels of services in the Internet. The new approach, called Differentiated Services, is significantly different from Integrated Services. Instead of making per-flow reservations, Differentiated Services architecture uses a combination of edge policing, provisioning, and traffic prioritization to achieve service differentiation.

In the Differentiated Services architecture, users' traffic is divided into a small number of *forwarding classes*. For each forwarding class, the amount of traffic that users can inject into the network is limited at the edge of the network. By changing the total amount of traffic allowed in the network, service providers can adjust the level of resource provisioning and hence control the degree of resource assurance to the users.

The edge of a Differentiated Services network is responsible for mapping packets to their appropriate forwarding classes. This packet classification is typically done based on the *service level agreement* (SLA) between the user and its service provider. The nodes at the edge of the network also perform traffic policing to protect the network from misbehaving traffic sources. Nonconforming traffic may be dropped, delayed, or marked with a different forwarding class.

The forwarding class is directly encoded into the packet header. After packets are marked with their forwarding classes at the edge of the network, the interior nodes of the network can use this information to differentiate the treatment of the packets. The forwarding classes may indicate drop priority or resource priority. For example, when a link is congested, the network will drop packets with the highest drop priority first.

Differentiated Services do not require resource reservation setup. The allocation of forwarding classes is typically specified as part of the SLA between the customer and its service provider, and the forwarding classes apply to traffic aggregates rather than to individual flows. These features work well with transaction-orientated Web applications. The Differentiated Services architecture also eliminates many of the scalability concerns with Integrated Services. The functions that interior nodes have to perform to support Differentiated Services are relatively simple. The complex process of classification is needed only at the edge of the network, where traffic rates are typically much lower.

The Differentiated Services approach relies on provisioning to provide resource assurance. The quality of the assurance depends on how provisioning is carried out and how the resources are managed in the network. These issues are explored in the next section, where we discuss performance optimization in the networks. Because of the dynamic nature of traffic flows, precise provisioning is difficult. Thus it generally is more difficult, and certainly more expensive, to provide deterministic guarantees through provisioning rather than reservation.

1.2   Performance Optimization

Once the resource allocation architecture and service models are in place, the second issue in resource allocation is performance optimization; that is, how to organize the resources in a network in the most efficient way to maximize the probability of delivering the commitments and minimize the cost of delivering the commitments.

The connection between performance optimization and QoS support may seem less direct compared with resource allocation. Performance optimization is, however, an important building block in the deployment of QoS. Implementing QoS goes way beyond just adding mechanisms such as traffic policing, classification, and scheduling; fundamentally, it is about developing new services over the Internet. Service providers must make a good business case so that customers are willing to pay for the new services and the new services will increase the return of their investment in the networks. The cost-effectiveness of the new services made possible by QoS capabilities is a major factor in the rollout of these services.

The Internet's datagram routing was not designed for optimizing the performance of the network. Scalability and maintaining connectivity in the face of failures were the primary design objectives. Routing protocols typically select the shortest path to a destination based on some simple metrics, such as hop count or delay. Such simple approaches are clearly not adequate for supporting resource allocation. For example, to make a reservation, we need to find a path with certain requested resources, such as bandwidth, but IP routing does not have the necessary information to make such decisions. Simply using the shortest-path algorithm for selecting paths is likely to cause high rejection rate and poor utilization. The shortest-path routing does not always use the diverse connections available in the network. In fact, traffic is often unevenly distributed across the network, which can create congestion hot spots at some points while some other parts of the network may be very lightly loaded.

Performance optimization requires additional capabilities in IP routing and performance management tools. To manage the performance of a network, it is necessary to have explicit control over the paths that traffic flows traverse so that traffic flows can be arranged to maximize resource commitments and utilization of the network.

MPLS has a mechanism called *explicit routing* that is ideal for this purpose. MPLS uses the label-switching approach to set up virtual circuits in IP-based networks. These virtual circuits can follow destination-based IP routing, but the explicit routing mechanism in MPLS also allows us to specify hop by hop the entire path of these virtual circuits. This provides a way to override the destination-based routing and set up traffic trunks based on traffic-engineering objectives.

The process of optimizing the performance of networks through efficient provisioning and better control of network flows is often referred to as *traffic engineering.* Traffic engineering uses advanced route selection algorithms to provisioning traffic trunks inside backbones and arrange traffic flows in a way that maximizes the overall efficiency of the network. The common approach is to calculate traffic trunks based on flow distribution and then set up the traffic trunks as explicit routes with the MPLS protocol. The combination of MPLS and traffic engineering provides IP-based networks with a set of advanced tools for service providers to manage the performance of their networks and provide more services at less cost.

1.2.1   Multiprotocol Label Switching

MPLS was originally seen as an alternative approach for supporting IP over ATM. Although several approaches for running IP over ATM were standardized, most of the techniques are complex and have scaling problems. The need for more seamless IP/ATM integration led to the development of MPLS in 1997. The MPLS approach allows IP routing protocols to take direct control over ATM switches, and thus the IP control plane can be tightly integrated with the rest of the IP network.

The technique that MPLS uses is known as *label switching.* A short, fixed-length label is encoded into the packet header and used for packet forwarding. When a *label switch router* (LSR) receives a labeled packet, it uses the incoming label in the packet header to find the next hop and the corresponding outgoing label. With label switching, the path that a packet traverses through, called the *label switched path* (LSP), has to be set up before it can be used for label switching.

In addition to improving IP/ATM integration, MPLS may also be used to simplify packet forwarding. Label lookup is much easier compared with prefix lookup in IP forwarding. With MPLS, packet forwarding can be done independent of the network protocols, and so forwarding paradigms beyond the current destination-based one can be easily supported. However, the driving force behind the wide deployment of MPLS has been the need for traffic engineering in Internet backbones. The explicit route mechanism in MPLS provides a critical capability that is currently lacking in the IP-based networks. MPLS also incorporates concepts and features from both Integrated Services and Differentiated Services. For example, MPLS allows bandwidth reservation to be specified over an LSP, and packets can be marked to indicate their loss priority. All these features make MPLS an ideal mechanism for implementing traffic-engineering capabilities in the Internet.

The purpose of MPLS is not to replace IP routing but rather to enhance the services provided in IP-based networks by offering scope for traffic engineering, guaranteed QoS, and virtual private networks (VPNs). MPLS works alongside the exiting routing technologies and provides IP networks with a mechanism for explicit control over routing paths. MPLS allows two fundamentally different data-networking approaches, datagram and virtual circuit, to be combined in IP-based networks. The datagram approach, on which the Internet is based, forwards packets hop by hop based on their destination addresses. The virtual circuit approach, used in ATM and Frame Relay, requires connections to be set up. With MPLS, the two approaches can be tightly integrated to offer the best combination of scalability and manageability.

MPLS control protocols are based on IP addressing and transport and therefore can be more easily integrated with other IP control protocols. This creates a unified IP-based architecture in which MPLS is used in the core for traffic engineering and IP routing for scalable domain routing. In several recent proposals extending the MPLS protocols to the optical transport networks has even been considered. MPLS may well become the standard signaling protocol for the Internet.

1.2.2 Traffic Engineering

The basic problem addressed in traffic engineering is as follows: Given a network and traffic demands, how can traffic flows in the network be organized so that an optimization objective is achieved? The objective may be to maximize the utilization of resources in the network or to minimize congestion in the network. Typically the optimal operating point is reached when traffic is evenly distributed across the network. With balanced traffic distribution, both queuing delay and loss rates are at their lowest points.

Obviously these objectives cannot be achieved through destination-based IP routing; there simply is not sufficient information available in IP routing to make possible such optimization. In traffic engineering, advanced route selection techniques, often referred to as *constraint-based routing* in order to distinguish them from destination routing, are used to calculate traffic trunks based on the optimization objectives. To perform such optimization, the traffic-engineering system often needs networkwide information on topology and traffic demands. Thus traffic engineering is typically confined to a single administrative domain.

The routes produced by constraint-based routing are most likely different from those in destination-based IP routing. For this reason these constraint-based routes cannot be implemented by destination-based forwarding. In the past, many service providers used ATM in the backbones to support constraint-based routing. ATM virtual circuits can be set up to match the traffic patterns; the IP-based network is then overlaid on top of these virtual circuits. MPLS offers a better alternative since it offers similar functions yet can be tightly integrated with IP-based networks.

The existing Internet backbones have used the so-called *overlay model* for traffic engineering. With the overlay model, service providers build a virtual network comprising a full mesh of logical connections between all edge nodes. Using the traffic demands between the edge nodes as input, constraint-based routing selects a set of routes for the logical connections to maximize the overall resource utilization in the network. Once the routes are computed, MPLS can be used to set up the logical connections as LSPs exactly as calculated by constraint-based routing.

The downside of the overlay model is that it may not be able to scale to large networks with a substantial number of edge nodes. To set up a full-mesh logical network with N edge nodes, each edge node has to connect to the other $(N-1)$ edge nodes, resulting in $N \times (N-1)$ logical connections. This can add significant messaging overheads in a large network. Another problem is that the full-mesh logical topology increases the number of peers, neighbors that routers talk to, that a routing protocol has to handle; most current implementations of routing protocols cannot support a very large number of peers. In addition to the increased peering requirements, the logical topology also increases the processing load on routers during link failures. Because multiple logical connections go over the same physical link, the failure of a single physical link can cause the breakdown of multiple logical links from the perspective of IP routing.

Traffic engineering without full-mesh overlaying is still a challenge. One heuristic approach that some service providers have used is to adjust traffic distribution by changing the link weights in IP routing protocols. For example, when one link is congested, the link weight can be increased in order to move traffic away from this link. Theoretically one can achieve the same traffic distribution as in the overlay model by manipulating the link weights in the Open Shortest Path First (OSPF) routing protocol. This approach has the advantage that it can be readily implemented in existing networks without major changes to the network architecture.

1.3 Summary

The need for QoS capabilities in the Internet stems from the fact that best-effort service and datagram routing do not meet the needs of many new applications, which require some degree of resource assurance in order to operate effectively. Diverse customer requirements also create a need for service providers to offer different levels of services in the Internet.

The Internet community has developed a number of new technologies to address these issues. Integrated Services and Differentiated Services provide new architectures for resource allocation in the Internet. Integrated Services use reservation to provide guarantee resources for individual flows. The Differentiated Services architecture takes a different approach. It combines edge policing, provisioning, and traffic prioritization to provide different levels of services to customers.

MPLS and traffic engineering address the issues of bandwidth provisioning and performance optimization in Internet backbones. The explicit route mechanism in MPLS adds an important capability to the IP-based network. Combined with constraint-based routing in traffic engineering, MPLS and traffic engineering can help network providers make the best use of available resources and reduce costs.

Further Reading

The following Web site has a collection of articles related to the early history of the Internet: *www.bookshelf.org/hist/*.

The basic principles of datagram networks and a detailed design were first described by Paul Baran in his 1964 RAND report "On Distributed Communications." Although the report was discovered after the ARPANET had already started, the current Internet is remarkably close to what Paul Baran originally had in mind. This 12-volume historical report is now available on-line at *www.rand.org/publications/ RM/baran.list.html*.

For a general introduction about data networking and the Internet, we recommend the following:

Peterson, L., and B. Davie. *Computer Networks: A Systems Approach.* San Francisco: Morgan Kaufmann, 1999.

2

Integrated Services

2.1 Introduction

The Integrated Services work was the first major attempt to enhance the Internet with QoS capabilities. Researchers were motivated in part by the experiments over the MBONE, a multicast network built on the Internet for audio and video conferencing. The MBONE experience showed that significant enhancements to the Internet architecture are necessary in order to support real-time applications over the Internet.

In the early 1990's, the networking research community also made substantial progress in developing algorithms and mechanisms for supporting advanced resource allocation in the network. In particular, the work on packet scheduling by a number of researchers demonstrated that it is quite feasible to provide delay and bandwidth guarantees with a class of scheduling algorithms, generally referred to as fair queuing (FQ). These schemes can be used to enforce strict resource allocation and at the same time maintain high resource utilization.

The development of Integrated Services was a major technical challenge to the Internet community. The new approach represents a significant departure from the datagram model on which the Internet was built. Many new concepts, mechanisms, and protocols had to be developed, including new service models, flow specifications, resource reservation protocols, routing mechanisms, admission control, and scheduling algorithms. The IETF established several working groups to standardize the service models and protocols for Integrated Services. The main working groups and their functions were as follows:

○ The Integrated Services (INTSERV) working group is responsible for defining the overall architecture, service models, flow specifications, and framework for all other related components in Integrated Services, such as admission control, flow identification, and scheduling.

○ The Integrated Services over Specific Link Layers (ISSLL) working group defines the specifications and techniques needed to implement Integrated Services capabilities within specific link layer technologies such as Ethernet and ATM.

○ The Resource Reservation Setup Protocol (RSVP) working group standardizes a resource reservation setup protocol that installs reservation state inside the network.

In this chapter we present the architecture, mechanisms, and protocols of Integrated Services. We begin with an analysis in Section 2.2 of the requirements of real-time applications that have influenced several aspects of the development of Integrated Services. In Section 2.3 we present an overview of the Integrated Services architecture and the basic approaches behind it, followed by a discussion in Section 2.4 of the new service models that Integrated Services support. Section 2.5 describes RSVP, the resource reservation protocol for supporting Integrated Services. In Sections 2.6 and 2.7 we move from Internet standards to mechanisms and algorithms for implementing Integrated Services in routers and switches. Section 2.6 describes the problem of identifying reserved flows, and Section 2.7 discusses packet scheduling algorithms that support delay and bandwidth guarantees. In Sections 2.8 and 2.9 we discuss the use of Integrated Services in enterprise networks and the mapping of Integrated Services to ATM networks.

2.2 Real-Time Applications

In the early 1990s considerable interest arose in multimedia communications over the Internet. Multimedia personal computers (PCs) became more powerful and affordable, and the development of the DVMRP multicast protocol provided efficient point-to-multipoint data distribution over the Internet. Real-time applications, such as audio and video conferencing, were considered by many people as possible killer applications for the Internet. In 1993 an experimental multicast backbone, MBONE, was set up for testing real-time applications. Many large-scale experiments were carried out, including broadcasting of IETF meetings, space shuttle launches, and even doctors operating on patients. Many research groups regularly used the MBONE for project meetings and seminars.

2.2.1 Playback Applications

Real-time applications refer to a group of applications that have stringent delay requirements. Typically they have a deadline for data to arrive by, after which the data become less useful. An example of real-time applications is audio and video conferencing. Consider a typical audio-streaming application. The source packetizes the voice signal and sends the packets to the network. Since individual packets experience a variable amount of delay in the network, the original timing between packets is no longer preserved when the packets get to the destination. The variation in delay (the difference between the largest and the smallest delay) is called *delay jitter* (Figure 2.1). Because of the distortion of timing caused by the delay jitter, the quality of the voice signal would not be good if the receiver simply sent the data to the audio device as the packets came in.

A common technique for removing delay jitter is to use a *play-out buffer*. With this approach the incoming packets are stored in the play-out buffer, and the delay jitter is smoothed out by adding extra delay to the packets that experienced less delay in the network (Figure 2.2). The data are sent out to the output device at a fixed delay offset from the original departure time; this way the original timing of the signal is faithfully reconstructed. The term *playback point* refers to the point in time that is offset from the original departure time; the

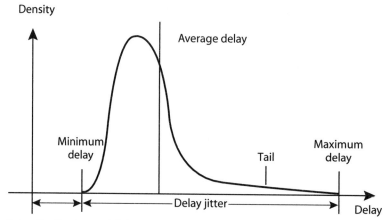

Figure 2.1 Delay distribution and delay jitter.

applications that use play-out buffers to reconstruct the original signal are called *playback applications*.

The playback point plays a crucial role in playback applications—the data arriving before the associated playback point are simply stored in the play-out buffer, waiting for the play-out point; the data arriving after the playback point are too late for the reconstruction of the original signal. In order to set a proper playback point, an application must know the maximum delay that a packet will experience. This delay bound could be provided by the network as a service commitment or estimated based on delays experienced by previously arrived packets.

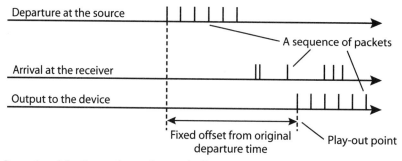

Figure 2.2 Removing delay jitter using a play-out buffer.

2.2.2   Tolerant and Intolerant Playback Applications

Latency and *fidelity* are two important performance measures for play-back applications. Latency is the delay between the time when the signal at the sender is generated and the time when the signal is played out at the receiver; for playback applications, it is exactly the delay offset. Some applications, mostly human-to-human interactions such as telephone conversations, are very sensitive to latency; the interaction will be hampered if the latency exceeds some limit (typically 100 to 300 ms). Other playback applications, such as broadcasting a lecture, can tolerate much longer latency.

Packet losses and distortion of timing between packets can cause degradation in the fidelity of the playback signal. When a packet arrives after its playback point, the receiver has two options: it can either discard the late packet or move the playback point farther out to accept the packet. The choice depends on individual applications, but either way, the fidelity is decreased because of the lost data or the distorted timing.

There is a general trade-off between latency and fidelity. We can use the worst-case delay as the delay offset from the original departure time; no packets will miss their play-out points, but latency is longer. If the delay offset is smaller than the worst delay, some packets will arrive after their playback points, which degrades fidelity.

Playback applications can be generally classified as *intolerant* or *tolerant*, depending on their requirements for fidelity. Intolerant applications require strictly faithful playback, either because the nature of an application demands it (e.g., high-fidelity music) or because the applications cannot deal with lost packets or distortion of timing. Intolerant applications must use a fixed delay offset and the delay offset must be larger than the worst-case delay a packet will experience so that no packets miss the playback point. To meet such requirements, the network must guarantee a delay bound and one that is sufficiently small to meet the latency requirement of the applications.

Many playback applications are designed to tolerate some degree of packet losses and adapt to changing delay by adjustment of the playback point. Several techniques have been developed and successfully tried over the Internet. For example, an application can use the data from adjacent packets to fill the gaps when a packet is lost or late. The playback point can be moved during the silent periods with less impact on the fidelity.

Although adaptive playback applications allow more flexibility in the service commitments that a network has to provide, the adaptation itself does not eliminate the need for controlling delay in the network. The performance of playback applications is dominated by the small percentage of packets that experience longer delay (the small tail or the right portion of the plot line in Figure 2.1); reducing the delay of those packets can substantially improve performance.

2.2.3 Lessons from MBONE

Experiments over the MBONE demonstrated the enormous potential of Internet video conferencing but also showed that real-time applications do not work well across the Internet, due to the variable queuing delays and congestion losses. Unlike traditional applications such as TELNET, FTP, and email, real-time applications have much stringent delay requirements. Most real-time applications are built on top of UDP and so do not react to congestion like TCP. Heavy packet losses during congestion often make these applications unusable. Although some real-time applications have incorporated close-loop feedback and can adapt to changing conditions, these mechanisms can only work within a very limited range.

The MBONE experience also highlighted the need for better traffic policing. Multicast in particular, if misused, can potentially cause tremendous disruption to a large portion of the Internet. Applications such as digital video are capable of generating very high rates of traffic, in the 1990s high enough to saturate many backbones. A malicious or careless user can spread congestion to many places by simply blasting a video stream to some multicast group. There were in fact several such incidents on the MBONE, caused by misconfiguration. For example, a feature in a video application was turned on by accident and the entire computer screen of a user was transmitted over the MBONE. The congestion that it caused was so bad that others could not contact the senders via the Internet and had to use the good old telephone system!

The lack of explicit traffic control inside the network can cause UDP-based applications to starve TCP-based applications in their competition for bandwidth. When a TCP-based application detects congestion in the network, the congestion control mechanism in TCP backs off and reduces the transmission rate. However, most UDP-based real-time applications do not react to congestion signals (or react less aggressively). Consequently TCP-based applications tend to suffer most of the congestion losses.

2.3 Integrated Services Architecture

Integrated Services developed a new architecture for resource allocation to meet the requirements of real-time applications. The basic approach is per-flow resource reservation. Although this idea is not new—it has been used in other networking technologies, such as ATM —it is still a significant challenge to integrate resource reservation into the existing Internet architecture. The goal of Integrated Services is to preserve the datagram model of IP-based networks and at the same time support resource reservation for real-time applications.

2.3.1 Basic Approach

In the Integrated Services architecture a set of mechanisms and protocols is used for making explicit resource reservation in the Internet. To receive performance assurance from the network, an application must set up the resource reservation along its path before it can start to transmit packets.

Figure 2.3 shows a simple example of an application making a reservation. The sender starts the setup of a reservation by first describing the characteristics of the flow and the resources requirements to the network. The network can accept this new application flow only if there are sufficient resources to meet the requested resources. Once the reservation is established, the application can send its packets along the reserved path, and the network will honor its commitment.

An implicit assumption of resource reservation is that the demand for bandwidth still exceeds supply. Although some people have argued for some time that bandwidth will become abundant in the future, with the expansion of fiber optic networks, this has not happened. In the near future bandwidth usage is likely to be controlled, and any fat pipes are likely to be filled immediately once broadband access (xDSL, cable modem, and fixed wireless) takes off.

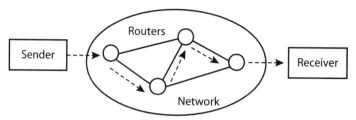

Figure 2.3   Making a resource reservation.

The Integrated Services architecture assumes that the main quality of service about which the network makes commitments is the *per-packet delay;* more specifically, the worst-case delay bound only. There are a number of reasons for this assumption. Time of delivery is one of the most important quantities of interest for applications. Playback applications, which we discussed in the previous section, are more sensitive to the packets that have experienced maximum delay. If the network can provide a delay bound, the playback delay offset can be set a priori at some appropriate level. In addition, providing worst-case delay bound is much easier than other delay quantities, such as average delay bound.

2.3.2   Key Components

Figure 2.4 shows the key components in the reference model for Integrated Services. The model can logically be divided into two parts: the *control plane* and the *data plane.* The control plane sets up resource reservation; the data plane forwards data packets based on the reservation state.

To set up a resource reservation, an application first characterizes its traffic flow and specifies the QoS requirements, a process often referred to in Integrated Services as *flow specification.* The reservation setup request can then be sent to the network. When a router receives the request, it has to perform two tasks. First, it has to interact with the routing module to determine the next hop to which the reservation request should be forwarded. Second, it has to coordinate with the admission control to decide whether there are sufficient resources to meet the requested resources. Once the reservation setup is successful, the information for the reserved flow is installed into the resource

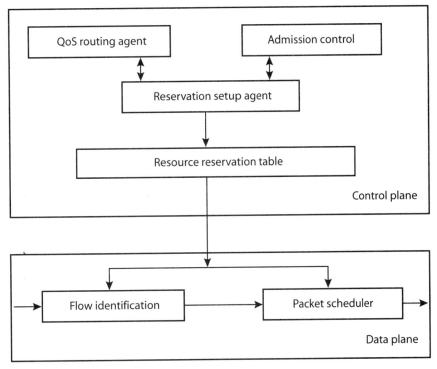

Figure 2.4   Integrated Services reference model.

reservation table. The information in the resource reservation is then used to configure the flow identification module and the packet scheduling module in the data plane. When packets arrive, the flow identification module selects packets that belong to the reserved flows and puts them on the appropriate queues; the packet scheduler allocates the resources to the flows based on the reservation information.

Route Selection
At each node the network must determine which path to use for setting up the resource reservation. The path must be selected so that it is likely to have sufficient resources to meet the requirement. For example, suppose that an application needs to reserve a path of 25 Mbits/sec bandwidth to a particular destination. It is important that the network select a path that meets such a bandwidth, but optimal route selection is difficult with existing IP routing. Currently routing protocols typically use a simple metric such as delay, hop count, or

administrative weight to compute the shortest paths to all destination networks. Therefore these routing protocols do not have the necessary information about the available resources to make an intelligent decision. The shortest path is often not the one that meets the resource requested. For example, the shortest path to the requested destination may not have the 25 Mbits/sec that the application has asked for, but a satellite link, although a longer path, may.

The issue is further complicated by the fact that applications may have multiple requirements; for example, both bandwidth and packet loss requirements. The problem of finding a path that satisfies multiple constraints is a difficult one and in many cases is NP complete. A number of interesting schemes have been proposed to resolve this problem, but none have been implemented in commercial products. We will discuss some related issues in Chapter 5 when we talk about traffic engineering and constraint-based routing.

Because routing for supporting resource reservation is still a difficult problem, the Integrated Services architecture deliberately decouples routing from the reservation process. The architecture assumes that the routing module in a router will supply the next hop. The route selection can initially be done based on current IP routing or using a centralized server until a better system is deployed.

Reservation Setup

To set up a reservation, we need a reservation setup protocol that goes hop by hop along the path to install the reservation state in the routers. The protocol also carries the information about traffic characterization and resource requirements so that at each node along the path it can be determined whether the new reservation request can be accepted or not. The reservation setup protocol must deal with changes in the network topology. For example, if a link goes down, the reservation protocol should set up a new reservation and tear down the old reservation.

Resource reservation usually involves financial transactions; thus there is a whole set of issues related to authorization, authentication, and billing. Before a reservation can start, it may have to be authorized by whoever will pay for the reservation. The user who requests a reservation must be authenticated, and the reservation is recorded for accounting.

In Integrated Services, the RSVP protocol has been developed as the reservation setup protocol for the Internet. RSVP is based on a receiver-initiated approach and is designed to work with IP multicast. The RSVP protocol allows a different reservation style and uses the "soft state" approach to deal with route changes. We will describe the details of the RSVP protocol in Section 2.5.

Admission Control

In order to offer guaranteed resources for reserved flows, a network must monitor its resource usage. It should deny reservation requests when no sufficient resources are available. An admission control agent performs this task as part of the reservation process; before a reservation request can be accepted, it has to pass the admission control test. Admission control has two basic functions. The first function is to determine if a new reservation can be set up based on the admission control policies. The second function is to monitor and measure the available resources.

There are two basic approaches to admission control: *parameter based* and *measurement based.* In the *parameter-based approach,* a set of parameters is used to precisely characterize traffic flows; the admission control agent then calculates the required resources based on these parameters. However, it is difficult in most cases to give accurate, tight traffic models. For example, the traffic rate from a video codec depends on the motion of objects; shaking heads will generate a lot more packets than just moving lips. Allocation of resources to meet the worst-case requirements will inevitably lead to low network resource utilization, particularly with bursty traffic sources.

An alternative is the *measurement-based approach.* Instead of relying on a priori traffic characterization, the network measures the actual traffic load and uses that for admission control. Since the traffic sources are not static, the measurement-based approach is probabilistic in nature and cannot be used to provide tight guarantees on resource commitments. Nevertheless, for bursty sources and applications that can tolerate some degree of delay fluctuation, the measurement-based approach offers a good trade-off between the level of resource guarantees and resource utilization. By allowing statistical multiplexing, network utilization can be substantially improved when there is a large number of flows in the network.

Several different methods have been proposed for deciding whether a new flow, with a different level of reliability, can be admitted to the network. The following algorithms are the most common ones:

○ **Simple sum.** The simplest approach is to ensure that the sum of requested bandwidth for all current flows and the new flow does not exceed the link capacity. The simple sum is the most conservative approach.

○ **Measured sum.** The measured sum approach uses the measured load of existing flows rather than the bandwidth requested by them. The measured load approach takes into account the fact that the actual traffic load is usually lower than the sum of all requested bandwidth.

○ **Acceptance region.** The acceptance region approach maximizes the reward of utilization increases against packet losses. Given the statistical models of traffic sources, the acceptance region for a type of traffic can be calculated.

○ **Equivalent bandwidth.** Equivalent bandwidth is another approach based on statistical modeling. The equivalent bandwidth for a set of flows is defined as the bandwidth $C(p)$ such that the stationary bandwidth requirement of the set of flows exceeds this value with a probability of at most p.

For measurement-based approaches, the traffic load of existing flows must be measured. The measurement can be done in a number of ways. One commonly used approach, exponential averaging over consecutive measurements, can be expressed as the following:

New estimation = $(1 - w) \times$ old estimation + $w \times$ new measurement

Exponential averaging provides a way of adjusting the speed at which the averaging process forgets the history. A small w gives a smooth average; a large w allows the averaging process to adapt to changes more quickly.

Time window is another approach for measurement of traffic load. In this approach the average arrival rate is measured over a sampling interval. At the end of a measurement period the highest average is used as the estimated rate. Suppose there are n sampling intervals in a measurement period T and C_i is the average rate measured over sampling interval I; then

$$\text{Estimated rate} = \max [C_1, C_2, C_3, \ldots C_n]$$

The measurement periods may overlap with each other so that some sampling intervals are used in two consecutive periods; this way we get a more frequent and smoother estimation with the same number of sampling intervals.

Flow Identification

In packet processing a router must examine every incoming packet and decide if the packet belongs to one of the reserved RSVP flows. An IP flow is identified by the five fields in the packet header: source IP address, destination IP address, protocol ID, source port, and destination port. The five fields are often referred to as the *five-tuple*. To determine if a packet matches an RSVP flow, the flow identification engine must compare the five-tuple of the incoming packet with the five-tuple of all flows in the reservation table. If there is a match, the corresponding reservation state is retrieved from the reservation table and the packet is dispatched to the packet scheduler with the reservation state associated with the flow.

Flow identification must be performed on every packet, so it has to complete the lookup within the time budget for processing a single packet. At high speeds the amount of time available for processing a packet is small, and the number of flows over backbone trunks can run into the hundreds of thousands. Performing flow identification at high speeds with a large number of flows is a challenging task. We will present a complete design of flow identification in Section 2.6.

Packet Scheduling

The last step of resource reservation, and probably also the most important one, is packet scheduling. The packet scheduler is responsible for enforcing resource allocation. It directly affects the delay that packets will experience and impacts, although less directly, on which packet is dropped when the buffer is getting full. The central task of a packet scheduler is to select a packet to transmit when the outgoing link is ready.

As we discussed in Chapter 1, the FCFS scheduling used for the best-effort model cannot support resource guarantees. More advanced scheduling algorithms are necessary to support the Integrated Services model. Weighted fair queuing (WFQ) is probably the most well known scheduling algorithm developed in recent years and is the one on which the Integrated Services model is based. In fact, WFQ presents a class of scheduling algorithms that share a common approach but differ in implementation details. Packet scheduling is discussed in depth in Section 2.7.

2.4   Service Models

Service models describe the interface between the network and its users in resource allocation architecture; that is, what services users can ask from the network and what kind of resource commitments the network can offer. Integrated Services standardized two basic service models: guaranteed service and controlled-load service. In this section we first look at the characterization of traffic flows and service requirements and then describe the two service models.

2.4.1   Flow Specification

To make a reservation, an application must characterize the traffic that it will inject into the network and specify the service requirements for the flow. In Integrated Services these are described in a so-called *flow specification*. The flow specification is in essence a service contract that specifies the traffic that the source will send and the resources and services the network promises to commit. If the source violates its traffic description (for example, by sending at a higher rate than the agreed-on one), the network will obviously not be able to keep its promises. Typically traffic is policed before it enters the network to ensure that the traffic conforms to the agreed-on traffic description.

A flow can be characterized in many ways; the exact form may depend on what admission control and packet scheduling mechanisms are used. The following parameters are common:

○ **Peak rate.** The highest rate at which a source can generate traffic. The peak rate is limited by the speed of the hardware devices. For example, we cannot generate packets faster than 10 Mbits/sec over a 10 Mbits/sec Ethernet. In some cases traffic is deliberately shaped to reduce the peak rate from the source; the peak rate can be calculated from the packet size and the spacing between consecutive packets.

○ **Average rate.** The average transmission rate over a time interval. The average rate can be calculated in many ways, and the results can be quite different. It is important to know the exact method and the time interval used in the calculation. Typically the average rate is calculated with a moving time window so that the averaging time interval can start from any point in time.

○ **Burst size.** The maximum amount of data that can be injected into the network at the peak rate. The burst size reflects the burstiness of the traffic source. To avoid packet losses, the first hop router may have to allocate a buffer for the source larger than its burst size.

In Integrated Services, traffic is described in terms of *leaky bucket parameters.* A leaky bucket is a popular class of traffic regulators. It has two parameters: the token arrival rate r and the bucket depth b (Figure 2.5). In a leaky bucket regulator, tokens drop into the bucket at a constant rate r and are consumed by the incoming packets. When a packet arrives, the regulator will send the packet only if the bucket has enough tokens. When a packet leaves the leaky bucket, the regulator removes the amount of tokens equal to the size of the outgoing packet. If a packet arrives and no sufficient tokens are available, the packet is stored in the packet buffer, waiting for more tokens. Once enough tokens have accumulated, the packet will be sent from the packet buffer. The depth b is the limit on the maximum amount of tokens that can be accumulated. Once the token bucket reaches the depth b, the regulator will discard further tokens until the size of the token bucket is less than the depth b.

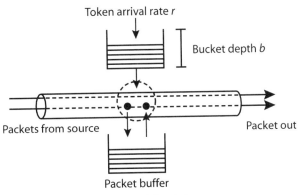

Figure 2.5   A leaky bucket with rate r and depth b.

The leaky bucket regulator has a number of interesting properties. First, the total number of bits that a leaky bucket allows a source to send is bounded by a linear function. Let $A(t)$ be the amount of bits transmitted during any interval of length t; then $A(t) \leq r \times t + b$. Second, the token arrival rate r corresponds to the long-term average rate of the traffic. Third, the source is allowed to sent bursts into the network, but the maximum burst size cannot be larger than the depth of the bucket b. When the source transmits at a rate less than the token rate r, tokens will start to accumulate in the bucket, which eventually become full. If the source then sends a burst of packets, a whole bucket's worth of packets will be able to pass the regulator as fast as the hardware allows.

Service requirements are application-specific. For example, an audio program would be sensitive to round-trip delay; a bulk file transfer application is more sensitive to the average transmission rate or the total amount of time for transferring the data. The following common parameters have been widely used to describe QoS requirements:

○ **Minimum bandwidth.** The minimum amount of bandwidth required by an application flow. The time interval for measuring bandwidth should also be specified since different measurement intervals may yield different results. Bandwidth allocation is guaranteed by the packet-scheduling algorithms. The WFQ class of scheduling algorithms is capable of providing minimum bandwidth guarantees over very small time intervals.

○ **Delay.** The delay requirement can be specified as the average delay or worst-case delay. The delay a packet experiences has three components: propagation delay, transmission delay, and queuing delay. Propagation delay is caused by the speed of light, and so is a function of distance. Transmission delay is the time to send a packet onto a link, and queuing delay is the waiting time a packet experiences. As we will show later in Section 2.4.2, transmission delay and queuing delay can be converted into a bandwidth requirement.

○ **Delay jitter.** A delay-jitter requirement specifies the maximum difference between the largest and smallest delays that packets experience. In any case, the delay jitter should not be larger than the worst-case transmission and queuing delay.

○ **Loss rate.** Loss rate is the ratio of lost packets and total packets transmitted. Packet losses in the Internet are often caused by congestion, and such losses can be prevented by allocating sufficient bandwidth and buffers for traffic flows.

A set of general characterization parameters is defined in RFC 2215 for any network elements that support Integrated Services. Each parameter is assigned a machine-oriented ID that can be used within protocol messages. The parameter ID consists of two numerical fields, one identifying the service associated with the parameter (the <service_number>) and the other identifying the parameter itself (the <parameter_number>). The textual form

<service_number, parameter_number>

is used to write a service_number/parameter_number pair. Service number 1 is reserved to indicate the default value. A parameter value identified by the ID

<1, parameter_number>

is a default value, which applies to all services unless it is overridden by a service-specific value for the same parameter.

Service numbers 2 through 254 are allocated to individual services. For example, guaranteed service is allocated number 2 and controlled-load service number 5. Parameter numbers in the range 1 through 127 are reserved for general parameters that apply to all services; parameter numbers in the range 128 through 254 should be used for parameters specific to a particular service.

Table 2.1 lists the general characterization parameters in Integrated Services. The definition of each parameter used to characterize a path has two types of values: local and composed. A *local value* gives information on a single network element; a *composed value* reflects the running composition of local values along a path with the specific composition rule for the parameter. For example, NON_IS_HOP is assigned the local number 1 and the composed parameter 2. The composition rule can be used to calculate the composed parameter of a path with individual local parameters. With AVAILABLE_BANDWIDTH as an example, the composed parameter is calculated as the minimum of all local values.

| Table 2.1 | | Integrated Services parameters |
Parameter	Numbers	Description
NON_IS_HOP	1, 2	A flag that provides information about the presence of network elements that do not implement QoS control services along the data path. The composition rule is an OR function.
NUMBER_OF_IS_HOPS	3, 4	A counter that is the cumulative total of the Integrated Services-aware hop. The composition rule is to increment by 1 for each qualified hop.
AVAILABLE_BANDWIDTH	5, 6	The amount of bandwidth available along a path followed by a data flow. The composition rule is the MIN function.
MINIMUM_PATH_LATENCY	7, 8	The minimum packet delay of a hop or a path. The latency includes fixed delay, such as propagation delay and processing delay, but not queuing delay. The composition rule is summation. The latency is reported in microseconds. The maximum value is $(2^{32} - 1)$. If the sum is larger than $(2^{32} - 1)$, it is set to $(2^{32} - 1)$, and is regarded as indeterminate latency.
PATH_MTU	9, 10	The maximum transmission unit (MTU) along a path. The value is used to invoke services that require packet size to be limited to a specific MTU. The current MTU discovery mechanism cannot be used because it reports only to the sender and does not allow service elements to set a value smaller than the physical MTU. The composition rule is the MIN function. The value is measured in bytes, with a maximum of $(2^{32} - 1)$ bytes.
TOKEN_BUCKET_TSPEC	127	Traffic parameters based on token bucket parameters. Note that this parameter is a data structure definition and is used only by the sender and the edge node. There are five parameters: token rate (r), bucket depth (b), peak rate (p), minimum policed unit (m), and maximum packet size (M).

2.4.2 Guaranteed Service

Guaranteed service provides guaranteed bandwidth and strict bounds on end-to-end queuing delay for conforming flows. The service is intended for applications that require the highest assurance on bandwidth and delay; for example, intolerant playback applications. Guaranteed service can also be used for applications that have hard real-time requirements, such as mission control systems.

End-to-End Behavior

Intuitively, the end-to-end behavior of a path that supports guaranteed service can be viewed as a virtual circuit with guaranteed bandwidth. This virtual circuit is more flexible than a real circuit; the partition of bandwidth between virtual circuits is logical, and so the boundaries of partitions can expand. For example, best-effort traffic flows may opportunistically use the bandwidth not consumed by reserved flows.

Let us illustrate this with an example. Suppose there are only two flows on a link and flows *A* and *B* both reserve 10 Mbits/sec. If both flows *A* and *B* are sending 10 Mbits/sec or more, both will get 10Mbits/sec, the amount they have reserved. Now suppose that for a while, flow *B* is sending only 5 Mbits/sec and flow *A* increases its rate to 15 Mbits/sec. If real circuits were used to guarantee the bandwidth, the 5 Mbits/sec bandwidth would be wasted. However, the virtual bandwidth partition allows other flows to access any unused bandwidth. For example, flow B can use the residual bandwidth. But as soon as flow *A* starts sending at 10 Mbits/sec, it will get all reserved 10 Mbits/sec.

Guaranteed service also provides strict delay bounds. It does not control the minimal or average delay but the *maximal queuing delay*. The maximal queuing delay guarantee assumes that the incoming traffic conforms to the specified token bucket parameters. The applications therefore must take into account the additional delay: the propagation delay of the path and the shaping delay to make the traffic flows conform to the token bucket parameters. In general, it is difficult to determine the token bucket parameters a priori for any traffic flow. Unless the token bucket parameters are chosen in a conservative way, some packets from an application flow may violate the token bucket parameters. This may result in extra shaping delay at the token bucket regulator.

TSpec and RSpec

An application invokes guaranteed service by specifying a traffic descriptor (TSpec) and a service specification (RSpec) to the network. Guaranteed service uses the `TOKEN_BUCKET_TSPEC` parameter.

TSpec describes traffic sources with the following parameters:

- **Bucket rate (*r*) (bytes/second).** The rate at which tokens arrive at the token bucket.

○ **Peak rate (*p*) (bytes/second).** The maximum rate at which packets can transmit.
○ **Bucket depth (*b*) (bytes).** The size of the token bucket.
○ **Minimum policed unit (*m*) (bytes).** Any packet with a size smaller than *m* will be counted as *m* bytes.
○ **Maximum packet size (*M*) (bytes).** The maximum packet size that can be accepted.

RSpec is specific to the guaranteed service. It describes the service requirements with two parameters:

○ **Service rate (*R*) (bytes/second).** The service rate or bandwidth requirement.
○ **Slack Term (*S*) (microseconds).** The extra amount of delay that a node may add that still meets the end-to-end delay requirement. We will discuss the Slack Term when we discuss the RSVP protocol in detail.

Delay Calculation

Given the TSpec and RSpec, the worst-case end-to-end queuing delay for a flow can be calculated. A simple approach is to use the *fluid model.* The fluid model for a service at rate R is in essence the service that would be provided by a dedicated wire with bandwidth R between the source and the destination. Suppose that the traffic source is constrained by a token bucket with parameters (r, b, p) and the token bucket is full when the flow starts to be served at time T_0. Normally the reserved bandwidth R is no less than the token rate r and the peak rate p is the speed of the output device, which is usually much larger than R and r. If we assume that p is infinite, the delay can then be expressed as the following simple equation:

$$\text{End-to-end worst-case queuing delay} = \frac{b}{R} \quad (p \rightarrow \infty \text{ and } R \geq r)$$

The above equation indicates that the queuing delay is determined only by the depth of the token bucket and the service rate. Intuitively the burst of packets that a traffic source can send is constrained by the depth of the token bucket, so the queue length will never exceed b. Note that the token bucket is full at time T_0. Suppose that the traffic source sends a burst of packets through the token bucket at peak rate p. The amount that the source can get through is no more than the depth of token bucket b. Since all packets arrive almost instanta-neously (since p is very large), the maximum queue length is b. In fact, the packet that experiences the worst-case queuing delay is the last packet in a burst of size b.

If the peak rate p is comparable to R and r, the worst-case delay is reduced because some packet will be serviced by the time the last packet of the burst enters the network. In this case the delay is

$$\text{End-to-end worst-case queuing delay} = \frac{b(p-R)}{R(p-r)} \quad (p > R \geq r)$$

If the peak rate p is less than the service rate R, there will be no queuing delay since the network can provide service faster than the source can transmit. On the other hand, if the token rate r is larger than the service rate R, the queuing delay becomes unbounded.

In a real network the services a flow receives cannot be exactly that of a real point-to-point link. Two error terms have been introduced to represent how the actual implementation of the guaranteed service deviates from the fluid model.

The error term C is the rate-dependent error term and represents the delay that a packet experiences due to the rate parameter and packet length. In the Internet packets are *stored* and *forwarded;* an intermediate node will wait until the last bit of the packet arrives before sending the packet out again. This packetization delay depends on the packet length and the transmission rate.

The error term D is the rate-independent, per-element error term and represents the worst-case non-rate-related delay. It is generally determined at configuration time. An example of D is the pipelining delay in a router. Typically packets are processed in a pipeline by different modules, such as route lookup and flow identification. Each module will introduce a fixed amount of delay; the total delay at one hop is decided by the length of the pipeline.

The end-to-end sums of C and D over a path are *Ctot* and *Dtot,* respectively, and the partial sums of C and D to a point are *Csum* and *Dsum*. Since the calculation of delay involves these quantities, they need to be made available to end nodes and service interfaces. The parameters C, D, *Ctot, Dtot, Csum,* and *Dsum* are summarized in Table 2.2. The use of *Csum* and *Dsum* are discussed later in this section.

Incorporating the error terms and packet lengths, the end-to-end worst-case queuing delay can be calculated as follows:

Table 2.2	Error terms for delay calculation	
Parameters	Parameter ID	Description
C	<2, 131>	Rate-dependent error term, measured in bytes
D	<2, 132>	Rate-independent error term, measured in units of 1 microsecond
Ctot	<2, 133>	The sum of C over a path
Dtot	<2, 134>	The sum of D over a path
Csum	<2, 135>	The partial sum of C between shaping points
Dsum	<2, 136>	The partial sum of D between shaping points

$$\frac{(b-M)(p-R)}{R(p-R)} + \frac{M+Ctot}{R} + Dtot \quad (p > R \geq r)$$

$$\frac{M+Ctot}{R} + Dtot \qquad\qquad (R \geq p \geq r)$$

The queuing delay is, however, only a component of the total delay. The total end-to-end delay that an application experiences must take into account the propagation delay, shaping delay, and other processing delays inside the end systems.

Policing and Shaping

Traffic flows that receive guaranteed service must conform to the token bucket and the peak rate parameters over all periods. For any period T, the amount of data sent cannot exceed $M + MIN\ [pT, rT + B - M]$. For the purpose of this calculation, packets smaller than the minimum policing unit m are counted as m. Nonconformant packets are subject to policing and shaping.

Policing is done at the edge of the network by comparing the traffic to the agreed TSpec parameters. Nonconforming packets are treated as best-effort datagrams and may be marked with a drop priority. Typically the application should make sure that the traffic entering the network conforms to the TSpec. Service providers, however, also need to monitor the flows and enforce TSpec.

Shaping is performed at all heterogeneous branch points and all merging points. A heterogeneous branch point is a spot where a multicast distribution tree has multiple outgoing branches that have different TSpecs. Shaping is necessary if the TSpec of the outgoing link is less than the TSpec reserved for the immediate upstream link. A merge point is where two distribution trees merge and share the same reservation (shared reservation is discussed in Section 2.5). Shaping is done by buffering packets until they conform to the token bucket parameters.

2.4.3 Controlled Load Service

The strict bandwidth assurance and delay bound provided by the guaranteed service come at a price: the resources have to be reserved for the worst case. For bursty traffic sources this will lead to low network utilization and increased cost for resource reservation. In addition, it is often difficult to know exactly the bandwidth and delay requirements for a given application. Consider the playback of a compressed digital movie. The peak rate of the movie could be substantially higher than the average rate, and the burst size is probably hard to quantify without detailed analysis of the traffic.

For some applications, a service model with less strict guarantees and lower cost would better serve their needs. The Integrated Services working group considered several proposals and standardized the controlled load service. The controlled load service does not provide any quantitative guarantees on delay bound or bandwidth. Instead it tries to emulate a lightly loaded network for applications that request the service. This service model allows statistical multiplexing and so can be implemented in a more efficient way than guaranteed service. Its characteristics fit well with adaptive applications that require some degree of performance assurance but not absolute bounds.

End-to-End Behavior

The end-to-end behavior of the controlled load service is somehow vague compared with guaranteed service; in some ways, this is intentional. The controlled load service attempts to create a service model between the best-effort service and guaranteed service through appropriate admission control and traffic isolation mechanisms. For this reason, it is also referred to as the *better-than-best-effort* service. The behavior visible to applications can be best described as similar to that of a lightly loaded best-effort network; more specifically:

○ A very high percentage of transmitted packets will be successfully delivered by the network to the receivers.

○ The transit queuing delay experienced by a very high percentage of delivered packets will not greatly exceed the minimum delay.

The controlled load service does not accept or make use of specific target values for control parameters such as delay and loss. The acceptance of a request for the controlled load service implies that the network has sufficient resources to accommodate the traffic without causing congestion.

Another way to define the controlled load service is to describe the events that are expected *not* to occur with any frequency:

○ Little or no average packet queuing delay over all time scales significantly larger than the burst time (the time required for transmitting the maximum burst size at the requested rate).
○ Little or no congestion losses over all time scales significantly larger than the burst time.

In essence, the controlled load service allows an occasional spike of delay or losses. However, the probability of such events must be sufficiently low so that the average queuing delay and average loss rate over a reasonable period is still close to zero.

Invocation and Policing

Applications can request the controlled load service by specifying the desired traffic parameters in the form of a TSpec to the network. The new request can be accepted only when all nodes over the path have sufficient resources available to accommodate the new flow. The admission control algorithm for deciding whether a flow can be accepted is left as a local matter and may be implementation specific; the controlled load standard specifies only the TSpec traffic parameters.

The controlled load service requires some policing mechanisms available for monitoring the conformance of flows and enforcing resource allocation in the presence of nonconformant packets. When nonconformant packets arrive, the network must ensure locally that the following requirements are met:

○ The network must continue to provide the contracted service guarantees to conforming flows.
○ The network should prevent the excessive controlled load traffic from unfairly impacting the best-effort traffic.

❍ The network must attempt to deliver the excessive traffic when it can do so without violating the previous two requirements.

When the enhanced services are offered, it may still be desirable to maintain some minimal level of services for all subscribers to the best-effort services. In such cases the excessive traffic from the controlled load services may be policed so that it does not cause starvation of best-effort traffic.

2.5   Resource Reservation Setup (RSVP)

With the best-effort model, an application can send packets whenever it wants to. However, the Integrated Services architecture requires an application to set up a reservation before it can transmit traffic. This necessitates a new protocol for setting up resource reservation in the network. RSVP is a resource reservation setup protocol developed by the IETF for this purpose. The RSVP protocol is used by hosts to communicate service requirements to the network and by routers in the network to establish a reservation state along a path.

2.5.1   Basic Features

The RSVP protocol was designed to be an add-on protocol to the existing IP protocol suite, and the architecture was in part influenced by the requirements of multicast-video-conferencing applications.

Simplex Reservation
The RSVP protocol is used to establish a resource reservation between a sender and a receiver. RSVP makes a reservation in only one direction (simplex flow). Although an application may act as both a sender and a receiver, RSVP treats a sender as logically distinct from a receiver. Thus in a two-way communication, the two ends must establish a reservation for both directions.

Receiver Oriented
The RSVP protocol supports multicast communications. In order to support large multicast groups, dynamic group membership, and heterogeneous receiver requirements, RSVP is receiver oriented; receivers are responsible for deciding what resources will be reserved and

initiating the reservation. The requests from receivers travel from the receivers toward the sender and gradually build up a reservation tree.

Routing Independent

RSVP is designed to operate with current and future unicast and multicast routing protocols. The decision to select a path for a flow is done separately by routing; the RSVP process simply consults the forwarding table and sends the RSVP messages accordingly. As we will discuss in Chapter 4, with traffic-engineering extensions to RSVP, an explicit route object can be carried in the RSVP message to specify the entire path over which the reservation should made. The explicit route is specified by the sender; RSVP just follows it.

Policy Independent

RSVP provides a general mechanism for creating and maintaining a reservation state over a multicast tree or a unicast path; the control parameters that are carried in the RSVP message are opaque from the RSVP perspective. The control parameters are passed on to the relevant control modules for processing. For example, the admission control will examine the reservation parameters and decide whether there are sufficient resources for a new reservation.

Soft State

RSVP uses the soft-state approach for maintaining a reservation state inside the network. The reservation state in the network has a timer associated with the state. When the timer expires, the state is automatically deleted. RSVP periodically refreshes the reservation state to maintain the state along the paths. This allows RSVP to adapt to changing multicast group membership and network topologies.

Reservation Style

RSVP provides a number of different reservation styles that characterize how a reservation should be treated. Reservation styles can be used to share a reservation among traffic streams from multiple senders or to select a particular sender that a receiver is interested in.

2.5.2 Operation Overview

In RSVP there are two types of messages: *PATH messages* and *RESV messages* (Figure 2.6). The PATH messages are sent from traffic sources

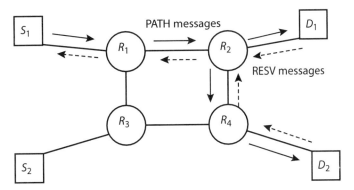

Figure 2.6   Basic RSVP operations.

toward the receivers, and these messages serve many purposes. First, they distribute information about the traffic source to the receivers. Second, the PATH messages are used to pass on characteristics of the path. Last, the PATH messages install the necessary state for the RESV messages to find out how to reach the senders from the receivers. The forwarding of the PATH messages is determined by the unicast and multicast routing protocols. After receiving the PATH messages, receivers can a request reservation by sending RESV messages upstream toward the source along the exact reverse path of the PATH messages. The RESV messages specify the resource requirements and set up the state in the routers along the path. After receiving the RESV messages, senders can start to transmit packets along the reserved paths.

2.5.3   RSVP Messages

We will now describe PATH and RESV messages in some detail and give an overview of other message types and object classes.

RSVP Message Transmission
RSVP messages are sent hop by hop between RSVP-capable routers as *raw* IP datagrams using protocol ID 46. Since RSVP is also used for end systems to request reservation to their first-hop routers, RSVP messages may be encapsulated in UDP packets if end systems cannot handle raw IP interfaces.

Path, PathTear, and *ResvConf* messages are not addressed to the immediate next-hop router; thus they must be sent with the Router Alert IP option [RFC 2113] in their packet headers. The Router Alert option will allow the next-hop router to detect such datagrams, which require special processing.

Each RSVP message must occupy exactly one IP datagram. If it exceeds the Maximum Transmission Unit (MTU), such a datagram will be fragmented by IP and reassembled at the receivers.

RSVP uses its periodic refresh mechanisms to recover from occasional packet losses. Under heavy congestion, however, substantial losses of RSVP messages could cause a failure of resource reservations. Ideally RSVP messages receive priority treatment during congestion.

PATH Message

RSVP *PATH messages* are sent downstream along the unicast or multicast routes that normal data packets will follow. The PATH messages install a *path state* in each node along the way. This path state includes at a minimum the unicast IP address of the previous hop node, which is used to route the corresponding RESV messages hop by hop in the reverse direction.

A *PATH message* contains the Previous Hop (PHOP), Sender Template, Sender TSpec, and the Adspec.

The *Sender Template* contains information that uniquely identifies the flow that the sender originates from other flows in the same session. It has exactly the same format as the *Filter Spec* that is used in RESV messages. Thus a Sender Template may specify only the sender IP address and optionally the UDP/TCP sender port, and it assumes the protocol ID specified for the session.

The *Sender TSpec* characterizes the traffic that the sender will generate. It can be used for deciding how much of the resources should be reserved and as part of the input to the admission control system. The Sender TSpec is not modified by the intermediate nodes.

The *Adspec* is an optional element in the PATH messages that is used to carry the OPWA (One Pass with Advertising; described in Section 2.5.5). The Adspec is passed to the local traffic control at each node, which returns an updated Adspec; the updated version is then forwarded in PATH messages sent downstream.

RESV Messages

RESV messages are reservation requests sent by the receivers toward the senders along the reverse direction of the PATH messages. An RESV message contains information about the reservation style, the *flow spec* object, and the *Filter Spec* object; the pair is referred to as a *flow descriptor.*

The flowspec specifies the desired QoS and parameters to be used in packet scheduling. The Filter Spec, together with a session specification, defines the flow to receive the QoS specified by the flow spec.

The flowspec in an RESV message may include a service class and two sets of parameters: a reservation spec (*RSpec*) that defines the desired QoS and a traffic spec (*TSpec*) that describes the traffic flow. The exact format depends on whether the receiver is requesting controlled load service or guaranteed service. Guaranteed service requires both the RSpec and the TSpec parameters; controlled load service needs only TSpec.

RSVP Message Formats

Each RSVP message begins with a common header followed by a series of variable-length RSVP objects. The format of the common header is shown in Figure 2.7, and each of the fields is described in Table 2.3.

The current protocol version number is 1. The *message type* defines the function of the message. Table 2.3 shows the seven types of messages that have been defined. The RSVP checksum is similar to the ones used in TCP, UDP, and IP.

The 4-bit *flags* and 8-bit *reserved* fields are currently not defined. The *send TTL* field records the TTL value used by the sender in the IP header. The *RSVP length* is the total length of the message in bytes, including the variable-length objects that follow.

Version	Flags	Message type	RSVP checksum
Send TTL		Reserved	RSVP length

Figure 2.7   RSVP message common header.

Table 2.3	RSVP common header fields
Message type	Description
PATH	Path message
RESV	Reservation message
PATHErr	Error indication in response to PATH message
RESVErr	Error indication in response to RESV message
PATHTear	Path tear-down message
RESVTear	Reservation tear-down message
RESVConf	Reservation confirmation message

Figure 2.8 shows the object header. The 16-bit *Length* field is the total length of the object in bytes. It must be a multiple of 4 and at least 4. The *Class-Num* identifies the object class. Table 2.4 lists the classes that an RSVP implementation must recognize. The *C type* is used to distinguish subtypes with the same Class-Num and is unique within Class-Num.

2.5.4 Reservation Styles

A reservation request can include a set of options collectively called *reservation styles*. Reservation styles determine how multiple requests are merged and which resource requests are forwarded to the upstream node.

The following three styles are currently defined (see Table 2.5):

○ **Wild-card-filter (WF) style.** The WF style implies *shared* reservation and *wild-card* sender selection. With a WF-style reservation, all receivers share a single reservation whose size is the largest of the resource requests from the receivers; all upstream senders can use the reservation. WF style can be represented as WF(*, {Q}), where the asterisk represents the wild-card sender selection and Q the flow spec.

○ **Fixed-filter (FF) style.** The FF style is the opposite of the WF style; it implies *distinct* reservation and *explicit* sender selection. With an FF-style reservation, a distinct reservation is established for the specific sender. FF style can be represented as FF($S_1(Q_1)$, $S_2(Q_2)$, . . . $S_n(Q_n)$), where S_1, S_2, . . . S_n are senders and Q_1, Q_2, . . . Q_n are corresponding flow specs.

Length	Class-Num	C type
Object content (variable length)		

Figure 2.8   RSVP object header.

Table 2.4	**RSVP object classes**
Object Class	**Description**
NULL	The rest of the fields are ignored.
SESSION	Defines the session: may contain destination address, protocol ID, and some generalized destination port, required in all messages.
RSVP_HOP	The sender of the message and a logical outgoing interface handle. This object is referred to as the PHOP (previous hop) object for downstream messages or as the NHOP (next hop) for upstream messages.
TIME_VALUE	The refreshing period, required in PATH and RESV messages.
STYLE	Defines the reservation styles and additional style-specific information that is not in FLOWSPEC and FILTER_SPEC, required by RESV messages.
FLOWSPEC	Defines the desirable QoS; in RESV messages.
FILTER_SPEC	Defines the flows from the session that should receiver the QoS specified by the FLOWSPEC in RESV messages.
SENDER_TEMPLATE	Holds the source address and multiplexing information to identify the sender; required in PATH messages.
SENDER_TSPEC	Defines the traffic characteristics of the sender's traffic; required in PATH messages.
ADSPEC	Carries path control data; in PATH messages.
ERROR_SPEC	Specifies errors in PATHErr, RESVErr, or RESVConf messages.
POLICY_DATA	Carries information for a local policy module to decide whether the reservation is permitted. May be in PATH, RESV, PATHErr, or RESVErr messages.
INTEGRITY	Carries information for authentication of the originating node and for verification of the content of the RSVP messages.
SCOPE	Carries an explicit list of senders to which the message is to be forwarded.
RESV_CONFIRM	Carries the address of a receiver that has requested a confirmation; in RESV and RESVConf messages.

Table 2.5   **Three reservation styles**

	Distinct reservation	Shared reservation
Explicit sender selection	Fixed filter (FF)	Shared explicit (SE)
Wild-card sender selection	(None defined)	Wild-card filter (WF)

○ **Shared explicit (SE) style.** The SE style implies shared reservation but explicit sender selection. An SE-style reservation creates a single reservation shared by specified senders. A receiver can explicitly list what senders are to be included in the reservation. SE style can be represented as $SE((S_1, S_2, \ldots S_n)\{Q_n\})$, where $S_1, S_2, \ldots S_n$ are senders and Q is the corresponding flow spec.

Shared reservation styles (WF and SE) are designed for multicast applications where it is unlikely that all sources can transmit simultaneously. For example, in audio conferencing, typically only one or two people can speak at the same time. An WF or SE reservation request for twice the bandwidth for one sender should be sufficient in such cases.

Let us illustrate with examples how reservation styles affect how much of the resources are reserved in the nodes and how the resource requests are constructed for upstream nodes. Figure 2.9 is a router with two incoming interfaces I_1, I_2, and two outgoing interfaces O_1, O_2. Suppose that there are three senders S_1, S_2, and S_3; packets from sender S_1 arrive through I_1 and packets from S_2/S_3 through I_2. Three receivers R_1, R_2, and R_3 are connected to the outgoing interfaces; packets bound for R_1 are routed through O_1 and packets for R_2/R_3 through O_2. Reservation requests come from the receivers toward

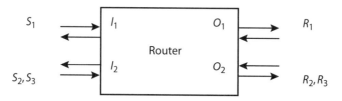

Figure 2.9   Router configuration.

the senders. For simplicity, we use B as the basic unit of resources to be reserved.

Figure 2.10 shows WF-style reservations. At the outgoing interface O_1 and O_2, resource reservations are made with the largest requests (4B on interface O_1 and 3B on interface O_2). The largest resource request (4B) is forwarded to the upstream node.

Figure 2.11 shows FF-style reservations. At the outgoing interfaces, a separate reservation is made for each sender that has been requested, and the reservation is shared by all receivers that made the request. For each sender, the largest resource request is forwarded to the upstream node.

Figure 2.12 shows SE-style reservations. When SE-style reservations are merged, the resulting filter is the union of the original filter specs, and the resulting flow spec is the largest flow spec.

In fact, the rules for the merging of resource requests from different receivers can be generalized as follows:

○ Merging takes place both at the outgoing interfaces before reservation is made and the incoming interfaces before the resource requests for upstream nodes are constructed.

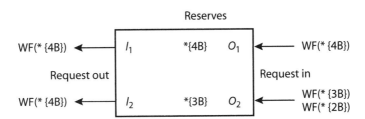

Figure 2.10   WF-style reservations.

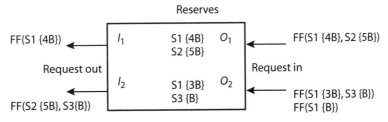

Figure 2.11   FF-style reservations.

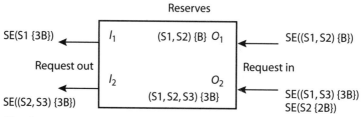

Figure 2.12 SE-style reservations.

○ The merged flow spec is always the largest of the individual requests for the set of senders specified.

Different reservation styles cannot be merged since they are based on completely different models.

2.5.5 Adspec, OPWA, and Slack Term

In this section we discuss some of the more advanced issues related to the operation of RSVP with the guaranteed service and controlled load services.

Adspec
As we described in Section 2.5.3, Adspec is an optional object for carrying OPWA information. This object is modified by an intermediate node and used to pass information to the next hop. The receiver can use the information in the Adspec to determine the characteristics of the end-to-end path.

The Adspec object has three components: a *default general parameters* fragment, a *guaranteed service* fragment, and a *controlled load service* fragment. If either a guaranteed service or a controlled load service fragment is not present in Adspec, the receiver should not try to use the omitted service. Currently RSVP does not allow heterogeneous service models within a session.

The default general parameters fragment contains the following fields:

○ **Minimum path latency.** The sum of fixed delay along the path that a packet may experience in addition to the queuing delay. The receiver needs this information in order to calculate the budget for end-to-end queuing delay.

○ **Path bandwidth.** The minimum bandwidth of the path.
○ **Integrated Services hop count.** The total number of hops that are capable of support the Integrated Services.
○ **Global break bit.** Set to 0 by the sender. If any node along the path does not support Integrated Services, the bit is set to 1 and the information is passed on to the receiver.
○ **Path MTU.** The maximum transmission unit of the path.

The guaranteed service fragment includes Ctot, Dtot, Csum, and Dsum for calculating the end-to-end delay, guaranteed service break bit, and optional values that override parameters in the default general parameters.

The controlled load service does not require extra data in the Adspec to function correctly. The controlled load service fragment contains only the controlled load service break bit and optional values that override parameters in the default general parameters.

One Pass with Advertising (OPWA)

The basic reservation model is called *One Pass*. With One Pass, the sender simply includes the Sender TSpec to inform the receiver what traffic to expect. It is not possible with this model to determine the characteristics of the path or whether the path is able to support the desired QoS.

The other model, *One Pass with Advertising* (OPWA), is a more sophisticated one that uses the Adspec. With OPWA, the sender includes an Adspec in its PATH message to collect the information about the path. The receiver can use the information in the Adspec to determine the end-to-end characteristics of the path and calculate the end-to-end delay.

Let us take guaranteed service as an example. The receiver uses the minimum path latency reported by the Adspec object to work out the queuing delay budget. The queuing delay value can then be used to calculate the amount of bandwidth that must be reserved. Together with the Ctot, Dtot, Csum, Dsum, and PATH MTU in the Adspec, the receiver can then construct an RSpec for the RESV message.

Slack Term

In the RSpec in an RESV message for guaranteed service, there is a field called the Slack Term. The Slack Term is added to allow more flexibility in allocating delay over multiple hops.

Recall that in the delay calculation for guaranteed service, the bandwidth reserved for a particular flow is identical at all hops along the path. For example, suppose that there are two links between the sender and the receiver and that to meet the delay bound, we need 2.5 Mbits/sec. Now, the amount of bandwidth available on the first link is 2 Mbits/sec and on the second is 10 Mbits/sec. This reservation will fail since the first link does not have sufficient bandwidth. However, one possible solution is to reserve different amounts of bandwidth on these two hops: increase the bandwidth reservation on the second hop and reduce the bandwidth reservation on the first hop. By doing so, we can reduce the delay in the second link to compensate for the increased delay in the first link. As long as we can meet the overall delay requirement, the reservation can go through.

The Slack Term signifies the difference between the desired delay and the actual delay obtained with current bandwidth reservation. In another words, the Slack Term is the credit in delay (the amount of delay that can be increased without violating the overall end-to-end delay) in the previous hops that may be used by other hops.

2.6   Flow Identification

In the previous three sections we presented the architecture and service models of Integrated Services and the RSVP protocol for setting up resource reservation. In this section and the next we will discuss the mechanisms for implementing Integrated Services in the packet-forwarding path.

In this section we focus on flow identification, one of the two main components for supporting Integrated Services in packet processing. We will use flow identification as an example to illustrate the design process: defining the problem, setting out requirements, examining design choices, and evaluating the final design.

2.6.1   Basic Requirements

In a network that supports Integrated Services, a router has to perform the following task: extract the five-tuple from an incoming packet and compare it against the reservation table. The router then decides whether the incoming packet matches one of the flows in the reservation table. If there is a match, the reservation state of the matched flow is retrieved. This process is often referred to as *flow identification*.

Since there is no information in the packet header to indicate if a packet belongs to a reserved flow or not, flow identification must be performed on every incoming packet. It has been suggested that a reservation bit should be allocated in the packet header so that the packets of reserved flows can be identified quickly and only those packets with the bit set need go through the flow identification component. However, modern routers must support wire-speed forwarding. To support that, a router must cope with the worst-case scenario rather than the average one. In the worst case, multiple packets that belong to reserved flows may arrive at the speed of the incoming link; that is, packets arrive back-to-back. A router must be able to deal with such a scenario.

Most routers are now designed with a pipelining architecture. Each packet passes through a sequence of processing modules like an assembly line; for example, from ingress header processing to IP lookup, then flow identification, and scheduling, and finally egress forwarding. Each module must complete its task within the amount of time available for processing a single packet. At high speeds the per-packet processing time is extremely small. For example, to support 64-byte packets at OC12 speed (622 Mbits/sec), the per-packet processing time is less than 1 microsecond. Most large service providers are expected to upgrade their backbone to OC48 (2.5 Gbits/sec) and OC192 (10 Gbits/sec) soon. As the Internet expands, the number of concurrent flows can also be very large. An OC12 backbone trunk currently may have tens of thousands of concurrent flows. Thus the design of a flow identification module must be able to perform lookup at high speeds with a large number of flows.

2.6.2   Design Choices

There are several possible approaches to the design of the flow identification module, all involving speed-versus-space trade-offs. One extreme is a direct memory lookup that requires only a single memory access. However, this approach is not practical since the five-tuple is 104 bits long. The other extreme is binary search. Binary search has the most efficient memory usage but is relatively slow. For example,

17 memory accesses and comparisons might be needed to support 64 K reserved flows.

A compromise we explore here is to use hashing-based schemes for flow identification. Hashing-based schemes are quite simple, involving calculation of a hash function and further comparison if there is collision. They offer a good trade-off between speed and memory requirements. Figure 2.13 illustrates how hashing-based flow identification works.

When an RSVP reservation is made, a router applies a hash function to the five-tuple that is used to identify the flow. If the output hash value has not been used by other reserved flows, the hash value is linked to the state of this flow in the reservation table. If other flows have been hashed into the same value, we refer it as *hash collision* and set a bit to indicate that there is a collision. The hash value points to a collision resolution table that holds the five-tuples of all reserved flows with the same hash value; each five-tuple in the collision resolution table has another pointer to the data in the reservation table.

In packet processing a router first applies the same hash function to the five-tuple of each incoming packet. If the hash value has no collision bit set, the hash value is used to find the entry in the reservation

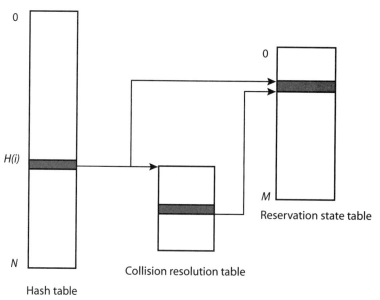

Figure 2.13   Hashing-based flow identification.

table and retrieve the reservation state for the flow. If the collision bit is set, another search in the collision resolution table is performed to find the exact match and its associated reservation state.

From the above description we can see that there are at most two steps in hashing-based flow identification. The first step is the computation of a hash function, then a lookup if there is a collision. It is therefore critical to reduce collisions to a minimum. Generally increasing the size of the hash table reduces the collision rate; this gives us a knob to fine-tune the trade-off between speed and space based on actual memory and speed requirements. For any design, there are two important performance metrics: the collision rate (the percentage of flows that have at least one collision), which determines average performance of the system, and the worst-case number of collided flows (the maximum number of flows may have the same hash value), which decides the performance of the system in the worst case. If the collision rate is extremely low, it may be acceptable to allow some small percentage of collisions so that we can skip the collision resolution step; this is another possible engineering trade-off between precision and speed. Before we can make the design decision, we need to look at the performance of the hashing-based schemes.

2.6.3 Hashing-Based Schemes

We now will describe four hash functions and a double-hashing scheme as possible candidates for flow identification.

XOR Folding of Source and Destination IP Addresses

This scheme concatenates source and destination IP addresses into a 64-bit string and performs XOR folding according to the hash table size. The computation is very simple and does not need access to the four-layer information in the packet. The hash function is as follows:

$$H(\bullet) = H_1 \oplus A_2 \oplus \ldots \oplus A_n$$

where A_i is the substring with i bit to $i + m$ bit of the 64-bit string. The last substring, A_n, may have zero padding to make it m bits long.

XOR Folding of Destination IP Addresses and Destination Port

For many Web-based applications, the data are delivered from the server toward the client. In such cases the source IP address and the port number may be the same while the destination address and port number change for each flow. Thus a simple variation of the previous one is to replace the source address with the destination port number. The mathematical formulation is identical to that of XOR folding of source and destination IP addresses, except that A_i is the substring with i bit to $i + m$ bit of the 48-bit string of the destination IP address plus the destination port number.

XOR Folding of the Five-Tuple

For a flow identified by the five-tuple, a scheme that uses the full five-tuple is likely to perform better. This hash function concatenates all bits of the five-tuple into a 104-bit string and performs XOR folding according to the hash table size (Figure 2.14). The mathematical formulation is identical to that of XOR folding of source and destination IP addresses except that A_i is the substring with i bit to $i + m$ bit of the 104-bit string of the five-tuple.

A hash table with 1 million entries can be implemented with the following code:

```
hash_index = srcIP >> 12;
temp = (srcIP << 8) | (destIP >> 24);
hash_index ^= temp;
temp = destIP >> 4;
hash_index ^= temp;
temp = (destIP << 16) | srcPort;
hash_index ^= temp;
temp = (destPort << 4 ) | (proto >> 4);
hash_index ^= temp;
temp = proto & 0xF;
hash_index ^= temp;
return hash_index;
```

32-Bit CRC

The 32-bit CRC algorithm (CRC32 for short) has been widely used for error detection in communication systems. It is known for exploiting

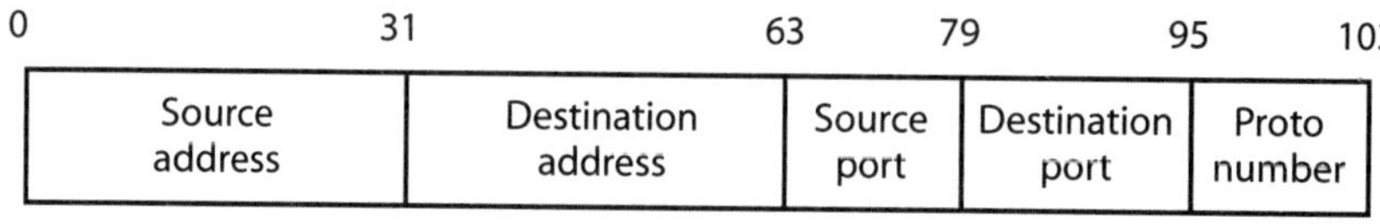

Source address	Destination address	Source port	Destination port	Proto number

0   31   63   79   95   103

Figure 2.14   The 104-bit string with five-tuple.

the randomness in traffic well and so can be a good hash function for flow identification. However, CRC32 is substantially much more complex than the hash functions previously described. The CRC32 algorithm should be considered only when it can add significant improvement to error detection.

The 32-bit CRC algorithm can be expressed as follows:

$$x^{32} + x^{26} + x^{23} + x^{22} + x^{16} + x^{12} + x^{11} + x^{10} + x^8 + x^7 + x^5 + x^4 + x^2 + x + 1$$

The hash table index is computed by applying the 32-bit CRC algorithm to the five-tuple of the incoming packet.

Double Hashing

Double hashing is one of the techniques for significantly reducing collision rate. It computes a second hash value with a different hash function if the first hashing causes a collision. In double hashing a flow is said to collide with another only when a hash collision is observed on both hash functions. The probability of a collision with two different hash functions is likely to be much smaller than with one hash function. Nevertheless, any performance improvement must justify the extra complexity.

2.6.4 Performance Evaluation

We use the following metrics to evaluate the performance of the hashing schemes:

○ **Collision rate.** The proportion of total active flows that are hashed into places that are already occupied by at least one flow.
○ **Worst-case number of collided flows.** The maximum number of flows that have the same hash value.

Let us first look at the theoretic performance limits of hash-based schemes. Suppose that we have a perfect hash function that can uniformly map flows into the hash table. Let N be the size of the hash table and m be the number of distinguished flows that are hashed into the table. The collision rate can be expressed as

$$C_r = 1 - \frac{N\left(1 - \left(\frac{N-1}{N}\right)^m\right)}{m}$$

Figure 2.15 shows the relationship between the collision rate C_r and the hash table size N for a given number of active flows m. The collision rate decreases quickly when the hash table size increases. The drop in the collision rate starts to level off after the hash table size is about 10 times larger than the number of flows.

Figure 2.16 shows the relationship between the collision rate C_r and the number of active flows m for a given hash table size. The collision rate increases almost linearly with the number of flows.

In practice, hash functions typically will not be able to match the performance of the perfect hash function we have described. The distribution of the bits in the five-tuple is not completely random; the port numbers in particular tend to concentrate on a small number of values (e.g., 80 for Web servers). However, a good hash function should be able to exploit all inherent randomness in the five-tuple.

In order to understand the performance of schemes in real networks, we will show some simulation results based on real packet traces collected on a major Internet backbone (over one OC12 trunk and one OC3 trunk) during summer 1998. The four sets of traces, containing complete packet headers and timing information for about 8 million packets, have 164 K, 112 K, 173 K, and 117 K distinct

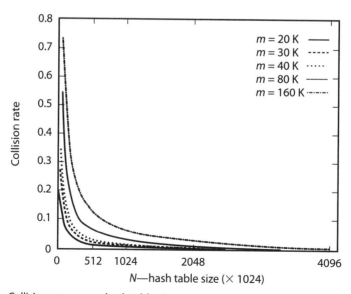

Figure 2.15   Collision rate versus hash table size.

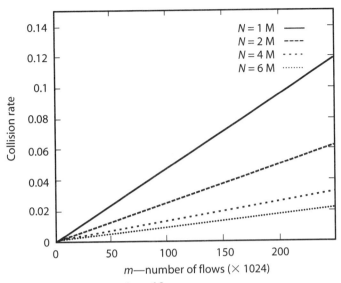

Figure 2.16   Collision rate versus number of flows.

flows. For collision rates and the maximum number of collided flows, the hash table size varies from 256 K to 4 M. Since the four sets of traces were collected over an interval of approximately 14 seconds each, it is assumed that all flows in the traces are active during the simulation.

Collision Rate

Figure 2.17 shows the collision rate with the first four hash functions we described in Section 2.3, together with that of the perfect hashing. Both the 32-bit CRC and the XOR folding of the five-tuple perform extremely well, close to the curve for the perfect hashing; the performance of the XOR folding of source and destination addresses and the XOR folding of destination address and destination port number is rather poor. The results are very consistent across the four sets of traces.

Figure 2.18 compares the 32-bit CRC and double hashing. Although the 32-bit CRC and double hashing both show an excellent performance, double hashing based on less complex functions outperforms the 32-bit CRC, although the difference is not significant.

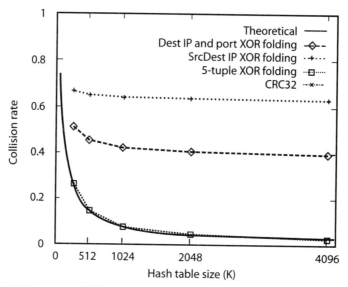

Figure 2.17   Collision rates with four hashing functions.

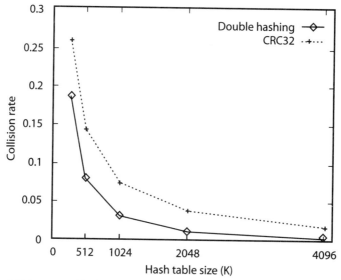

Figure 2.18   Collision rate with double hashing.

Number of Collided Flows

For collided flows it is important to know how many flows have been hashed into the same hash value. In particular, the worst-case number of collided flows determines the maximum number of comparisons that must be performed to find the exact match. Tables 2.6 and 2.7 show the average and worst-case number of collided flows. For the average numbers, all four hash functions perform well, although CRC32 and XOR folding of the five-tuple are slightly better than the other two. For the worst-case numbers, however, the difference between the worst and the best is huge: CRC32 and XOR folding of the five-tuple have worst-case numbers consistently below 7, whereas XOR folding of source and destination addresses and XOR folding of destination address and destination port are over 1000.

The simulation results show that hashing-based schemes with CRC32 and XOR folding of the five-tuple perform very well, both on the memory requirement for a collision rate target and on the number of collided flows on average and in the worst case. Given the

Table 2.6	Average number of collided flows			
Hash table size	SrcIP + DestIP	DestIP + DestPort	Five-tuple	CRC32
256 K	3.00	2.05	1.348	1.350
512 K	2,84	1.81	1.166	1.166
1024 K	2.76	1.71	1.081	1.080
2048 K	2.72	1.66	1.042	1.040
4096 K	2.70	1.64	1.022	1.020

Table 2.7	Worst-case number of collided flows			
Hash table size	SrcIP + DestIP	DestIP + DestPort	Five-tuple	CRC32
256 K	1284	2353	7	6
512 K	1284	2350	5	6
1024 K	1284	2350	4	5
2048 K	1284	2350	4	5
4096 K	1284	2351	4	4

implementation complexities of the two schemes, XOR folding of the five-tuple seems to be the ideal choice for the implementation of flow identification that can support hundreds of thousands of reserved flows at high speeds.

2.7 Packet Scheduling

The packet scheduler is responsible for enforcing resource allocation to individual flows. When the network resources cannot accommodate all traffic flows, queues will start to build up in the routers. The purpose of the scheduler is to decide which packets should get the resources. Intuitively, a packet scheduler works like a dispatcher: it keeps track of how many packets each flow has sent and compares that with the amount of resources the flow has reserved. Arriving packets from a flow are sent only when the flow has not used up the reserved resources.

In this section we first look at the basic requirements and design choices for packet scheduling and then describe some popular scheduling algorithms for supporting Integrated Services.

2.7.1 Basic Requirements

Before we describe the details of scheduling schemes, let us first look at the key requirements for supporting resource reservations.

Isolation and Sharing

The basic purpose of a scheduler is to allow sharing of common resources in a controlled way. In a circuit-switched network, such as the telephone system, all flows are completely isolated; each connection has dedicated resources. If some connections are not fully used, the resources are wasted. In a datagram-based Internet, all resources are shared on a per-packet basis without any form of isolation and protection between different flows. The resource utilization is maximized, but there is little isolation between flows. These two approaches are two extreme forms of resource allocation. The fair-queuing algorithms we will describe in Section 2.7.3 can maintain a good balance between the two conflicting forces of isolation and sharing. Fair-queuing algorithms emulate the traffic isolation in a circuit-switched network, but when resources are not used by some flows, they can be shared by others.

Delay Bounds

The Integrated Services approach requires scheduling algorithms to support delay bounds. Delay bounds can be either deterministic or statistical. For example, guaranteed service requires the network to provide a delay bound for the worst-case scenario. For controlled load service the performance would be acceptable as long as there was no sustained queuing over a time period, but occasional bursts would be allowed.

The deterministic and statistical bounds reflect the basic trade-off between isolation and sharing. Deterministic bounds give the best isolation but at the price of reduced statistical multiplexing. Typically overprovisioning is necessary in order to guarantee the worst-case bounds. Statistical bounds allow more efficient sharing and thus improve resource utilization. For deterministic delay bounds, the burstiness of the traffic sources must be limited.

Bandwidth Allocation

When there are not sufficient resources to satisfy all traffic demands, bandwidth must be allocated fairly to all competing flows. One form of fair-sharing policy that has been widely considered in the literature is called *max-min fair sharing*. The max-min fair sharing tries to maximize the minimum share of a flow whose demand is not fully satisfied. The basic principles are as follows:

○ Resources are allocated in order of increasing demands.
○ No flow is allocated more than its demand.
○ Flows with unsatisfied demands get an equal share of the resource.

The max-min fair share can be calculated as follows:

1. Calculate the initial fair share = (total capacity)/(total number of flows).
2. For all flows that have a demand equal to or less than the fair share, allocate the flows' actual demands.
3. Remove the satisfied flows and subtract the allocated capacities from the total available capacity.

4. Repeat steps 2 and 3 for the remaining flows with the current fair share = (remaining capacity)/(remaining number of flows) until all remaining demands are larger than the current fair share. All remaining demands will get the current fair share.

With max-min fair sharing, all flows with demands less than the fair share will be satisfied while the unused resources from those flows are allocated according to the same principles for the remaining flows with demands larger than the fair share.

In the above description, we assumed that all flows have an equal right to resources. If some flows should be allocated bigger share of the resources than others, for example, based on subscription fees, we can associate a weight to each flow to indicate the relative sharing. The max-min fair sharing can be easily extended by simply normalizing the demand with the corresponding weight for the flow.

2.7.2   Design Choices

We now examine some of the fundamental choices available for scheduling packets.

Work-Conserving versus Non-Work-Conserving Schedulers

Typically a scheduler is idle only when there are no packets waiting to be transmitted. Such schedulers are said to be *work conserving*. For example, FCFS is work conserving. In fact, most of the well-known queuing disciplines are work conserving. However, *non-work-conserving* scheduling algorithms have been proposed to reduce delay jitter and buffer size in the network. In a non-work-conserving scheduler a node can transmit a packet when the packet is eligible. If no packets are eligible for transmission, the node will become idle even when there are packets in the queue.

One potential application of non-work-conserving disciplines is to reduce delay jitter in the network. Recall that real-time applications must smooth out delay jitters introduced by the network. One way of reducing delay jitter is to maintain the interpacket intervals of consecutive packets from a flow inside the network. This may be achieved to some degree by non-work-conserving schedulers in which a packet becomes eligible for transmission only after a short period from the departure of the previous packet from the same flow.

The disadvantage of the non-work-conserving disciplines is that bandwidth may be wasted during the period that a node is idle when there are packets in the queue. In addition, the non-work-conserving disciplines reduce delay jitter at the expense of increasing the average delay of a flow.

Simple Priority

Simple priority has been widely used in many computer systems. In a simple priority system, there are a number of priority levels, and the higher priority always has precedence over the lower priority. When the outgoing link becomes available for transmission, a priority scheduler will always select packets from the queue with the highest priority. Packets with lower priorities are transmitted only when there are no packets in the queues of higher priorities.

Simple priority is easy to understand, and its implementation is straightforward. However, simple priority must be used with care. A large volume of higher-priority packets can easily starve lower-priority packets; lower-priority packets may never get a chance to transmit if higher-priority packets are always in the queue. Therefore simple priority is typically reserved for mission-critical traffic such as network control or used with strict admission control to ensure that the amount of higher-priority traffic is limited to a small portion of the total traffic.

Basic Approaches

Considerable progress on packet scheduling has been made over the past 10 years in both theory and implementation experience. Scheduling algorithms can be roughly divided into three categories: fair queuing, deadline based, and rate based.

In the *fair-queuing approach*, the share of bandwidth by a flow is represented by a real number, often referred to as a *weight*. Fair-queuing schemes try to allocate bandwidth proportional to active (or backlogged) flows based on their weights. Intuitively each flow is entitled to a share of the bandwidth based on its weight. However, if a flow does not consume all its entitled bandwidth, the excessive bandwidth is not wasted but is allocated to all backlogged flows in proportion to their weights. With fair queuing, a flow is guaranteed to get its entitled bandwidth and may get more. It has been shown that fair queuing is able to provide an end-to-end delay bound, and this has been used as the basis of the Integrated Services approach.

Deadline-based schemes schedule packets based on the earliest-deadline-first (EDF) principle. With EDF each packet is assigned a deadline, and the scheduler simply transmits packets in the order of the deadlines. The advantage of the deadline-based approach is that delay and bandwidth are decoupled; the delay bounds can be independent of bandwidth allocation. For example, a flow reserving a small amount of bandwidth can still obtain a small delay bound. However, the admission control process is much more complex. In general, two admission control tests must be performed. First, the total allocated bandwidth must not exceed the link capacity. Second, a schedulability test must be performed to ensure that deadlines will not be missed. Another problem is that the allocation of excessive bandwidth may not be fair; two connections with identical delay and bandwidth requirements may not receive the same level of service.

Rate-based scheduling is a general framework that may be used to construct different work-conserving and non-work-conserving scheduling disciplines. Rate-based schedulers have two components: a regulator and a scheduler. The regulator determines the eligibility time for the packet. Once a packet becomes eligible, the scheduler may select the packet for transmission. The traffic is in essence shaped by the regulator before arriving at the scheduler; packets may be delayed in the regulator. A variety of regulators may be used here, including token bucket regulators, peak rate regulators (limiting the rate to the scheduler within a peak rate), and jitter regulators (smoothing out jitter added by previous hops). The scheduler can also be FCFS, fair queuing, or EDF.

2.7.3   Weighted Fair Queuing

Weighted fair queuing (WFQ) is a class of scheduling algorithms that support bandwidth allocation and delay bounds. Since the original WFQ was proposed over 10 years ago, many different variations have been developed with different trade-offs between complexity and accuracy. WFQ has been widely implemented in routers for supporting QoS. We first look at the key properties of WFQ and then describe some variants that are designed for high-speed implementation.

Fluid Model

WFQ algorithms are often explained with the *fluid model.* In the fluid model we assume that traffic is infinitely divisible and a node can serve multiple flows simultaneously. In a real network, of course, packets are processed one at a time; thus packet size will affect the queuing system. However, the simplification in the fluid model allows us to visualize the operation of the queuing disciplines more easily, and in most cases, it is straightforward to derive the results for a pack-etized system from that of the fluid model.

Let us illustrate with some examples. Suppose that we have two flows that equally share an outgoing link and all packets are the same size (Figure 2.19). In the fluid model the two packets (colored gray and white) from the two flows are serviced simultaneously, and they start and finish at the same time. In the packetized model, however, the gray packet has to be serviced before the white packet or the other way around. It is important to note that although the gray packet in Figure 2.19 finishes earlier than the white packet, both packets finish no later than they did in the corresponding fluid system.

Generalized Processor Sharing (GPS)

GPS is an ideal fair-queuing algorithm based on the fluid model that provides an exact max-min weighted fair sharing. In GPS a connection is called *backlogged* when it has data in the queue. Suppose that there are N flows being served by a server with service rate R and the ith flow is assigned a weight ϕ_i, and let $S(i, \tau, t)$ be the amount of data serviced for flow I during an interval (τ, t). In GPS, for any backlogged flow i and for any other flow j, in (τ, t) we have

$$\frac{S(i, \tau, t)}{S(j, \tau, t)} \geq \frac{\phi_i}{\phi_j}$$

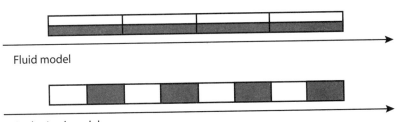

Fluid model

Packetized model

Figure 2.19   Fluid model and packetized model.

In the interval (τ, t) the flow i receives a minimum fair share proportional to its weight

$$\frac{\phi_i}{\sum_{j=1}^{V}\phi_j} \times R$$

where V is the set of flows that are backlogged during the interval. Intuitively, in a GPS system, all nonbacklogged flows (sending less than their fair shares) receive services without any queuing; the remaining bandwidth is shared by backlogged flows in proportion to their weights. In short, the minimum fair share is guaranteed for any flow and the excessive bandwidth is distributed proportionally to backlogged flows. GPS provides perfect fairness in bandwidth allocation. When the traffic source is constrained by a token bucket with burst size b and token rate

$$r \geq \frac{\phi_i}{\sum_{j=1}^{V}\phi_j} \times R$$

GPS can guarantee a delay bound of $\frac{b}{r}$. In essence, the service that a flow receives in a GPS system is no worse than an equivalent dedicated link with a capacity of

$$\frac{\phi_i}{\sum_{j=1}^{V}\phi_j} \times R$$

These results provide the basis for guaranteed services, which we discussed in Section 2.4.2.

Weighted Fair Queuing

Weighted fair queuing or *packet-by-packet generalized processor sharing* (PGPS) is a packetized approximation of GPS scheduling. WFQ tries to emulate a GPS system by calculating the departure time of a packet (called *finish time*) in a corresponding GPS system and using this virtual time stamp to schedule packets. Note that the finish time is not the real departure time of the packet but rather a number representing the order of the packets in the system. For example, if packet A finishes transmission before packet B under a GPS system, packet A will be selected for transmission before packet B in the corresponding WFQ.

It turns out that calculating the finish time in a GPS system for a general case is not straightforward. Let us first look at a simple case where all flows are backlogged all the time (always sending at higher rates than their reserved bandwidth). In this case, the finish time of packet k from flow i is equal to the finish time of the previous packet from the same flow plus the time for transmitting the current packet. Letting F_i^k represent the finish time of kth from flow i, we get

$$F_i^k = F_i^{k-1} + \frac{L_i^k}{\phi_i}$$

However, in a more general case flows may move from backlogged to nonbacklogged or vice versa, and so there will be idle time between two packets. The finish time can be calculated as

$$F_i^k = \max\left[F_i^{k-1}, V(t)\right] + \frac{L_i^k}{\phi_i}$$

where $V(t)$ is a linear function of real time t in each of the time intervals.

The calculation of finish time can be more clearly explained with arrival-departure curves. Suppose that we have two flows sharing a server equally, so that flow 1 and flow 2 are both served at a rate of 1/2. Figures 2.20 and 2.21 are the arrival-departure curves. The dashed line is the arrival process (the amount of data arrived versus time), and each arrow represents the arrival of a packet. The height of the arrow is the size of the packet. For example, in Figure 2.20, packets arrive at $t = 1, 2, 3,$ and 11 with packet size 1, 1, 2, 2, respectively. After the arrival of each packet, the arrival curve (dashed line) increases by the packet size. The solid line represents the amount of data that have been served. During the time interval (0, 1), flow 1 is idle and flow 2 sends a packet at $t = 0$. Therefore the first packet from flow 2 is served at the rate of 1 during the interval. At $t = 1$, the first packet from flow 1 arrives, and both flows are backlogged and are served at the rate of 1/2 until $t = 9$. At this time the three packets from flow 1 have left the system, and no more packets arrive. During the interval (9, 11), flow 2 again is served at the rate of 1. At $t = 11$, a packet from flow 1 arrives, and by this time all packets from flow 2 are finished. The fourth packet from flow 1 is then served at the full rate of 1 and finishes at $t = 13$. Using the arrival-departure curves, we can calculate the finish time of a packet in a GPS system. Let us look at flow 1 (Figure 2.20). The third packet from flow 1 arrives at $t = 3$, and the total amount of arrived data is 4 (dashed line). The solid line indicates that the amount of data that has been served reaches 4 at $t = 9$. Thus the third packet from flow 1 arrives at $t = 3$ and departs at $t = 9$; the total delay it experiences is 6.

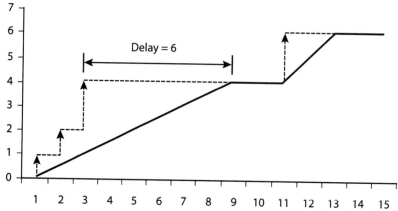

Figure 2.20   Arrival-departure curve for flow 1.

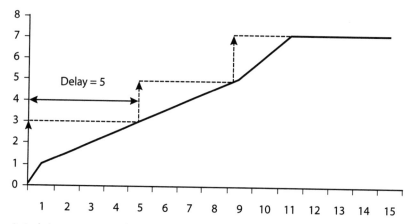

Figure 2.21   Arrival-departure curve for flow 2.

In fact, the distance between the dashed line and solid line along the *x* axis is the delay bound for the flow. The curves also show that the finish time of a packet in a GPS system is a piecewise function of time. The complexity of calculating the finish time in a GPS system lies in the fact that a newly arrived packet may move a flow from a nonbacklogged state to a backlogged state and change the finish time of previously arrived packets from other flows.

Due to the packetization effect, the worst-case delay for WFQ is slightly larger than for GPS. However, the difference is bounded. The worst-case delay in WFQ can be expressed as

$$\frac{b}{r_i} + \frac{(K-1)L_{max}}{r_i} + \sum_{m=1}^{K} \frac{L_{max}}{R^m}$$

where K is the number of hops, L_{max} is the maximum packet size, r_i is the reserved rate for flow i, and R^m is the service rate for each hop m. The first item in the equation is the delay bound of a GPS system. The second item is the extra delay a packet may experience if it arrives just after it would have been served under the GPS system. The third item reflects the fact that packets are served one by one, so a packet may have to wait after the current packet being served.

The theoretical results provide the foundation for calculating delay bounds in guaranteed service. The error terms C and D in guaranteed service were added to reflect the two items above.

Worst-Case Fair WFQ

In WFQ the scheduler chooses packets based only on the finish time of packets in the corresponding GPS system. The worst-case fair-weighted fair queuing (WF^{2}Q) is an enhancement to the WFQ scheduling. In WF^{2}Q the scheduler considers the start time of a packet as well as the finish time; the packet selected for transmission is the one that has the smallest finish time among all the packets that have already started service in the corresponding GPS system. Compared with WFQ, WF^{2}Q achieves the same delay bound and has better fairness. WF^{2}Q also achieves smoother packet interleaving and so can improve average delay, particularly in hierarchical link sharing.

Hierarchical WFQ

WFQ scheduling algorithms can be used in a hierarchical fashion to achieve more sophisticated hierarchical-link-sharing polices. For example, suppose a corporation has 10 divisions sharing a link in some fashion, and within each division its share of the link is further allocated to each class of applications (Figure 2.22). Hierarchical link sharing can be achieved by running fair-queuing algorithms at multiple levels; for example, one across all divisions and one within each of the divisions. In a hierarchical WFQ system excessive bandwidth will

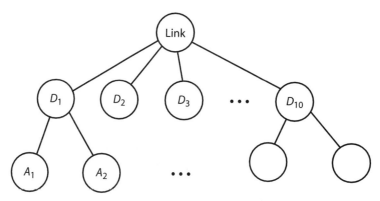

Figure 2.22   Hierarchical sharing.

first be redistributed within its own hierarchy group (within a division) and, if there is still excessive bandwidth, be redistributed among hierarchies (across divisions).

2.7.4   Variants of WFQ

Although the WFQ has many unique properties that make it an ideal scheduling discipline for support of QoS in the Internet, the calculation of the finish time in the corresponding GSP system is quite complex and impractical at high speeds. A number of variants of WFQ have been proposed that are less complex and are used in most implementations.

Self-Clocking Fair Queuing (SCFQ)

Close examination of the equation for the finish time in Section 2.7.3 reveals that the complexity lies in the calculation of the finish time for a flow that becomes backlogged after an idle period. In this case, it is necessary to compute the piecewise function $V(t)$ in order to assign the finish time for the newly backlogged flow. Thus one way of reducing the complexity is to make the calculation of finish time simpler.

SCFQ proposes a simple approach to approximate the finish time in a corresponding GSP system. When a packet from a nonbacklogged flow arrives, SCFQ uses the finish time of the packet *currently in service* as the $V(t)$. The calculation is as follows:

$$F_i^k = \max\left[F_i^{k-1}, F_{current}\right] + \frac{L_i^k}{\phi_i}$$

The approximation of $V(t)$ to the finish time of current packet leads to a larger worst-case delay, and the increase in the worst-case delay is linear to the number of flows in the system.

Weighted Round Robin (WRR)

A simpler way of emulating GPS scheduling is *weighted round robin*. The server simply visits the list of flows in turn and selects the number of packets for transmission based on the weights. For example, suppose that there are two flows A and B sharing a link with weights 1 and 2. The server first selects one packet from flow A and two packets from flow B and then one packet from flow A and two from flow B again, and so forth. WRR works particularly well when the packet size is fixed or the mean packet size is known for a flow. Otherwise WRR cannot allocate bandwidth fairly.

Deficit Round Robin (DRR)

Deficit round robin is similar to WRR but takes into account variable packet sizes. In DRR each flow is associated with a deficit counter, which is set to 0 at the beginning. The scheduler visits and serves a fixed number of bits (called quantum) from each flow. When a packet is transmitted, the quantum is reduced by the packet size. For each flow the scheduler transmits as many packets as the quantum allows. The unused quantum is recorded in the deficit counter representing the amount of quantum that the scheduler owes to the flow. At the next round of visiting, the scheduler will add the previously left quantum to the current quantum. The quantum can be assigned according to the weight of a flow to emulate WFQ, and when a flow is idle, the quantum is discarded since the flow has wasted its opportunity to transmit packets. A simple variation of the DRR is *credit round robin* (CRR). In CRR when a flow has a packet in the queue but not enough quantum, the scheduler still transmits the packet but records the extra quantum in the credit counter.

2.8 Integrated Services over Specific Link Layers

The Integrated Services standards are defined to extend the QoS capabilities of the IP layer. Since IP runs over many different subnet technologies, it is often necessary to map these standards onto those technologies. The IETF created a working group called Integrated Services over Specific Link Layers (ISSLL) to address these issues. The standards for mapping Integrated Services to specific link layers specify the following two mappings for each link layer:

○ **Service mappings.** Service mappings define the way that the link layer technology is used to provide a particular service in Integrated Services, such as controlled load or guaranteed services.
○ **Setup protocol mappings.** Setup protocol mappings define how an Internet-level setup protocol such as RSVP is implemented or mapped onto the link layer technology.

The simplest link layer to support is a point-to-point link since it has very simple and predictable characteristics. Ethernet and ATM are more challenging. The bandwidth arbitration over Ethernet is completely decentralized, whereas ATM has developed its own standards for QoS capabilities. In this section we briefly discuss the mapping of Integrated Services to LANs and ATM networks.

2.8.1   Local Area Networks

Shared and switched LANs are the most common networking technologies used in corporate and campus networks. These LANs do not currently have any capability to provide resource assurance. Access to the link bandwidth is arbitrated by media access protocols in a decentralized fashion.

To support resource allocation over LANs, the concept of a *Subnet Bandwidth Manager* (SBM) has been developed. An SBM is a centralized entity that provides all bandwidth management functions over a LAN segment; for example, admission control, traffic policing, scheduling, and reservation. For each LAN segment, a single SBM is designated to be the DSBM (Designated Subnet Bandwidth Manager). When a new host comes alive on the LAN, it attempts to discover whether a DSBM exists through a DSBM discovery-and-election algorithm. Once a host finds the DSBM, it becomes an SBM client to that DSBM. A host that is capable of serving as a DSBM may choose to participate in the election process.

SBM clients can communicate with DSBM using RSVP. When an SBM client sends a PATH message over a LAN interface, it actually transmits the message to the DSBM. After processing the PATH message, the DSBM forwards it to the actual destination of the RSVP message. The DSBM builds up the state for the session. When the RESV message comes back, it also goes to the DSBM. The DSBM determines if the request can be granted. If sufficient bandwidth is available, the DSBM forwards the RESV message to its destination. An SBM client needs to implement flow identification and packet scheduling to support Integrated Services in packet forwarding.

In addition to the SBM proposal, the IEEE 802.1 Interworking Task Group developed a set of enhancements that would provide a mechanism for distinguishing 802-style frames based on a simple priority. The current 802.1p specification defines a 3-bit *user_priority* field and a way to transport this value across the subnet using an extended frame format. Ethernet switches, for example, can use this field to provide preferential queuing and access to the media.

Table 2.8 presents the default mapping from delay targets to IEEE 802.1p user_priority classes. However, these mappings must be viewed as defaults and must be changeable. The delay-bound numbers were proposed to address the needs of current video and voice technology and are only guidelines—there is no requirement to adhere to these values.

With this example set of mappings, delay-sensitive, admission-controlled traffic flows are mapped to user_priority values in ascending order of their delay-bound requirement. Since the 802.1p specification provides only eight classes, a straightforward mapping for the

Table 2.8	IEEE 802.1p default service mapping
User-priority value	Service mapping
0	Default, assumed to be best effort
1	Reserved, less-than-best-effort
2	Reserved
3	Reserved
4	Delay sensitive, no bound
5	Delay sensitive, 100 ms bound
6	Delay sensitive, 10 ms bound
7	Network control

Integrated Services traffic does not exist. One approach is to map the traffic of guaranteed service to user_priority class 5 and 6 and the traffic of controlled-load service to class 4. Through strict admission control, the delay bound for each class can be controlled within the specified limits.

2.8.2   ATM Networks

The ATM forum developed a framework for traffic management for ATM networks. Since many Internet backbones are built over ATM, it is important that we compare Integrated Services and ATM traffic management and look at ways of running Integrated Services over ATM networks.

The service models in Integrated Services and the service model in the ATM networks have many similarities. The mapping between the two is relatively straightforward (Table 2.9). Guaranteed service shares many characteristics with the CBR (constant bit rate) and rt-VBR (real-time variable bit rate) classes. Controlled load service is closer to the nrt-VBR (non-real-time variable bit rate) or ABR (available bit rate) classes. The best-effort traffic can be mapped to the UBR (unspecified bit rate) classes.

The ATM traffic management specification also makes use of the token bucket parameters. Thus the peak rate, token rate, and maximum burst size in TSpec can be easily mapped to the corresponding parameters in ATM: PCR (peak cell rate), SCR (sustained cell rate), and MBS (maximum burst size).

Since ATM PVCs emulate dedicated point-to-point circuits in a network, RSVP should be able to operate normally by treating ATM PVCs as point-to-point links. However, the service models of the PVCs

Table 2.9	Mapping of Integrated Services and ATM service classes
Integrated services	**ATM service class**
Guaranteed service	CBR or rt-VBR
Controlled load service	nrt-VBR or ABR
Best effort	UBR

must be consistent with the Integrated Services. RSVP can also be mapped to ATM SVCs, although it is less straightforward. The ingress node of an ATM network must be able to find the egress node appropriate for the RSVP connection and set up an SVC from the ingress to the egress so that RSVP can traverse the ATM network toward the final destination.

Major differences exist in how ATM and RSVP set up reservations. ATM is sender oriented, and RVSP is receiver oriented. But since RSVP actually includes the sender's TSpec in the PATH message toward the receivers, the ingress of the ATM network can use the TSpec to set up a connection across the ATM network. When the RESV message comes back from the receivers, it can use the ATM connection that was already established during the processing of the PATH message.

2.9 Summary

The Integrated Services architecture developed a framework, new service models, the RSVP protocol, and a set of mechanisms so that applications can make resource reservations in the Internet. Guaranteed service provides deterministic bandwidth assurance and delay bound for applications that require stringent resource commitments, and controlled load service is designed for adaptive applications that can tolerate some degree of delay variation.

RSVP is a receiver-oriented reservation protocol for setting up resource reservations in the Internet. The sender describes the characteristics of the traffic source in the PATH message to the receivers, and the receivers make a reservation by sending the RESV message backward to the sender. RSVP is based on the soft-state approach, and the reservation must be refreshed periodically.

To implement Integrated Services in the Internet, routers must support flow identification and packet scheduling. A packet classifier maps each incoming packet to the corresponding entry in the reservation table, and the packet scheduler is responsible for enforcing resource allocation. WFQ is a class of scheduling algorithms that support bandwidth allocation and delay bound. Many variants of WFQ have been developed for high-speed implementation.

Further Reading

The following two papers give an excellent discussion on the rationale and architecture of Integrated Services:

Braden, R., D. Clark, and S. Shenker. "Integrated Services in the Internet Architecture: An Overview." RFC 1633, Internet Engineering Task Force, June 1994.

Clark, D., S. Shenker, and L. Zhang. "Supporting Real-Time Applications in an Integrated Services Packet Network: Architecture and Mechanism." Proc. of ACM SIGCOMM'92, August 1992.

A good overview of the RSVP protocol and design considerations can be found in

Zhang, L., S. Deering, D. Estrin, S. Shenker, and D. Zappala. "RSVP: A New Resource Reservation Protocol." *IEEE Network,* 7 (September 1993).

A wealth of material exists on packet scheduling. For a more comprehensive discussion on the subject, we recommend the following two theses:

Parekh, A. K. "A Generalized Processor Sharing Approach to Flow Control in Integrated Services Networks." Ph.D. diss., Massachusetts Institute of Technology, 1992.

Stiliadis, D. "Traffic Scheduling in Packet Switched Networks: Analysis, Design and Implementation." Ph.D. diss., UC Santa Cruz, 1996.

The full details of the scheduling algorithms described in this chapter can be found in the following papers:

Bennett, J. C. R., and H. Zhang. "WF2Q: Worst-Case Fair Weighted Fair Queueing." Proc. of IEEE INFOCOM '96, March 1996.

Kalmanek, C. R., H. Kanakia, and S. Keshav. "Rate Controlled Servers for Very High Speed Networks." Proc. of IEEE Globecom'90, December 1990.

Golestani, S. J. "A Self-Clocked Fair Queueing Scheme for Broadband Applications." Proc. of IEEE INFOCOM'94, June 1994.

Parekh, A. K., and G. R. Gallager. "A Generalized Processor Sharing Approach to Flow Control—The Single Node Case." Proc. of IEEE INFOCOM'92, April 1992.

Shreedhar, M., and G. Varghese. "Efficient Fair Queueing Using Deficit Round Robin." Proc. of ACM SIGCOMM'95, September 1995.

For a good overview of router architectures and mechanisms, we recommend:

Kumar, V. P., T. V. Lakshman, and D. Stiliadis. "Beyond Best Effort: Router Architectures for the Differentiated Services of Tomorrow's Internet." *IEEE Communications,* 36, no. 5 (May 1998).

The following is a list of Internet standards related to Integrated Services and the RSVP protocol:

RFC 2215, General Characterization Parameters for Integrated Service Network Elements (Standard Track). Defines a set of general control and characterization parameters for network elements supporting the Integrated Services framework.

RFC 2212, Specification of Guaranteed Quality of Service (Standard Track). Specifies the network element behavior required to support guaranteed service.

RFC 2211, Specification of the Controlled-Load Network Element Service (Standard Track). Specifies the network element behavior required to support controlled-load service.

RFC 2216, Network Element Service Specification Template (Informational). Defines a framework for specifying services provided by network elements and available to applications.

RFC 2205, Resource ReSerVation Protocol (RSVP)—Version 1 Functional Specification (Standard Track). Specifies version 1 of the RSVP protocol.

RFC 2209, Resource ReSerVation Protocol (RSVP)—Version 1 Message Processing Rules (Informational). An algorithmic description of the rules used by an RSVP implementation for processing messages.

RFC 2210, The Use of RSVP with IETF Integrated Services (Standard Track). Describes the use of the RSVP protocol with controlled-load and guaranteed service.

RFC 2208, Resource ReSerVation Protocol (RSVP)—Version 1 Applicability Statement—Some Guidelines on Deployment (Informational). Describes the applicability of RSVP along with the Integrated Services protocols and other components of resource reservation and offers guidelines for deployment of resource reservation.

RFC 2815, Integrated Service Mappings on IEEE 802 Networks (Standard Track). Describes mappings of IETF Integrated Services over IEEE 802 LANs and describes parameter mappings for supporting controlled load and guaranteed service using the inherent capabilities of relevant IEEE 802 technologies.

RFC 2382, A Framework for Integrated Services and RSVP over ATM (Informational). Outlines the issues and framework related to providing IP Integrated Services with RSVP over ATM networks.

3

Differentiated Services

3.1 Introduction

The Differentiated Services architecture was developed in response to the need for relatively simple, coarse methods of providing different levels of service for Internet traffic, to support various types of applications and specific business requirements. The Differentiated Services approach to supporting QoS capabilities in the Internet employs a small, well-defined set of building blocks from which a variety of aggregate behaviors can be built.

The Differentiated Services architecture differs from that of Integrated Services in many respects. The Integrated Services architecture allocates resources to individual flows, whereas the Differentiated Services model divides the traffic into a small number of classes and allocates resources on a per-class basis. The Differentiated Services approach offers a simpler solution from the viewpoint of implementation and deployment. The core of a Differentiated Services network must distinguish a small number of forwarding classes rather than individual flows. The forwarding classes can be directly carried in the packet header; no resource reservation setup is required. In addition, complex per-flow classification and scheduling used in Integrated Services, which have caused scalability concerns, are no longer needed.

In this chapter we present the architecture and mechanisms of Differentiated Services. In Section 3.2 we describe the main concepts and the overall architecture of Differentiated Services and explain the key differences between Differentiated Services and Integrated Services. We then move on in Section 3.3 to the standard for encoding forwarding behaviors in a packet header. Section 3.4 discusses the traffic classification and conditioning functions at the edge of a Differentiated Services network. The two standardized forwarding behaviors are described Sections 3.5 and 3.6, followed by a discussion on interoperability issues in Section 3.7. We then look at the mechanisms and algorithms for implementing Differentiated Services. Section 3.8 discusses the algorithms for classifying packets based on a set of rules, and Section 3.9 describes the token bucket traffic-policing mechanism. Finally we discuss end-to-end resource allocation architecture in Section 3.10 and some performance issues with Differentiated Services in Section 3.11.

3.2 Differentiated Services Framework

In this section we first examine the basic principles behind Differentiated Services and contrast them with those of Integrated Services. We then discuss the important concepts in some detail.

3.2.1 Basic Approach

The best-effort model and the Integrated Services architecture represent two extremes of the resource allocation spectrum: the best-effort model works on a per-packet basis, whereas the Integrated Services architecture deals with individual flows. The Differentiated Services approach lies somewhere in between these two extremes; it tries to take one small step further from the best-effort model to offer a "better than best-effort" service.

With Differentiated Services (DS), traffic is divided into a small number of groups called *forwarding classes*. The forwarding class that a packet belongs to is encoded into a field in the IP packet header. Each forwarding class represents a predefined forwarding treatment in terms of drop priority and bandwidth allocation.

In a Differentiated Services network, the nodes at the boundary of the network (boundary nodes or edge nodes) and nodes inside the network (interior nodes or core nodes) have different responsibilities (Figure 3.1). When traffic arrives at the boundary of two administrative domains, the boundary node performs two basic tasks: packet classification and traffic conditioning. They include mapping packets to different forwarding classes, checking whether the traffic flows meet the service agreements, and dropping nonconformant packets. Within the interior of the network, packets are forwarded based solely on the forwarding classes in the packet header.

The approach that Differentiated Services uses for resource allocation is quite different from that of Integrated Services. Let us look at the basic principles behind Differentiated Services and compare them to those in Integrated Services.

○ **Resource allocation to aggregated traffic rather than individual flows.** In Differentiated Services, resources are allocated to individual classes that represent aggregated traffic. The performance assurance to individual flows in a forwarding class is provided through prioritization and provisioning rather than per-flow reservation. The Integrated Services approach allocates resources to individual flows, which can run into tens of thousands in a large network.

○ **Traffic policing on the edge and class-based forwarding in the core.** In Differentiated Services, only boundary nodes at the edge of the network classify traffic and mark packets. Once the packets are

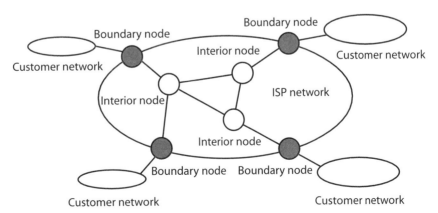

Figure 3.1   Boundary and interior nodes.

marked, the interior nodes use the forwarding classes encoded in the packet header to determine the treatment of the packets. Integrated Services, in contrast, requires all nodes to perform packet classification to identify packets from reserved flows and schedule them with per-flow queuing.

○ **Define forwarding behaviors not services.** The Differentiated Services standards define forwarding treatments, not end-to-end services. Each forwarding class represents a treatment rather than a service. The services, however, can be constructed by combining forwarding classes and admission control. The Integrated Services model takes the opposite approach: it defines services; for example, the guaranteed service and the controlled load service. The treatment of packets is not part of the standards, although some reference models are given.

○ **Guarantee by provisioning rather than reservation.** Differentiated Services provides resource assurance through provisioning combined with prioritization rather than per-flow reservation, as in Integrated Services. By allocating resources to forwarding classes and controlling the amount of traffic for these classes, Differentiated Services creates different levels of services and resource assurance but not absolute bandwidth guarantees or delay bounds for individual flows.

○ **Emphasis on service level agreements rather than dynamic signaling.** The purpose of Differentiated Services is to ensure that the service level agreements (SLAs) between customers and service providers are honored. SLAs are typically long-term contracts and can be enforced by the boundary nodes that connect customers to service providers. In Integrated Services, applications set up resource reservation on demand using the RSVP protocol. This dynamic reservation requires more support infrastructure, such as authentication and billing in the network.

○ **Focus on a single domain vs. end to end.** The deployment of Differentiated Services in the Internet can be incremental. Forwarding classes can be defined for a single domain, and between different domains service providers may extend or map their definitions through bilateral agreements. The Integrated Services model is inherently end to end. The resource reservation for a particular flow will fail if some part of the path does not support Integrated Services.

3.2.2 Service and Forwarding Treatment

Service and forwarding treatment are two important concepts in the Differentiated Services architecture. The difference between them is quite subtle, and people often confuse them. In the Differentiated Service context, *forwarding treatment* refers to the externally observable behavior of a specific algorithm or mechanism that is implemented in a node. In contrast, *service* is defined by the overall performance that a customer's traffic receives.

Services and forwarding treatments are not the same but are closely related. Let us illustrate the difference with an example. Priority queuing is a common mechanism that allows higher-priority packets to get transmitted before packets with lower priority. Let us call this forwarding treatment for the packets with higher priority *express forwarding*. Express forwarding is a treatment, not a service. This forwarding treatment, however, can be used to construct services. For example, suppose that we define a service called *no-loss service*, which guarantees no packet losses for the customers of this service. The no-loss service can be implemented with the express forwarding by assigning high priority to the packets from the customers using the no-loss service. However, the express forwarding alone is not sufficient to guarantee the no-loss service. If too many high-priority packets arrive at a link, they will also be dropped. The no-loss service must be constructed with proper admission control to limit the amount of traffic in the no-loss service.

A service and a forwarding treatment do not necessarily have a one-to-one mapping. Typically there are multiple ways of implementing a service with different forwarding treatments. For example, it is possible, at least in theory, to implement the no-loss service with First Come First Serve (FCFS) queuing. To do that, all traffic into the network must be limited to a very small percentage of the link bandwidth so that the network is always highly loaded. This is, of course, much more difficult to implement than the approach we described using express forwarding. Thus services constructed with different forwarding treatments may result in different provisioning, admission control, and efficiency. For the no-loss service implemented with FCFS, the network must be provisioned so that in the worst case resources are sufficient to meet all traffic demands. In contrast, when the no-loss service is implemented with express forwarding, the network must only be provisioned to accommodate all high-priority traffic; the low-priority traffic can fill in the gaps of the traffic demands.

Services tend to change over time, whereas forwarding treatments are relatively stable. The merit of a service cannot be judged purely from a technical perspective; the success of a service in the marketplace depends on many business-related factors, such as marketing, usability, pricing, and cost. Services must evolve as the market and the competition landscape change. In contrast, forwarding treatments are implemented in products; they cannot be easily changed. In addition, the actions that a node can do to a packet are limited and typically involve marking, dropping, or reordering. To sum up, forwarding treatments are the underlying mechanisms for creating services.

3.2.3 Per-Hop Behaviors (PHBs)

In Differentiated Services, externally observable forwarding treatments at a single node are described by the term *per-hop behavior* (PHB). Each PHB is represented by a 6-bit value called a *Differentiated Services codepoint* (DSCP). All packets with the same codepoint are referred to as a *behavior aggregate*, and they receive the same forwarding treatment.

In the Differentiated Services architecture, PHBs are used as the basic building blocks for resource allocation to different behavior aggregates. Distinctive forwarding treatments can be observed when different behavior aggregates compete for resources at a node. End-to-end services can be constructed by combining PHBs with traffic conditioning and network provisioning.

PHBs may describe the forwarding treatments in either relative or absolute terms. For example, PHBs may be specified in terms of guaranteed minimal bandwidth for a behavior aggregate. An example of PHBs with relative forwarding treatments is a PHB that allocates link bandwidth proportionally.

A set of PHBs may form a *PHB group*. A PHB group must be defined meaningfully and implemented simultaneously as a group that shares a common constraint. A PHB group may describe resource allocation in relative terms among themselves in terms of bandwidth allocation and drop priority. For example, a PHB group may be defined as a set of drop priorities for each PHB in the group. A single PHB may be viewed as a special case of a PHB group. When multiple PHB groups coexist in the same DS domain, it is necessary to specify the interaction and relationship among them.

PHBs are typically implemented by means of buffer management and packet scheduling. Although many PHBs are closely associated with certain well-known mechanisms (such as WFQ), the definition of PHBs is meant to be a more generic description of forwarding treatments rather than the specifics of the implementation. For a particular PHB, a variety of implementation mechanisms may be used to achieve the same desired forwarding treatment.

3.2.4 Services

A *service* describes the overall treatment of a customer's traffic within a DS domain or end to end. Services are what is visible to customers, whereas PHBs are hidden inside the network elements. Creating a service requires that many components work together: mapping of traffic to specific PHBs, traffic conditioning at the boundary nodes, network provisioning, and PHB-based forwarding in the interior of the network.

In the Differentiated Services architecture, services are defined in the form of a *Service Level Agreement* (SLA) between a customer and its service provider. An SLA specifies the details of services to be provided to the customer. One of the important elements in an SLA in terms of Differentiated Services is the *traffic conditioning agreement* (TCA). The TCA details the service parameters for traffic profiles and policing actions. These may include

○ Traffic profiles, such as token bucket parameters for each of the classes
○ Performance metrics, such as throughput, delay, and drop priorities
○ Actions for nonconformant packets
○ Additional marking and shaping services provided by the service provider

In addition to the TCA, an SLA may also contain other service characteristics and business-related agreements such as availability, security, monitoring, auditing, accounting, pricing, and billing.

SLAs may be static or dynamic. Most SLAs are negotiated between customers and service providers before the services are started, with only occasional changes from time to time. SLAs can also be dynamically changed and renegotiated. For example, a customer may want to request additional bandwidth for special events or for special traffic flows. Such dynamic SLAs require management systems that can automate these changes and negotiations based on agreed policies and rules.

Services can be defined in either quantitative or qualitative terms. Quantitative services specify the parameters in absolute terms; for example, minimum bandwidth. Qualitative services typically use relative terms, such as lower delay or higher-loss probability.

Services may have different scopes:

○ All traffic from ingress node A and any egress nodes
○ All traffic between ingress node A and egress node B
○ All traffic from ingress node A to a set of egress nodes

Note that the egress node may or may not be in the same domain as the ingress node. If the egress point is in a different domain, the ingress provider needs to negotiate an SLA with the service provider that the egress node is connected to so that the service offered can be extended to the egress node.

In general, service definition applies only to the outgoing traffic from a customer to its service provider, that is, from an ingress point to multiple egress points. A special case of service scope is a service that covers incoming traffic from a service provider to a customer's network. Such services are desirable in many cases but are more difficult to implement. When the traffic goes from a customer into a service provider, the node that the customer network is connected to is responsible for policing the traffic to enforce the SLA specification. However, when the traffic is coming from the service provider to the customer, the network has to figure out which customer the traffic is destined for. For IP-based networks, this requires complicated classification. In addition, to police the traffic coming to a customer, the traffic profile must be stored at any point that the traffic may enter the service provider's network. If there are multiple entry points, a traffic profile must be divided for each of them.

3.3 Differentiated Services Field

The Differentiated Services approach uses 6 bits in the IP packet header to encode the forwarding treatment. We now describe the Internet standards that define the Differentiated Services field.

3.3.1 Structure of DS Field

The current IP packet header includes an 8-bit field called the *IP TOS field*. It is composed of a 3-bit precedence, a 3-bit type of service (TOS), and 2 unused bits that must be zero (Figure 3.2). The precedence bits represent the priorities for the traffic, whereas the TOS bits indicate the preference for throughput, delay, and loss (Table 3.1).

The Differentiated Services standard redefines the existing IP TOS field to indicate forwarding behaviors. The replacement field, called the *DS field*, supersedes the existing definitions of the TOS octet and also the IPv6 traffic class octet. The first 6 bits of the DS field are used

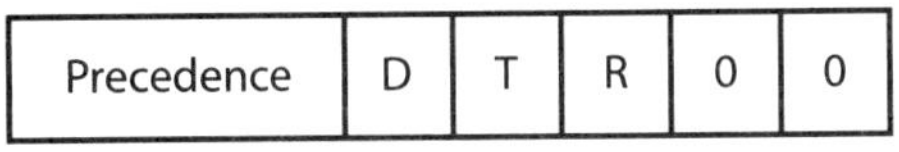

Precedence	D	T	R	0	0

Figure 3.2 IP TOS field.

Table 3.1	IP TOS field definition
Bit	**Description**
0–2	Precedence
3	0 = Normal delay 1 = Low delay
4	0 = Normal throughput 1 = High throughput
5	0 = Normal reliability 1 = High reliability
6–7	Reserved for future use

as a DSCP to encode the PHB for a packet at each DS node (Figure 3.3). The remaining 2 bits are currently unused (CU). The DSCP should be treated as an index, and the mapping of DSCPs to PHBs must be configurable.

We use the notation <xxxxxx> to represent the 6 bits of a DSCP value. The leftmost bit signifies bit 0 of the DS field, and the rightmost bit signifies bit 5. The DS field can have at most 64 distinct values. Considerable debate took place on the allocation of these codepoints. Some people proposed to have one set of globally unique PHBs and its corresponding codepoints; others argued that flexibility should be built into the allocation so that new and experimental PHBs and codepoints could be added in an incremental fashion. The final decision was to divided the space into three pools for the purpose of codepoint assignment and management: a pool of 32 recommended codepoints (pool 1) to be standardized, a pool of 16 codepoints (pool 2) to be reserved for experimental or local use, and a pool of 16 codepoints (pool 3) that are available for experimental and local use but may be subject to standardization if pool 1 is ever exhausted (Table 3.2).

DSCP	CU

Figure 3.3 DS field.

Table 3.2   Codepoint allocation

Pool	Codepoint space	Assignment policy
1	xxxxx0	Standards action
2	xxxx11	Experimental and local use
3	xxxx01	Experimental and local use but may be subject to standards action

3.3.2 Historical Codepoint Definition

Although the IP Type of Service (TOS) field was defined in the original IP specifications, few applications actually make use of them. Some vendors, however, do use the precedence field (the first 3 bits) for filtering control traffic; for example, routing updates and giving them higher priorities. The allocation of the DSCP values provides some limited backward compatibility with the current best-effort forwarding and the use of the precedence field for control traffic.

Default PHB Codepoint

The default PHB is defined for backward compatibility with the current best-effort forwarding treatment. All DS-compliant nodes must support the default PHB. Packets belonging to the default forwarding class may be sent into a network without any policing, and the network will try to deliver as many of these packets as possible and as soon as possible. In general, packets in other forwarding classes have higher priorities to network resources than the packets in the default forwarding class. However, some minimal bandwidth must be reserved for the default forwarding class so that the packets in this class are not completely starved. Any packets sent out by senders that do not support Differentiated Services today receive default forwarding treatment. The special codepoint <000000> is assigned to the default PHB, which is compatible with existing practice.

Class Selector Codepoints

To maintain partial backward compatibility with known current use of the IP precedence field, Differentiated Services has specified a set of PHBs that are compatible with current common practice. This set of PHBs is referred to as *class selector* PHBs. In addition, the codepoints <xxx000> are reserved as the class selector codepoints that must meet the requirements of the class selector PHBs. Other codepoints may also be mapped to the class selector PHBs, but they must meet the class selector requirements:

❍ The eight class selector PHBs must yield at least two different forwarding classes. Any implementation therefore must have at least two forwarding treatments that meet the requirements.

❍ The PHB mapped by a codepoint with the larger numerical value should receive better or equal forwarding treatment than the one with a lower numerical value. For example, packets with codepoint <100000> should be treated better than (or at least equally to) packets with codepoint <010000>.

○ PHBs selected by codepoints <111000> or <110000> must receive preferential forwarding treatment over the default PHB <000000> to preserve the common use of IP precedence value 110 and 111 for routing traffic.

○ Each PHB can be independently forwarded, and so packet ordering may not be maintained between different PHB forwarding classes.

The class selector PHBs are in essence eight forwarding classes with descending levels of treatments. They can be implemented with priority queuing or some form of WFQ with different weights. Although this set of PHBs is specified for maintaining backward compatibility with current practice, they may also be used for constructing other services that require different forwarding behaviors.

3.3.3 Current Codepoint Allocation

Apart from the default PHB codepoint and the class selector codepoints, two new PHBs, assured forwarding (AF) and expedited forwarding (EF), have been standardized; the codepoints for them are allocated from the standard action space. The AF and EF PHBs will be discussed in detail in Sections 3.5 and 3.6. We summarize the current codepoint allocation in Table 3.3.

Table 3.3	Current codepoint allocation
DSCP	**PHB**
000 000	CS0 (DE)
000 001	EXP/LU
000 010	-
000 011	EXP/LU
000 100	-
000 101	EXP/LU
000 110	-
000 111	EXP/LU

Table 3.3 *(continued)*

001 000	CS1
001 001	EXP/LU
001 010	AF11
001 011	EXP/LU
001 100	AF12
001 101	EXP/LU
001 110	AF13
001 111	EXP/LU
010 000	CS2
010 001	EXP/LU
010 010	AF21
010 011	EXP/LU
010 100	AF22
010 101	EXP/LU
010 110	AF23
010 111	EXP/LU
011 000	CS3
011 001	EXP/LU
011 010	AF31
011 011	EXP/LU
011 100	AF32
011 101	EXP/LU
011 110	AF33
011 111	EXP/LU
100 000	CS4
100 001	EXP/LU
100 010	AF41
100 011	EXP/LU
100 100	AF42
100 101	EXP/LU
100 110	AF43
100 111	EXP/LU

(continued)

Table 3.3 *(continued)*

DSCP	PHB
101 000	CS5
101 001	EXP/LU
101 010	-
101 011	EXP/LU
101 100	-
101 101	EXP/LU
101 110	EF
101 111	EXP/LU
110 000	CS6
110 001	EXP/LU
110 010	-
110 011	EXP/LU
110 100	-
110 101	EXP/LU
110 110	-
110 111	EXP/LU
111 000	CS7
111 001	EXP/LU
111 010	-
111 011	EXP/LU
111 100	-
111 101	EXP/LU
111 110	-
111 111	EXP/LU

AFxy: Assured Forwarding PHB (class x, drop precedence y)
CSx: Class Selector PHB x
DE: Default PHB (CS0)
EF: Expedited Forwarding PHB
EXP/LU: Experimental/local use

3.4 Traffic Classification and Conditioning

In Differentiated Services, boundary nodes are responsible for mapping packets to one of the forwarding classes supported in the network, and they must ensure that the traffic conforms to the SLA for the specific customer. Once the packets pass the boundary nodes into the interior of the network, resource allocation is performed based solely on forwarding classes.

These functions that boundary nodes perform are often referred to as *traffic classification* and *traffic conditioning* (Figure 3.4). The classification module contains a classifier and a marker. The classifier selects packets based on some predefined rules. These classification rules may specify that a selected packet be marked with a particular codepoint. The output of the classification module is then steered to the traffic-conditioning module.

The boundary nodes translate the TCA into a *traffic profile* for each customer that they are directly connected to. The traffic profile specifies the temporal properties of the traffic stream from a customer in terms of traffic-conditioning parameters and provides a set of rules for determining whether a particular packet is considered within the specified profile or not. The traffic-conditioning module measures the traffic streams from the classification module and compares them against the customers' traffic profiles. For example, suppose a traffic profile specifies that traffic from a particular customer should conform to a token bucket with rate r and burst size b. The meter uses this traffic profile to measure the traffic from the customer. When the traffic stream is within the profile, the packets will be allowed to enter the network. If the customer sends more packets than allowed, actions will be taken to ensure that traffic flow is fully consistent with the traffic profile.

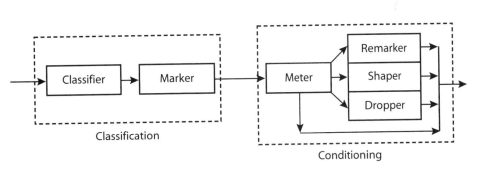

Figure 3.4 Classification and conditioning.

3.4.1 Classifier

A classifier divides an incoming packet stream into multiple groups based on predefined rules. There are two basic types of classifiers: *behavior aggregate* (BA) or *multifield* (MF). The simplest Differentiated Services classifier is the BA classifier. A BA classifier selects packets based solely on the DSCP values in the packet header. BA classifiers are generally used when the DSCP has been set (also referred to as marked) before the packet reaches the classifiers.

The DSCP value of a packet can be marked in many different ways. If the customer's network supports Differentiated Services, it is desirable for the packets to be marked by the source or the first-hop router on the LAN. Only the customer knows how the packets should be treated in the network and will mark the packets consistently with the customer's resource allocation polices. However, many customer networks are expected to be unable to perform these markings at an early stage of deployment. Such customers may use services provided by their service providers to mark the packets.

The MF classifier uses a combination of one or more fields of the five-tuple (source address, destination address, source port, destination port, and protocol ID) in the packet header for classification. It can be used to support more complicated resource allocation policies from customers. For example:

○ Marking packets based on the application types (port numbers), such as TELNET or FTP
○ Marking packets based on particular source and destination addresses or network prefixes, such as CEO's traffic or some mission-critical servers
○ Marking packets based on the *t*-tuple that determines an application flow, such as a video stream

The classification policies may specify a set of rules and the corresponding DSCP values for marking the matched packets. The MF classifier can be very versatile in expressing resource allocation policies. However, multifield classification is in essence a multidimensional, difficult matching problem. We will discuss some classification schemes in detail in Section 3.8. A BA classifier is much simpler: it can be implemented as a direct lookup based on DSCP values. Once the classification is done, the classifier sends the packets to the traffic conditioner for further processing.

3.4.2 Traffic Conditioner

Traffic conditioners perform traffic-policing functions to enforce the TCA between customers and service providers. A traffic conditioner consists of four basic elements: meter, marker, shaper, and dropper. The meter monitors and measures the traffic streams; marking, shaping, and dropping are actions that can be taken on nonconformant packets.

Meter

For each forwarding class a *meter* measures the traffic flow from a customer against its traffic profile. The in-profile packets are allowed to enter the network, while the out-of-profile packets are further conditioned based on the TCS. The actions that a traffic conditioner may take include shaping, marking, and dropping. Since traffic profiles are typically described in terms of token bucket parameters, most meters are implemented as token buckets. We will discuss the implementation of a meter using a dual token bucket in Section 3.9.

Marker

Markers set the DS field of a packet to a particular DSCP, adding the marked packet to the forwarding class. Markers may act on unmarked packets or remark previously marked packets. Marking may occur at many different locations. If the customer networks support Differentiated Services marking, packets can be marked by the applications or the first-hop routers on LAN. The boundary nodes of a service provider may also mark packets on behalf of the customers. Such marking is often associated with an MF classifier.

Marking is also one of the actions that can be taken on nonconformant packets. When a traffic stream passes a meter, some packets may be marked with a special DSCP to indicate their nonconformance. These packets should be dropped first if the network experiences congestion.

Since packets may pass many different domains, packets that have been previously marked may be remarked. When a packet stream violates traffic profiles at any administrative boundary, packets may be remarked to a different DSCP. Remarking is also necessary at the boundary of two administrative domains that use different DSCPs. The DSCPs must be translated when the packet crosses the domain boundary.

When a packet remarked with DSCP receives worse forwarding treatment than from the previous DSCP, this is referred to as *PHB demotion*. If the new DSCP represents a better forwarding treatment than the previous one, it is referred to as *PHB promotion*. Typically boundary nodes demote out-of-profile packets to a DSCP with worse forwarding treatment.

Shaper

Shapers delay the nonconformant packets in order to bring the stream into compliance with the agreed-on traffic profile. The difference between a shaper and a marker is that a marker simply marks a packet and lets it into the network whereas a shaper prevents the packet from entering the network until the stream conforms to the traffic profile. Thus shaping is a much stronger form of policing than marking. For some services strict admission control is necessary; shaping ensures that excessive packets are not allowed into the network.

Shaping may also be needed at a boundary node to a different domain. Traffic profiles tend to change when packets traverse the network. The egress node may need to shape the outgoing traffic stream so that it conforms to the appropriate traffic profile for the next domain.

Dropper

Dropping is another action that may be applied to out-of-profile packets. Compared with shaping, which must buffer packets temporarily, dropping is much easier to implement. Since a shaper has a finite-size buffer, it also drops packets when the buffer overflows.

3.4.3   Location of Traffic Classifiers and Conditioners

Traffic classifiers and conditioners are usually situated with DS ingress and egress nodes where traffic goes across domains. They may also be present within the interior of a DS domain or within a non-DS-capable domain.

Within a Source Domain

The *source domain* is the domain where a packet originates. Traffic sources and intermediate nodes within the source domain may also perform classification and marking before the packets leave the source domain. This is referred to as *premarking* to distinguish it from the marking done by boundary nodes.

Premarking allows the source domain to classify packets based on local polices. For example, a corporation may have a policy that traffic from hosts (such as a CEO's PC, or mission-critical servers) should receive better treatment. This can be done by marking the packets within the hosts. Alternatively, the first-hop routers from these hosts can classify and mark them with an appropriate codepoint. In addition, the traffic may be conditioned to limit the amount of high-priority traffic.

Another advantage of premarking is that classification is much simpler before the traffic has merged with packets from other sources. Also, since the classification is done in a distributed fashion, the number of classification rules is typically small and manageable.

Since premarking may be distributed across multiple nodes, the source domain should ensure that the aggregate of each forwarding class conforms to the TCS. Some additional mechanisms for allocating resources within the source domain may be needed to facilitate dynamic allocation. We will come back to this issue later in this chapter (Section 3.10.1) when we discuss the Internet working between Integrated Services and Differentiated Services.

At the Boundary of a DS Domain

Traffic streams may be classified, marked, and conditioned at the boundary of two domains (the DS egress node of the upstream domain or the DS ingress node of the downstream domain). The SLA may specify which domain is responsible for marking the packets with appropriate DS codepoints. However, a DS ingress node must assume that the incoming traffic may not conform to the TCS and must be prepared to enforce the TCS.

If the upstream domain is not capable of classification and marking, the ingress node of the downstream domain must perform all necessary classification and conditioning. ISPs may also offer such value-added services to customers who want to outsource the classification and marking to their ISP. To support such services, the ingress node connecting to the customers may need to do complex MF classification.

If two domains use different codepoints for a PHB, any premarked packets must be remarked at the boundary. Either the egress node of the upstream domain or the ingress node of the downstream domain may perform the mapping.

In Interior DS Nodes

Although classification and conditioning are typically done at the boundary of the network, these functions are not precluded in the interior of a DS domain. For example, at some heavily congested hot spots, additional traffic policing may be applied or the traffic may be shaped at some points to ensure arrival patterns. In general, however, such use should be limited to special handling, and other services should not be affected.

3.4.4   Configuring Traffic Classifiers and Conditioners

Most configuration information is specified in the TCS for a customer. In a simple case where an interface is dedicated to a single customer, the configuration information applies to all traffic arriving at the interface. If multiple customers share the same interface, the classifier must be able to identify which customer a packet comes from and selects the corresponding TCS to use.

The classifier should be configured with a set of rules and associated actions. The rules may contain a list of fields from the packet header (source address, destination, source port, destination port, protocol ID, and DS field) and additional information such as the incoming logical interface ID. The actions may include the marking of the packet with a particular DSCP, the selection of a traffic conditioner for the packet, and the allocation of bandwidth for a forwarding class.

The configuration information for the traffic conditioner includes the traffic profile for the meter and the actions for the in-profile and out-of-profile packets. Typically token bucket parameters are used to describe traffic profiles.

3.5   Assured Forwarding

The AF PHB group is one of the two PHB groups that have been standardized by the IETF.

3.5.1 AF PHB Group

The basic idea behind AF came from the RIO scheme [CLARK98], one of the early proposals that influenced the Differentiated Services work. In the RIO framework a service profile specifies the *expected capacity* for the user. The boundary nodes monitor the traffic flows and tag the packets as being *in* or *out* of their profiles. During congestion the packets tagged as *out* will be dropped first. In essence, the *in/out* bit indicates drop priorities. The service providers should provision their networks to meet the expected capacities for all in-profile packets and allow out-of-profile packets only when excessive bandwidth is available.

The AF standard extended the basic *in* or *out* marking in RIO into a structure of four *forwarding classes* and, within each forwarding class, three *drop precedences*. Each forwarding class is allocated a minimum amount of buffers and bandwidth. Customers can subscribe to the services built with AF forwarding classes and their packets will be marked with the appropriate AF DSCPs.

The three drop priorities within each forwarding class are used to select which packets to drop during congestion. When backlogged packets from an AF forwarding class exceed a specified threshold, packets with the highest drop priority are dropped first and then packets with the lower drop priority. Drop priorities in AF are specific to the forwarding class; comparing two drop priorities in two different AF classes may not always be meaningful. For example, when a DS node starts to drop the packets with the highest drop priority in one forwarding class, the packets in other forwarding classes may not experience any packet dropping at all. Each forwarding class has its bandwidth allocation. Dropping takes place only in the forwarding class in which traffic exceeds its own resources.

A DS node must implement all four AF classes. For each AF class the minimum amount of forwarding resources (buffers and bandwidth) that are allocated to an AF class must be configurable. The bandwidth allocation must be guaranteed over both short and long time scales.

Although the AF standard does not specify how excessive bandwidth above the minimum allocation should be shared, implementations must describe the exact algorithm for allocation and configuration.

Within an AF class a DS must forward a packet in accordance with the drop priority of the packet. Any DS node must accept all three drop priorities and must implement at least two of the three drop priorities.

In general, a DS node may reorder packets of different AF classes but should not reorder packets with different drop priorities but in the same class. The boundary nodes should avoid splitting traffic from the same application flow into different classes since it will lead to packet reordering with a microflow.

The recommended codepoints for AF are listed in Table 3.4. The first 3 bits of the DS field encode the class. The next 2 bits encode the drop priorities. AF classes are sometimes represented in the form AFxy, where x is the forwarding class and y is the drop priority within the forwarding class.

3.5.2   Implementation Guideline

The AF PHB group can be implemented as a bandwidth partition between classes and drop priorities within a class. The bandwidth partition is specified in terms of minimum bandwidth, and so many different implementations are available. One common approach is to use variants of WFQ and assign weights according to minimum bandwidth requirements. Such implementations also distribute excessive bandwidth proportional to backlogged classes.

Let us look at an example. Suppose that we have four AF classes with a minimum bandwidth of 2, 4, 8, and 16 Mbits/sec, respectively. In order to meet the bandwidth guarantees, each link needs at least 30 Mbits/sec capacity available to the AF traffic. With WFQ-like implementations, the four AF classes can be mapped to four queues with weights of 1, 2, 4, and 8, respectively.

Table 3.4	AF PHB codepoints			
	Class 1	Class 2	Class 3	Class 4
Low drop precedence	001010	010010	011010	100010
Medium drop precedence	001100	010100	011100	100100
High drop precedence	001110	010110	011110	100110

The AF standard also specifies certain properties for the implementation of the drop mechanisms. First, an AF implementation must attempt to minimize long-term congestion while allowing short-term fluctuation. Some smoothing functions should be used to measure the long-term congestion level for the dropping decision. Second, the dropping mechanism must be insensitive to the short-term traffic characteristics and discard packets from flows of the same long-term characteristics with equal probability. One way to achieve this is to use some random function in the dropping. Third, the discard rate for a flow within a drop priority must be proportional to the flow's percentage of the total amount of traffic passing through that drop priority level. Finally, the level of discard must be gradual rather than abrupt in relation to the level of congestion. The AF specification allows many dropping implementations, including the Random Early Discard (RED) [CLARK98].

DS boundary nodes should condition traffic that enters the network for a specific AF class based on the provisioning requirement and the amount of resources allocated to the class. In the interior of a network, nodes must be able to dispatch the packets to the queue provisioned for the class using the first 3 bits of the DS field. The dropping mechanism must make use of the next 2 bits of the DS field in its dropping decision.

The recommended AF codepoint mappings do not interfere with the local use space or the class selector codepoints. A PHB group may coexist with other PHB groups. In particular, the default PHB with codepoint <000000> may remain for use with best-effort traffic. When the AF PHB group provides similar forwarding treatment to some of the class selector PHBs, it may be appropriate within a DS domain to use some or all of the class selector codepoints as aliases of AF codepoints.

The AF standard does not specify the exact relationship between the AF group and other implemented PHBs; it requires only that the relationship be configurable and the following aspects be documented:

○ **Any PHB groups that may preempt any AF PHB group.** Such preemption must not happen in normal network operation but may be appropriate under some unusual circumstances such as high volume of control traffic generated by network emergency handling.

○ **How excessive resources are allocated between the AF PHB group and other implemented PHBs.** For example, between the AF PHB group and the default PHB, all excessive bandwidth may be allocated to the default PHB once all AF requirements are fulfilled. Alternatively AF traffic may have priority over all resources and only the remaining resources can be used by the default PHB traffic.

3.5.3   Example Services

In a DS node the forwarding assurance that a packet receives depends on three factors:

○ The amount of resources allocated to the AF class
○ The amount of traffic admitted into the AF class
○ The drop priority of the packet

The first two factors determine the resource allocation between AF classes, and the third factor assigns internal priorities to the resource within an AF class. By combining the two levels of allocation, different services can be constructed.

The AF PHB group could be used to provide simple services based on drop priority, such as the expected bandwidth service, as outlined in RIO. A customer for the expected bandwidth service is assigned a traffic profile. The traffic profile specifies the amount of bandwidth the service provider is prepared to accept based on the subscription fee. At the boundary nodes of the network, a customer's traffic stream is measured against its traffic profile and marked as in profile and out of profile. The expected bandwidth service can be implemented with two codepoints for one of the four AF classes; for example, <001010> for in profile and <001100> for out of profile.

When the network is provisioned to accommodate all traffic of expected bandwidth from all customers under normal operation, a customer of this service can expect that all in-profile packets will have a high probability of being delivered within the network. In addition, during less busy periods some of the out-of-profile packets may get through. Typically most networks are not provisioned for the worst-case scenario since the cost of such provisioning can be prohibitively high in a large network. The expected bandwidth is not an absolute guarantee but rather an assurance based on past experience; the amount of bandwidth that a customer gets may be less than the expected bandwidth under unusual circumstances. In essence, the quality of the assurance is determined by the level of provisioning.

Another possible use of AF is to construct several services with different provisioning levels. For example, we can create a service with three service classes: bronze, silver, and gold, with different subscription fees. The three service classes can be mapped to three AF forwarding classes with different bandwidth allocation. The gold service class has the best provisioning in terms of the ratio between the amount of traffic allowed to this class and the amount of bandwidth reserved for it. Thus under normal operation, the load for the gold service class is always lower than that for the silver and bronze services. Packets within each class may be further separated by giving them different drop priorities.

3.6 Expedited Forwarding

In this section we describe EF PHB, which can be used to create low loss, low latency, and assured bandwidth services.

3.6.1 EF PHB

EF PHB was originally proposed to characterize a forwarding treatment similar to that of a simple priority queuing, but the formal definition in the standard is somehow ambiguous about this intention. EF PHB is defined as a forwarding treatment for a traffic aggregate where the departure rate of the aggregate's packet from any DS node must equal or exceed a configurable rate. The EF traffic should receive this rate independent of the intensity of any other traffic attempting to transit the node. We can argue that such a forwarding treatment also falls into the definition of an AF class. However, it is implicitly assumed that the EF traffic can preempt other traffic within a certain limit, thus providing a forwarding treatment for constructing low-delay and low-loss services. The codepoint <101110> is recommended for EF PHB.

3.6.2   Implementation Guideline

Several types of queue scheduling mechanisms may be employed to implement EF PHB. A simple approach is a priority-queuing scheme with a token bucket. The queue for the EF traffic must be the highest-priority queue in the system in order to preserve the properties of the EF treatment. The token bucket is there to limit the total amount of EF traffic so that other traffic will not be starved by bursts of EF traffic.

Another way to implement EF is to use a variant of WFQ and configure the weights in such a way that the EF traffic has relative priority. In a typical use of the WFQ schemes, the weight is proportional to the allocated bandwidth, referred to as *rate-proportional allocation*. For example, if flows A and B are allocated 1 Mbits/sec and 2 Mbits/sec, the weights for flow A and B in a WFQ system should have a ratio of 1/2. For a link with a capacity of 3 Mbits/sec or more, flows A and B will get a minimum of 1 Mbits/sec and 2 Mbits/sec bandwidth. However, the WFQ algorithm itself does not require rate-proportional allocation. In fact, non-rate-proportional allocation, although less well known, may be used to provide controlled priority at fine granularity. Suppose we assign a weight of 1 to both flows A and B; the ratio of weights is 1/1. If all conditions remain the same, flows A and B will be allocated 1.5 Mbits/sec, respectively. If flows A and B continue to send 1 Mbits/sec and 2 Mbits/sec of traffic over the link of 3 Mbits/sec, flows A and B will still get 1 Mbits/sec and 2 Mbits/sec bandwidth, respectively. The only difference is that flow A experiences a shorter delay than flow B. In other words, the queuing delay is reallocated while the bandwidth allocation remains unchanged. The reason is that the WFQ algorithm is a work-conserving scheme. The excessive bandwidth left by flow A will be consumed by flow B rather than wasted. Therefore, as long as the total amount of traffic is within the capacity of the link, the bandwidth allocation can be the same; the ratio of the weights indicates the priority and delay allocation.

It is possible to emulate simple priority queuing with non-rate-proportional allocation in WFQ. We can simply assign a very large weight for the queue that carries priority traffic; the resulting behavior is very close to that of simple priority queuing. As in the simple priority implementation of EF, the queue that has the largest weight should be rate limited to prevent starvation of other traffic.

3.7 Interoperability with Non-DS-Compliant Networks

A *non-DS-compliant node* is a node that does not implement some or all of the standardized PHBs. A special case of a non-DS-compliant node, which we call the *legacy node,* implements IPv4 Precedence classification and forwarding as defined in RFC791 and RFC1812 but is otherwise not DS compliant. The class selector codepoints were designed to maintain some backward compatibility with the precedence bits in the IP TOS field. Nodes that are non-DS compliant and are not legacy nodes may exhibit unpredictable forwarding behaviors for packets with nonzero DS codepoints. Differentiated Services depends on the resource allocation mechanisms provided by per-hop behavior implementations in nodes. The level of assurance for the service may break down in the event that traffic transits a non-DS-compliant node or a non-DS-capable domain.

3.7.1 Non-DS-Compliant Node within a DS Domain

During the initial deployment of Differentiated Services, non-DS-compliant nodes may be quite common within a DS domain. When the links connected to a non-DS-compliant node are lightly loaded, the worst-case packet delay, jitter, and loss may be negligible. In general, however, the lack of PHB forwarding in a node may make it impossible to offer low-delay, low-loss, or provisioned bandwidth services across paths that traverse the node.

The use of a legacy node may be acceptable if the DS domain restricts itself to using only the class selector codepoints and if the precedence implementation in the legacy node is compatible with the services offered along paths that traverse the node. Note that it is important to restrict the codepoints in use to the class selector codepoints since the legacy node may or may not interpret bits 3 to 5 in accordance with RFC1349, resulting in unpredictable forwarding results.

3.7.2 Transit Non-DS-Capable Domain

When a flow traverses several domains, some of the transit domains may be non-DS capable. If a non-DS-capable domain does not deploy traffic-conditioning functions on domain boundaries, even a domain that consists of legacy or DS-compliant interior nodes may not be able to deliver some types of services across the domain. A DS domain and a non-DS-capable domain may negotiate an agreement that governs how egress traffic from the DS domain should be marked before entry into the non-DS-capable domain. This agreement might be monitored for compliance by traffic sampling instead of by rigorous traffic conditioning. Alternatively, when the non-DS-capable domain consists of legacy nodes, the upstream DS domain may map the traffic to one or more of the class selector codepoints. Where there is no knowledge of the traffic management capabilities of the downstream domain and no agreement in place, a DS domain egress node may choose to remark DS codepoints to zero, under the assumption that the non-DS-capable domain will treat the traffic uniformly with best-effort service. In the event that a non-DS-capable domain peers with a DS domain, traffic flowing from the non-DS-capable domain should be conditioned at the DS ingress node of the DS domain according to the appropriate SLA or policy.

3.8   Packet Classification

In the preceding sections we have described the architecture and key components in Differentiated Services. In this section we look at the details of packet classification for supporting Differentiated Services.

3.8.1   Basic Requirements

Packet classification is the process of identifying packets based on specified rules (also referred to as *packet filtering*). It has been widely used in the Internet for security filtering and service differentiation. In Differentiated Services, packet classification is one of the key components that determines what forwarding class a packet belongs to. The classification is based on rules that can be specified by administrators to reflect policies for network operations and resource allocation. An example of classification rules is that packets from and to a mission-critical server must be identified and given a preferable forwarding treatment. Another rule could be that traffic of a particular application such as audio be put on a separate queue with guaranteed bandwidth. An example of packet classification used for security filtering would be that in most large enterprise networks, packets in and out typically go through a fire wall. A packet filter will allow only traffic from specified hosts or applications to pass the fire wall and block all other unauthorized access.

Packet classifiers must be able to identify packets by examining the fields in the packet headers; these fields typically include source address, destination address, source port, destination port, and protocol ID. The classification rules may apply to a whole range of addresses or port numbers and not just hosts or applications. For example, customers may want to block all packets from a specific network or to put all flows between a set of source and destination networks into a special queue with bandwidth guarantees. For packets that match a particular filtering rule, the classifier may apply the set of actions associated with the match. The range of actions that the classifier may take depends on the specific implementation. Examples of actions include discarding of packets, placing packets on a special queue with bandwidth provisioning, setting a buffer limit for matched packets, setting DS codepoints, and overriding destination-based routing decisions.

The classification algorithms must meet the speed and scalability requirements of large Internet backbones. In a typical Internet backbone today, there may be as many as 500 K flows over an OC12 trunk, and the number of filter rules can be in the thousands. Since the classification determines the resource allocation priority, it is important that the classification be performed at the speed of the interface. Because a packet will be identified as high priority after the classification stage, any queuing before the classifier may introduce unacceptable latency to high-priority traffic. To operate at very high speeds, the classification algorithm must be amenable to hardware implementation and have reasonable memory requirements.

When there are a large number of rules, a packet will likely match more than one rule. When there are multiple matches, the algorithm must allow arbitrary policies to select one match that is applicable to the packet. Priority levels can be assigned to the rules so that among all matches, the one with the highest priority is considered the best match.

Packet classification is somewhat related to the flow identification that we discussed in Chapter 2 (Section 2.6). Flow identification groups packets into flows based on the five-tuples in the packet headers; therefore it can be viewed as a special case of packet classification where the rules are a set of five-tuples. The packet classification we describe in this section is more generic in the sense that the rules can be expressed as a range of values; for example, IP address prefix. Such a range match is more expressive but requires more complex algorithms than the hashing-based schemes for flow identification.

3.8.2 Classification Algorithms

Packet classification is in essence a problem of multidimensional range match. Transitionally, caching has been used to speed up classification. Since a flow typically has a certain lifetime, we can expect that when a packet from a new flow arrives, more packets from the same flow will come shortly. In the caching approach the information about the flows that has been seen recently is kept in a cache. When a new packet arrives, the forwarding engine first checks with the cache to determine if it belongs to one of the flows in the cache. If the cache has the information for the flow, the packet will pass through this *fast path*. Otherwise the packet must be sent to the *slow path* for complete header examination and match, and then the information about the new flow is inserted into the cache.

The caching approach is sensitive to traffic patterns; thus the performance is not deterministic. In the worst case many packets may have to be processed by the slow path, which can cause temporary overload in the router. The queue formed as packets waiting to be processed in the slow path can lead to violation of QoS guarantees such as bandwidth and delay bounds. Therefore to provide deterministic QoS guarantees, the classifier must be able to process the packets at wirespeed independent of the traffic patterns.

We now describe two basic approaches for multidimensional range match that do not depend on traffic patterns: the *geometric approach* and the *tries approach*.

Geometrically, a k-dimension filter can be viewed as a rectangular box in k-dimensional space. The extent in dimension j spans the range of matching values in the jth field. A packet maps to a point in the k-dimensional space. Thus the problem of multidimensional range match can be viewed as a point location problem in multidimensional space. Let us illustrate this with a 2D example. Suppose we want to filter packets based on their source and destination addresses. The ranges of source and destination addresses in the filter rules can be represented as rectangles that are arbitrarily overlapped (Figure 3.5). Each packet can be represented as a point in the same space. If a point falls into a rectangle, there is a match for that corresponding rule. For example, Figure 3.5 has three rules, A, B, and C and two packets, P_1 and P_2. P_1 matches rule A, whereas P_2 matches both rules B and C. If a cost has been assigned to the rules, we will use the match with least cost among the multiple matches. An algorithm for implementing the geometric scheme is presented in [LAKSH98]. In the preprocessing step of the algorithm, the edge of the rectangles is projected to the corresponding axis. In the example shown, the three rectangles create five intervals on both the destination axis and the source axis. For each interval a bitmap is used to indicate which rectangles fall into this interval. The bit is set to 1 if the corresponding rectangle falls in the interval. For example, both rectangles B and C overlap with destination interval X_4; thus the bitmap for X_4 is (011). Similarly, interval Y_3 has a bitmap of (111). When a packet arrives, the first step is to find the corresponding source and destination intervals that contain the point for the packet. In the second step we perform a logical AND of the two bitmaps, and any bit that is set in the result represents a match. For example, packet P_2 falls into the interval Y_3 and X_4. After a logical AND of (111) and (011), we find that both rectangles B and C match P_2. If all rectangles are ordered by their priority, the first match should be the one with the highest priority.

Another approach is based on tries, which have been widely used for the longest prefix match in IP address lookup. A *trie* is a binary

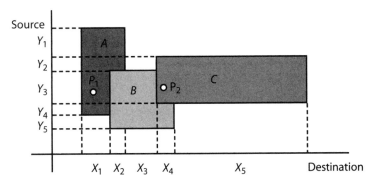

Figure 3.5   Geometric view.

branching tree, with each branch labeled 0 or 1. In [SRINI98], a simple scheme called grid of tries is proposed for handling a two-dimensional longest-prefix match, such as source address and destination address. The idea is that we first build the destination trie and then attach the corresponding source tries to each valid destination prefix.

To achieve a match with the grid of tries, we first traverse the destination trie for a match to the destination address. Once we find the longest destination match, we then traverse the associated source trie to find the longest source match. As we search the source tree, we keep track of the cost in order to find the lowest cost match.

Let us illustrate the tries-based approach with the following example. Table 3.5 shows an example database of seven filters. Each filter consists of a pair of source and destination prefixes (the * indicates the wild card field).

Figure 3.6 shows the destination trie and source tries for the database in Table 3.5. The top half is the destination trie and the bottom half the source trie. The source tries are linked to the destination trie where there is a value match for the destination address prefix. Take the destination filter 0*, for example. The source prefixes associated with this destination prefix include 10*, 01*, and 1*. In addition, the wild card destination prefix * of F7 matches whatever 0* matches. Thus the source tries under 0* have filters {F1, F2, F3, F7}.

A memory blowup problem affects the simple scheme described here since many filters must be stored in multiple places. For exam-

Table 3.5	An example with seven source and destination filters	
Filter	Destination	Source
F1	0*	10*
F2	0*	01*
F3	0*	1*
F4	00*	1*
F5	00*	11*
F6	10*	1*
F7	*	00*

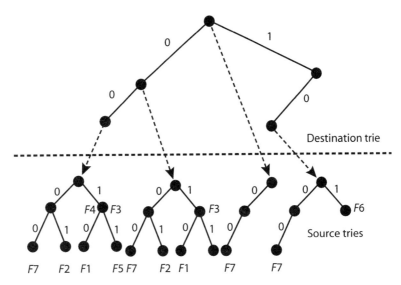

Figure 3.6 Destination trie and source tries.

ple, *F7* is under four different points in the tries. Improvement can be achieved by using precomputation and switch pointers to speed up the search for a later source trie based on the search in an earlier source trie. Refer to [SRINI98] for details of the complete algorithm.

3.9 Traffic Policing

In this section we describe the traffic-policing mechanisms for supporting the metering and marking functions in a traffic conditioner.

3.9.1 Metering and Marking

One important part of the traffic conditioner in Differentiated Services is measuring the traffic against the traffic profile and then marking the packets accordingly. These functions are often implemented as token bucket policers since traffic profiled is often described in terms of the token bucket. When a packet arrives at a token bucket, the number of tokens in the bucket is examined. If there are not enough tokens for the packet to pass, the packet will be regarded as out of profile. Therefore a token bucket can be used to determine whether a traffic flow is in or out of the token bucket profile. How-ever, to support Differentiated Services, we need to divide traffic into more than two groups and so may need to use multiple token bucket policers. For example, for each AF class we use two token buckets to divide the traffic into three drop priorities.

For AF, the two-rate three-color marker (trTCM) has been proposed for metering and marking. The trTCM meters a traffic stream and marks its packets with one of three colors: green, yellow, or red. The trTCM has four configurable token bucket parameters: a peak rate and its associated peak burst size, and a committed rate and its associated committed burst size. A packet is marked as red if it exceeds the peak rate. Otherwise it is marked as either yellow or green, depending on whether it exceeds the committed rate or not.

Metering operates in two modes: color blind or color aware. In the color-blind mode the packets are assumed to be uncolored. In the color-aware mode the packets may have been previously colored before arriving at the meter. For precolored packets the policer can demote the color by remarking them with a "worse" color than their current one. For example, the policer can change the color from yellow to red but not from yellow to green.

3.9.2   Dual Token Bucket Algorithm

The dual token bucket policer consists of two token bucket regulators: P and C (Figure 3.7). The token bucket P is regulated by two parameters, peak information rate (PIR) and peak burst size (PBS), and the token bucket C by the committed information rate (CIR) and committed burst size (CBS). Generally PIR and PBS are larger than (or at least equal to) the CIR and CBS, respectively.

Each packet will pass through the two token buckets. A color will be assigned to the packet depending on the results of tests by the two token buckets:

○ The packet is marked as green if it passes the tests of both token buckets P and C.
○ The packet is marked as yellow if the packet passes the P bucket but not the C bucket.
○ The packet is marked as red if it fails both tests.

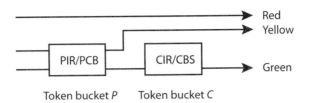

Figure 3.7   Marking packets as red, yellow, and green.

When the packet is precolored by previous entities, the rule is that we can leave the color unchanged or change the color to a worse one; that is, marking a green packet to yellow or red or a yellow packet to red.

The dual token bucket algorithm can be divided into two parts: token size calculation and packet coloring. We use the following notations:

```
PIR: Peak Information Rate
PBS: Peak Burst Size
CIR: Committed Information Rate
CBS: Committed Burst Size
pkt_size: packet size
pkt_arrival: the arrival time of previous packet
p_tk: the token counter for bucket P
c_tk: the token counter for bucket C
```

Token Size Calculation
When a packet arrives, first the number of tokens available in buckets C and P is calculated:

```
elapsed_time = Time_Now() - ptk_arrival;
p_tk = min[(p_tk + elapsed_time * PIR), PBS];
c_tk = min[(c_tk + elapsed_time * CIR), CBS];
pkt_arrival = Time_Now(t);
```

Packet Coloring
Once the tokens in buckets P and C are calculated, the color for the packet is determined:

```
If the packet is precolored as RED
    mark the packet as RED;
```

```
    else if the packet is precolored as YELLOW
        if p_tk(t) < pkt_size
            mark the packet as RED;
        else
            mark the packet as YELLOW;
            p_tk = p_tk - pkt_size;
        endif

    else if the packet is precolored as green
        if p_tk(t) < pkt_size
            mark the packet as RED;
        else if c_tk(t) < pkt_size
            mark the packet as YELLOW;
            p_tk = p_tk - pkt_size;
        else
            mark the packet as GREEN
            p_tk = p_tk - pkt_size;
            c_tk = c_tk - pkt_size;
        endif

    else /* packet is not pre-colored or the color is not
    recognized */
        if p_tk(t) < pkt_size
            mark the packet as RED;
        else if c_tk(t) < pkt_size
            mark the packet as YELLOW;
            p_tk = p_tk -  pkt_size;
        else
            mark the packet as GREEN
            p_tk = p_tk - pkt_size;
            c_tk = c_tk - pkt_size;
        endif
    endif
```

In the above scheme the packets that are not precolored or whose colors are not recognized are treated the same way as those that are precolored green. Thus the packets for customers who do not precolor packets will be assigned to green whenever possible.

Observant readers may notice a subtlety with the precolored packets that may cause green packets to be marked as red even though tokens are available in token bucket C. Note that a packet precolored yellow can be marked only as yellow or red but not green. Let us illustrate this with an example. Suppose that at a point token buckets P and C have 10 and 8 packets' worth of tokens. Then a burst of 10 yellow packets arrives at the dual token bucket. The yellow packets consume all the tokens in bucket P but none of the tokens in bucket C since they cannot be marked as green. A small interval later a burst of 10 green packets arrives. Suppose that during this period the token buckets P and C increase their tokens by 2 and 1 packets, respectively; thus buckets P and C have 2 and 10. The first two arriving green packets will pass both buckets P and C. However, at this point bucket P has no tokens left and bucket C has 8. Thus 8 of the green packets will be marked as red since there are no tokens left in bucket P. Given that the green packets are the ones we are try to protect from congestion, it is undesirable to mark them red when bucket C still has 8 tokens. If the green packets arrive before the yellow packets, all packets will pass with their colors unchanged and the yellow packets will be marked as red.

One possible alternative is to allow the green packets to "borrow" future tokens from the bucket P; namely, bucket P can go negative if bucket C has sufficient tokens to pass the green packets. This will protect the green packets from being marked as red because the yellow packets ahead of them exhaust bucket P. This may, however, cause the peak rate to be exceeded over a short period. To implement this, the marking of the packets that have been precolored should be separated from that of the packets not precolored. The algorithm for packets precolored green is

```
If the packet is precolored as green
   if c_tk(t) > pkt_size
      mark the packet as GREEN
      p_tk = p_tk - pkt_size;
      c_tk = c_tk - pkt_size;
   else if p_tk(t) > pkt_size
      mark the packet as YELLOW;
      p_tk = p_tk - pkt_size;
   else
      mark the packet as RED;
   endif
endif
```

3.10   End-to-End Resource Management

Differentiated Services focuses on resource management for a single domain, particularly backbone domains. Experience shows that this is necessary to bootstrap deployment in the Internet. However, the question of end-to-end resource management is unresolved—users are able to experience enhanced services only when there is QoS support all the way between sender and receiver.

Currently no consensus exists on how to achieve end-to-end resource management. A number of approaches have been proposed, but none of them has moved beyond the proposal stage. In this section we briefly discuss some of the proposals to illustrate the issues in end-to-end resource management.

One proposal is to run Integrated Services over Differentiated Services core networks. In this mode Integrated Services are supported around the edge of the Internet, customer networks and small regional service providers, and the backbone networks are based on Differentiated Services. From the Integrated Services perspective, the Differentiated Services clouds are virtual links connecting Integrated Services customer networks.

Another approach to interdomain bandwidth management is called *Bandwidth Broker* (BB). The BB proposal presents a framework for dealing with resource allocation between different backbone service providers. A BB is an agent that keeps track of current bandwidth consumption and applies usage policies within an administrative domain. Externally a BB sets up bilateral service agreements with neighboring BBs for border-crossing traffic. In this framework BBs act as central management entities responsible for managing the bandwidth resources within their own domains and for coordinating bandwidth allocation between domains.

3.10.1 Integrated Services over Differentiated Services

In the Integrated Services over Differentiated Services approach end-to-end resource management is provided by applying the Integrated Services model end to end across a network containing one or more Differentiated Services regions. The Differentiated Services network is treated as a link layer medium like ATM or LAN. At the boundary of the network the Integrated Services requests are mapped onto the underlying capabilities of the Differentiated Services network. Aspects of the mapping include

○ Selecting an appropriate PHB or a set of PHBs for the requested services

○ Performing appropriate policing at the edge of the Differentiated Services network

○ Exporting Integrated Services parameters from the Differentiated Services network

This framework creates a two-tier resource allocation model: Differentiated Services distributes aggregated resources in the core networks to customer networks; Integrated Services then further allocates the resources at finer granularity to individual users or flows on an as-needed basis. Since Differentiated Services only allocates bandwidth in aggregate, a mechanism is needed to allocate the aggregate to individual flows and users. For example, suppose that a customer network subscribes to 10 Mbits/sec of the assured service: which flow in the customer network should be allowed to use the assured service?

Let us look at an example of how this works. Figure 3.8 shows an enterprise network with four routers and two LANs connecting to the users. The access router connects the enterprise network to its ISP and is also responsible for the classification of traffic into different forwarding classes. When a sender initiates a transaction, it exchanges RSVP PATH and RESV messages with the receiver. The RSVP messages are ignored through the ISP that supports only Differentiated Services. When the RSVP RESV messages pass through the access router,

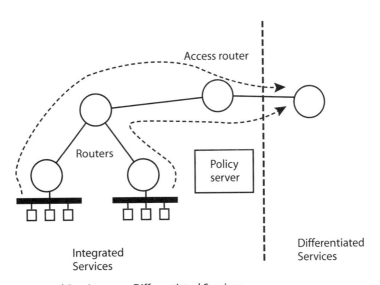

Figure 3.8   Integrated Services over Differentiated Services.

the access router must consult with the policy server in order to decide about admission control. Suppose that the enterprise has paid for 10 Mbits/sec assured service from its ISP and 9 Mbits/sec of that has been allocated. If the new reservation asks for less than 1 Mbits/sec bandwidth, the access router will pass the reservation request, and the policy server then records the amount of bandwidth the new reservation will consume. If the user wants to reserve more than 1 Mbits/sec, the reservation request will fail since sufficient assured service bandwidth is not left.

Another important function of the policy server is to apply administrative policies to the reservation requests. Based on the defined rules and confirmation, the policy server can decide how the Integrated Services requests should be mapped to the Differentiated Services model. The admission control policy can allow critical packets to get priority to the assured service bandwidth over other traffic. Sophisticated policies, such as who can use which forwarding classes and when, may be implemented.

3.10.2   Interdomain Bandwidth Allocation

Another issue in end-to-end resource allocation is how a multiple Differentiated Services network can coordinate to provision bandwidth across multiple administrative domains. Different domains are usually separately owned and administrated, and the relationship between any two different domains is governed by their SLA. When Differentiated Services is supported, the SLA must specify the profiles of border-crossing traffic. During initial deployment, the traffic profiles are likely to be static and change relatively infrequent and limited. However, as deployment expands, it is desirable to allow more dynamic negotiation on resource allocation between domains. For example, a customer may want to adjust bandwidth requirements based on estimated traffic growth or to accommodate a one-off event.

The BB approach can be used to achieve dynamic interdomain resource negotiation. Figure 3.9 shows a backbone consisting of three ISPs and an enterprise network that can communicate with many receivers in any of the ISPs. The BB of the enterprise network performs admission control for reservation requests from its own users. When the enterprise network wants to increase (or decrease) the amount of bandwidth for a certain forwarding class, its bandwidth

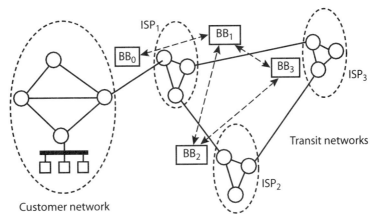

Figure 3.9   Interdomain bandwidth management.

broker BB_0 talks to BB_1, the bandwidth broker of ISP_1. To determine whether the new request can be accepted or not, BB_1 may communicate with BB_2 and BB_3.

In essence, bandwidth brokers act as resource management agents for their ISPs and perform the following three main functions:

○ **Admission control.** The bandwidth brokers are the central repositories for all bandwidth resources and current allocation. The admission control decisions are based on the predefined provisioning algorithms for the networks.

○ **Policy control.** Administrative and pricing policies can also be part of the admission control process. For example, some customers may have higher priority for the resources or special restrictions may apply.

○ **Reservation aggregation.** Instead of making a reservation for each request from the end users, bandwidth brokers can collect multiple requests from users and make a single request for resources. Such aggregation will improve the scalability of the system.

One disadvantage of the BB approach is that the bandwidth brokers must know where the new traffic is going in order to make accurate bandwidth requests. For example, if BB_0 asks BB_1 for additional bandwidth for its assured service allocation, BB_1 has to decide whether it needs to ask for more bandwidth on the links to BB_2 and BB_3. Thus ideally BB_0 should break down its bandwidth request by destination domains. This requires close interaction with interdomain routing protocols such as Border Gateway Protocol (BGP) and adds considerable complexity. A less optimal but much simpler solution is to use measurement-based allocation. Each BB monitors its current level of resource utilization and make requests for additional bandwidth when resource utilization reaches some thresholds. To make use of this approach effectively, it is necessary to use tools and algorithms for network traffic engineering, which we will discuss in Chapter 5.

3.10.3 End-System Congestion Control

In the discussion so far, we have focused on network-centric mechanisms; that is, the network takes the responsibility of resource allocation. However, the end systems or hosts actually generate the traffic and so can also help alleviate congestion inside the network by reducing the transmission rates when longer delay or packet losses are experienced. TCP congestion control is an end-system mechanism that has been implemented to avoid congestion collapse in the best-effort Internet. The network-centric approach and end-system mechanisms are not mutually exclusive in any way. In fact, resource allocation works most efficiently when both end systems and the network work together.

TCP uses a window-based scheme for congestion control. The sending window size represents the maximal number of packets in flight; that is, the number of packets that have been sent but not yet acknowledged by the receiver. The sender can adjust the window size to control the transmission rate. The TCP connection control mechanism treats packet losses as an indication of congestion. When the sender of a TCP connection detects a packet loss, it goes into slow start. The sender shrinks the window size to one packet and then potentially increases it to half the previous size. This slowdown gives the network time to recover from the congestion. If the congestion persists, the process repeats until the congestion is eased. When the sender experiences no congestion, it attempts to increase the window size slowly to find an optimal window size.

It usually takes some time for the sender to detect a packet loss and adjust sending-window size. Dropping packets only when the buffer is full often causes an overshoot in queue length and consequently a dropping of many packets in a row. The performance of TCP congestion control can be improved if packets are actually dropped before the buffer overflow occurs. If the packet drop is sufficiently early for the sender to react in time, the queue length stabilizes around an operating point.

RED has been developed for use in conjunction with TCP to give early warning of potential congestion. RED computes a queue length $Q_{average}$ using a weighted running average as follows:

$$Q_{average} = (1 - weight) \times Q_{average} + weight \times Q_{current}$$

The averaging process smooths out temporary traffic fluctuations and gives a stable indication of long-lived congestion trends. RED maintains two queue thresholds: MinThreshold and MaxThreshold. Once the average queue length exceeds the MinThreshold, the arriving packet may be dropped with a probability p. The drop probability p increase linearly as the average queue length increases and becomes 1 when the average queue length exceeds MaxThreshold. These parameters give service providers knobs to fine-tune exactly when to act on congestion and how much.

When consecutive packets are dropped as a result of buffer overflow, one can observe synchronization of rate adjustment as many end systems detect the packet losses around the same time. Such synchronization can lead to increased fluctuation in queue length. The random dropping in RED helps reduce synchronization. It also improves the fairness property in packet discarding: since the dropping is random, the sender who transmits more packets tends to have more packets dropped in the event of congestion.

Weighted RED (WRED) is a variation of RED that works with Differentiated Services. When packets are marked with different dropping priorities, we can configure the RED parameters, MinThreshold, MaxThreshold, and p as the function of the queue length to yield distinct dropping behaviors for packets with different dropping priorities. For example, in the RIO scheme mentioned in Section 3.5, packets are classified as *in* and *out* based on the traffic profile. The packets marked *in* are subject to a set of RED parameters that are different from those for the packets marked *out*. In general, the DSCP value can be used to select a drop probability curve and produce different dropping behaviors.

3.11   Performance Issues in Differentiated Services

The Differentiated Services approach removes complexity in the core of the network by pushing all fine granularity operations to the edge of the network. The simplification, however, comes at a price. Since traffic is policed only at the edge of the network, performance assurance depends on the careful design and provisioning of the networks.

In this section we look at performance issues in Differentiated Services. We use a simple network as an example to illustrate the relationship between traffic profiles and bottleneck bandwidth and the protection from misbehaving sources. This discussion is intended for advanced readers who design and manage Differentiated Services networks and want to have a deeper understanding of the provisioning issues.

3.11.1   Network Configuration

The simple network we use to illustrate the performance issues is shown in Figure 3.10. In this network we have 10 sources (1 through 10, counting down) that communicate with one of two different destinations, X and Y. The sources are connected to destination X through a link of capacity 33 Mbits/sec and to destination Y through a link of capacity 155 Mbits/sec. Each of the links that connects a source to the first router in the diagram has a capacity of 30 Mbits/sec. The one-way propagation delays to both destinations X and Y for the sources (counting from the top down) were set at 20, 20, 40, 40, 50, 50, 70, 70, 100, and 100 ms, respectively. The sources are all TCP-Reno sources (unless specified otherwise) that use a packet size of 500 bytes, and each of them sends 500,000 packets to the destination. Each source is assigned an "expected bandwidth" as its traffic profile.

We examine two implementations of Differentiated Services: RIO and 2-bit. RIO is a simple AF-based scheme, described briefly in Section 3.5. In the simulation the first router that connects to the 10 sources tags the packets based on each source's traffic profile. Any packets that are out of profile are marked as *out* while those that conform to the user profile are marked as *in*. In the network core the in-profile and out-of-profile packets are treated with different drop priorities using RED. The in-profile traffic has less chance of getting dropped than out-of-profile traffic and so gets predictable levels of ser-

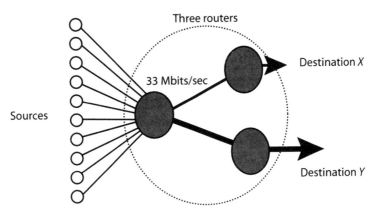

Figure 3.10   Network configuration.

vice as long as it stays within profile. The RIO scheme also makes it possible to use statistical multiplexing to utilize any excess bandwidth that may be available since it allows out-of-profile packets into the network.

In the simulation the routers use RED with values of 400 packets, 800 packets, and 0.02 for *min_in*, *max_in*, and P_{max_in}, and 100 packets, 200 packets, and 0.5 for *min_out*, *max_out*, and P_{max_out} [FLOYD 93], where *min_in* and *max_in* represent the upper and lower bounds for the average queue size for in-profile packets when RED kicks in and P_{max_in} is the maximum drop probability for an in-profile packet when the average queue size is in the [*min_in, max_in*] range. The corresponding parameters for the out-of-profile packets are the *min_out*, *max_out*, and P_{max_out} values. Note that total queue sizes are used when calculating the drop probability for out-of-profile packets.

The 2-bit scheme combines the RIO scheme and premium service to create three different classes of service: premium, assured, and best effort. Premium service is based on a simple EF model where premium traffic is transmitted prior to other traffic. Such a service is useful for time-critical applications that require minimum delay as well as applications that require explicit bandwidth and delay guarantees.

Premium traffic is strictly policed at the edge of the network: packets that are out of the service profile are dropped or delayed until they are within the service profile. The assured service class corresponds to the in-profile traffic in the RIO scheme and has a lower drop priority than ordinary best-effort service. When congestion occurs, chances are high that the assured packets will receive predictable levels of service if they conform to their service profile, which is typically based on average bandwidth utilization.

In order to compare performance, we also include the *user-share differentiation* (USD) scheme [WANG98]. The USD scheme combines Integrated Services and Differentiated Services in some fashion. It allocates link bandwidth in proportion to the share of active flows over the link; thus its performance can be considered optimal. The USD scheme is used here as a benchmark in evaluating the other two schemes.

3.11.2   Traffic Profiles and Bottleneck Bandwidth

To examine the relationship between traffic profiles and bottleneck bandwidth, we create three sets of traffic compositions, and for each composition, we perform two simulations, first directing traffic to destination X and then to destination Y.

In the simulations the odd-numbered sources (1, 3, 5, 7, 9) are assigned to the lower expected bandwidth and the even-numbered sources (2, 4, 6, 8, 10) to the higher expected bandwidth. In the first set of traffic composition we set the expected lower and higher bandwidths to 1 Mbits/sec and 5 Mbits/sec, respectively, such that the aggregate (i.e., sum of) expected bandwidth of all the flows matched the 33 Mbits/sec bottleneck bandwidth. In the second set the expected bandwidths were chosen to be 5 and 25 Mbits/sec, respectively, to match the 155 Mbits/sec bottleneck, and in the third set they were set to 3 and 15 Mbits/sec, respectively, which is the average of expected bandwidths in the first two sets.

The performance of the RIO scheme is shown in Figure 3.11. The figure consists of six clusters with 10 bars in each cluster. Each cluster has a label of the form x Mbits/sec (y,z), which means that the particular cluster represents the bandwidth allocation for the 10 sources when the bottleneck bandwidth is x Mbits/sec and the higher and lower expected bandwidths are y and z Mbits/sec, respectively.

The results indicate that if the aggregate expected bandwidth of all the flows passing through the bottleneck closely matches the bottleneck bandwidth, the RIO scheme can allocate bandwidth in accordance with the expected bandwidth profiles. This is clear from the graphs for the 33 Mbits/sec (1,5) and 155 Mbits/sec (5,25) cases. In

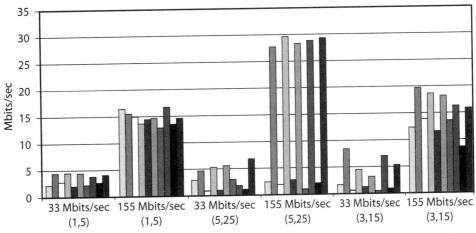

Figure 3.11 Two different bottleneck bandwidths and three different expected profiles using the RIO scheme.

the first case the sources with a lower expected bandwidth are allocated a slightly higher bandwidth than their expected profiles at the expense of sources with a higher expected bandwidth; the situation is reversed in the 155 Mbits/sec (5,25) case.

We expect that some tuning of the RED parameters is required to obtain a bandwidth allocation that is more commensurate with expected bandwidth profiles. If the bottleneck bandwidth is in excess of the aggregated expected bandwidth, the excess bandwidth is more or less evenly allocated among all the sources. This is evident in the 155 Mbits/sec (3,15) and 155 Mbits/sec (1,5) cases. In the 155 Mbits/sec (3,15) case the sources with the higher expected bandwidth do get more bandwidth than the others, but the relative difference is smaller than those in the 33 Mbits/sec (1,5) and 155 Mbits/sec (5,25) cases, where the bottleneck bandwidth matches the aggregate expected bandwidth. In the 155Mbits/sec (1,5) case (where the difference between the bottleneck bandwidth and the aggregated expected bandwidth is higher), the bandwidth allocation is fairly even among all the sources. This is because the excess bandwidth is allocated only to the out-of-profile packets, and the RED scheme for out-of-profile packets ensures that this excess bandwidth is allocated fairly.

If the aggregated expected bandwidth is less than the bottleneck bandwidth, the RIO scheme is able (for the most part) to allocate the existing bandwidth in a manner that is commensurate with existing user expectations. One exception is the 33 Mbits/sec (5,25) case, where the bandwidth allocated to source 8 is less than that allocated to sources 1 and 7, although the latter have lower expected bandwidths.

For the 2-bit scheme, the higher bandwidth traffic is tagged as premium traffic. For example, in the 33 Mbits/sec (1,5) case, the 5 Mbits/sec sources were all considered premium sources with a peak sending rate of 5 Mbits/sec. Network bandwidth for premium traffic was reserved at connection-setup time. The low-bandwidth sources were subjected to the RIO scheme, where all the in-profile packets had their A-bit set, whereas the out-of-profile packets did not. The RIO parameters in this case were the same as in the previous experiment. Figure 3.12 shows the bandwidth allocation for the 2-bit scheme. The bandwidth allocation matches the expected bandwidth in the 33 Mbits/sec (1,5) and 155 Mbits/sec (5,25) cases. This implies that the 2-bit scheme performs well when the bottleneck bandwidth matches the aggregate expected bandwidth. However, we see that in the 155 Mbits/sec (1,5) and the 155 Mbits/sec (3,15) cases, the bandwidth share allocated to the sources with the lower expected bandwidth is higher. This is because of how premium traffic is handled in the network: any out-of-profile premium packet is dropped by the profile

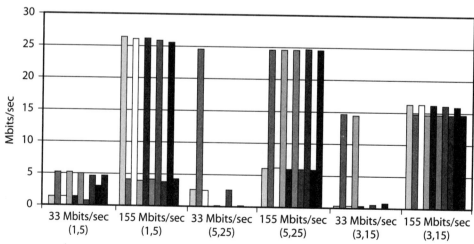

Figure 3.12   Two different bottleneck bandwidths and three different expected profiles using the 2-bit scheme.

meter. Consequently all the excess bandwidth in these cases goes to the sources with lower expected bandwidth. In this respect, the bandwidth allocation done by the RIO scheme is more in keeping with user expectations. In the 33 Mbits/sec (5,25) and 33 Mbits/sec (3,15) cases, some of the high expected bandwidth sources do not get any bandwidth at all. This is because their connection setup calls get rejected due to unavailable bandwidth. Thus for the 2-bit scheme with premium traffic, it is important that the aggregated expected bandwidth through the bottleneck match the bottleneck bandwidth, or else some premium traffic may get denied bandwidth because the network resources have been overcommitted.

The bandwidth allocation in USD is shown in Figure 3.13. As expected, the bandwidths allocated to all the sources remain the same in all cases and are proportional to their expected bandwidths.

3.11.3   Protection from Misbehaving Sources

We will look at how well Differentiated Services can protect networks from nonresponsive sources or malicious sources. The nonresponsive sources are simulated with CBR (constant bit rate) sources that send at a fixed rate and malicious sources that flood the network by sending

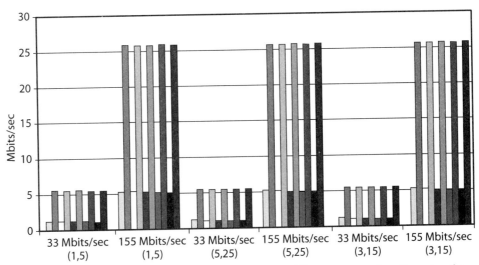

Figure 3.13   Two different bottleneck bandwidths and three different expected profiles using the USD scheme.

as fast as they can. In the simulations sources 1 and 2 were CBR sources transmitting at 5 Mbits/sec and the other sources were TCP-Reno sources, where the odd-numbered sources had an expected bandwidth of 1 Mbits/sec and the even-numbered sources had an expected bandwidth of 5 Mbits/sec. All CBR traffic was marked as out of profile.

Figure 3.14 shows the bandwidth allocation in each of the three schemes when the bottleneck bandwidth is 33 Mbits/sec, and Figure 3.15 shows the same when the bottleneck bandwidth is 155 Mbits/sec. In both figures the first two bars in each cluster are for the CBR sources and the rest are for the TCP-Reno sources. The numbers for the 33 Mbits/sec (1,5) case indicate that with RIO, the CBR sources are able to get close to their expected bandwidth (i.e., about 5 Mbits/sec) despite all of their traffic being marked out of profile (i.e., lower priority). However, the TCP-Reno sources perform reasonably well: the sources with higher expected bandwidth show a bandwidth share of about 4 Mbits/sec, which is close to the expected bandwidth profile. The sources with a lower expected bandwidth show bandwidth shares that are higher than their expected bandwidth profiles, closer to about 2 Mbits/sec rather than 1 Mbits/sec. In the 155 Mbits/sec (1,5) case the CBR sources get about 5 Mbits/sec, as in the previous case. All the other sources (that are all TCP-Reno sources) receive bandwidths that are in excess of their expected average bandwidths, and it is clear that the excess bandwidth at the bottleneck is allocated fairly evenly among the TCP sources by the RED mechanism.

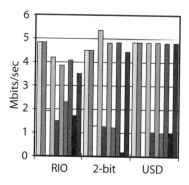

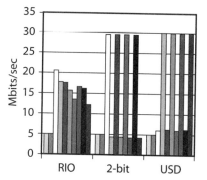

Figure 3.14 Two nonresponsive (CBR) sources with 33 Mbits/sec (1,5).

Figure 3.15 Two nonresponsive (CBR) sources with 155 Mbits/sec (1,5).

For the 2-bit scheme, the CBR sources get close to their expected bandwidth (about 4.5 Mbits/sec) in both the scenarios. The sources with the higher expected bandwidth, whose packets are all marked as premium traffic, also get close to the 5 Mbits/sec bandwidth (about 4.8 Mbits/sec from the graphs). In the 33 Mbits/sec (1,5) case three of the four sources that have a low expected bandwidth profile of 1 Mbits/sec get a slightly higher bandwidth allocation than their expected profiles. All of this comes at the expense of the fourth low bandwidth source, which gets close to zero bandwidth. Apparently in the 2-bit scheme, if there are noncooperative, bandwidth-hungry sources (even if all their packets are marked out of profile), other well-behaved, low-priority traffic may get starved. The situation is slightly different when there is excess bandwidth at the bottleneck; that is, the 155-Mbits/sec (1,5) case. In this scenario the premium bandwidth sources do not get any more than their expected bandwidths because premium traffic that is out of profile gets dropped. Consequently the excess bandwidth at the bottleneck is shared evenly by the low-bandwidth TCP-Reno sources, which now show a higher bandwidth allocation than the higher bandwidth sources. Finally, the results for the USD scheme show that the bandwidth allocations are commensurate with the expected bandwidth profiles and thus are effective in the presence of noncooperative CBR sources.

Malicious sources are different from CBR sources: they try to deliberately attack the network by flooding it at maximum speed. In the simulation sources 1 and 2 both declare an expected bandwidth of 1 Mbits/sec and then send as fast as they can. The other sources are TCP-Reno sources, where the odd-numbered sources have an expected bandwidth of 1 Mbits/sec and the even-numbered sources have an expected bandwidth of 5 Mbits/sec.

The results for the 33 Mbits/sec (1,5) scenario are shown in Figure 3.16. In the RIO case the low-bandwidth sources get very little bandwidth—sources 3 and 5 get nothing, and sources 7 and 9 get about 0.1 Mbits/sec. The high-bandwidth sources do not do well either; none of the sources are able to get more than 2.5 Mbits/sec. The reason for this is that the packets for the malicious sources fill up the queues on the bottleneck routers very quickly and cause packets from other sources to be dropped more often. Consequently the TCP windows do not open up to the extent required to get the expected average bandwidth.

For the 2-bit scheme, the low-bandwidth sources get very little bandwidth (as in the RIO case) for the same reason, and the bulk of the bandwidth goes to the malicious sources. However, in this case the malicious sources grab about 6 Mbits/sec each as opposed to 12 Mbits/sec each in the RIO case. The reason is that the packets from the high-bandwidth sources in the 2-bit scheme are queued in a separate, higher-priority, premium traffic queue. As a result the high-bandwidth sources are able to get close to their expected bandwidth of 5 Mbits/sec while the low-bandwidth sources get very little—sources 3, 5, and 7 get less than 0.2 Mbits/sec, and source 9 gets nothing. Thus in both RIO and 2-bit schemes a malicious source can easily deprive low-priority traffic of its fair share, but high-priority traffic tends to do better in the 2-bit scheme because such traffic is queued in a separate, high-priority queue. In the case of the USD scheme the malicious sources are penalized and actually receive slightly less than their average expected bandwidth (0.79 Mbits/sec in place of 1 Mbits/sec), while the other sources get slightly more than their expected bandwidth—the low-bandwidth sources get 1.31 Mbits/sec instead of 1 Mbits/sec and the high-bandwidth sources get 6.54 Mbits/sec instead of 5 Mbits/sec.

The results for the 155 Mbits/sec (1,5) scenario are shown in Figure 3.17. In this scenario the malicious sources for the RIO and the 2-bit schemes are able to grab almost the full bandwidth of their outgoing links, which is set to 30 Mbits/sec in the simulation. In the RIO case the TCP-Reno sources are able to get more than their expected band-

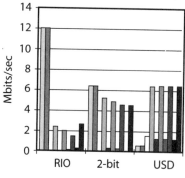

Figure 3.16   Two malicious sources with 33 Mbits/sec (1,5).

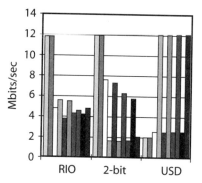

Figure 3.17   Two malicious sources with 155 Mbits/sec (1,5).

width profiles but not in proportion to their expected bandwidths. Again, the reason is that the excess bandwidth (the bandwidth consumed only by out-of-profile packets) is more or less evenly distributed by the RED scheme among all the sources. In the 2-bit case the premium sources are able to get slightly less than their expected bandwidths (in the range of 3.5 to 4 Mbits/sec instead of 5 Mbits/sec). This is because the malicious sources constantly fill up the lower-priority queues and therefore the routers spend more time processing the lower-priority queues than the higher-priority ones. Consequently the congestion windows for the higher-bandwidth premium traffic do not open up fast enough to utilize the requisite expected bandwidth. The excess bottleneck bandwidth is more or less evenly allocated only among the low-bandwidth sources because any premium traffic that is out of profile is dropped. This causes the low bandwidth sources to get a higher-bandwidth allocation than the high-bandwidth sources.

3.12 Summary

In Differentiated Services, traffic is divided into a small number of forwarding classes and resources are allocated on a per-class basis. The Differentiated Services architecture standardizes a set of per-hop-behaviors as the basic building blocks with which services can be constructed. The PHBs are encoded into the 6-bit DS field in the IP packet header.

In Differentiated Services networks, traffic is mapped to forwarding classes by packet classifiers and traffic conditioners at the boundary of administrative domains. Traffic conditioners measure traffic entering the service providers' network against the traffic profiles of the customers. Nonconformant packets are subject to policing actions such as marking, shaping, and dropping. Inside the interior of the network, packets are forwarded based solely on the DSCP in the packet header.

Two PHBs, assured forwarding (AF) and expedited forwarding (EF), have been standardized. The AF PHB specifies four forwarding classes, each with its own bandwidth allocation. Within each forwarding class, AF has three levels of drop priorities. The EF PHB provides a forwarding treatment of minimal delay and loss. With EF the arrival rate of the packets at any node must be limited to be less than the output rate.

Performance assurance in Differentiated Services networks is provided by a combination of resource provisioning, traffic prioritization, and admission control. It is important that the networks be carefully provisioned to avoid mismatch between traffic patterns and bottleneck bandwidth, and additional mechanisms may be needed to detect misbehaving and malicious traffic sources.

Further Reading

The following RFC gives an overview on the architecture for Differentiated Services:

Carlson, M., W. Weiss, S. Blake, Z. Wang, D. Black, and E. Davies. "An Architecture for Differentiated Services." RFC 2475, December 1998.

For further details on packet classification and traffic policing, we recommend the following papers:

Lakshman, T. V., and D. Stiliadis. "High Speed Policy-Based Packet Forwarding Using Efficient Multi-dimensional Range Matching." Proc. of ACM SIGCOMM'98, September 1998.

Srinivasan, V., and G. Varghese. "Fast IP Lookups Using Controlled Prefix Expansion." Proc. of ACM SIGCOMM'98, September 1998.

Heinanen, J., and R. Guerin. "A Single Rate Three Color Marker." RFC 2697, September 1999.

Heinanen, J., and R. Guerin. "A Two Rate Three Color Marker." RFC 2698, September 1999.

The RIO, 2-bit, USD, and RED schemes mentioned in Section 3.11 are described in

Clark, D., and W. Fang. "Explicit Allocation of Best Effort Packet Delivery Service." *IEEE/ACM Trans. on Networking* 6, no. 4 (1998).

K. Nichols, V. Jacobson, and L. Zhang. "A Two-Bit Differentiated Services Architecture for the Internet." Internet draft, November 1997.

Wang, Z. "USD: Scalable Bandwidth Allocation for the Internet." Proc. of High Performance Networking '98, September 1998.

Floyd S., and V. Jacobson. "Random Early Detection Gateways for Congestion Avoidance." IEEE/ACM Transactions on Networking, August 1993.

A compete discussion on the performance of Differentiated Services can be found in

Basu, A., and Z. Wang. "Fair Bandwidth Allocation of Differentiated Service." Proc. of Protocols for High-Speed Networks (PfHSN99), August 1999.

The following is a list of Internet standards related to Differentiated Services:

RFC 2474, Definition of the Differentiated Services Field (DS Field) in the IPv4 and IPv6 Headers (Standards Track). Defines the Differentiated Services field and class selector and default per-hop behaviors.

RFC 2598, An Expedited Forwarding PHB (Standards Track). Specifies expedited forwarding per-hop behavior.

RFC 2594, Assured Forwarding PHB Group (Standards Track). Describes assured forwarding per-hop behavior.

4

Multiprotocol Label Switching

4.1 Introduction

ultiprotocol Label Switching (MPLS) has emerged as an important new technology for the Internet. It represents the convergence of two fundamentally different approaches in data networking: datagram and virtual circuit. Traditionally IP forwarding in the Internet is based on the datagram model: routing protocols precalculate the paths to all destination networks by exchanging routing information, and each packet is forwarded independently based on its destination address. Asynchronous transfer mode (ATM) and Frame Relay (FR) technologies, on the other hand, are connection oriented; a virtual circuit must be set up explicitly by a signaling protocol before packets can be transmitted into the network.

ATM has been widely deployed in Internet backbones, and several approaches have been standardized for running IP over ATM networks. However, these techniques are cumbersome and have scaling problems. The need for more seamless IP/ATM integration led to the development of label switching. The first commercial product that gained significant attention was the *IP Switch,* from a start-up company called Ipsilon. The IP Switch uses a proprietary signaling protocol to set up an ATM connection on the fly for long-lasting IP flows. Toshiba had previously presented a similar scheme that was later implemented in their Cell Switching Router (CSR). Several other approaches were soon proposed, including Cisco's *Tag Switching* and IBM's *Aggregate Route-based IP Switching* (ARIS). Although these approaches differ in the details, they are all based on the same paradigm of label-based switching.

Label switching uses a short, fixed-length label inserted in the packet header to forward packets. A *label-switched router* (LSR) uses the label in the packet header as an index to find the next hop and the corresponding new label. The packet is sent to its next hop after the existing label is swapped with the new one assigned for the next hop. The path that the packet traverses through a network is defined by the transition in label values. Such a path is called a *label-switched path* (LSP). Since the mapping between labels is fixed at each LSR, an LSP is determined by the initial label value at the first LSR of the LSP.

The basic idea of label switching is not new. In fact, both ATM and FR use similar approaches. However, supporting the label-switching paradigm within IP allows unified IP routing and control across the Internet and makes easier seamless integration of IP over both ATM and FR. The purpose of label switching is not to replace IP routing but rather to enhance the services provided in the IP networks by offering scope for traffic engineering, guaranteed QoS, and virtual private networks (VPNs).

The potential of label switching was quickly recognized by the Internet community. A birds of feather (BOF) was organized at the IETF meeting in December 1996, and the MPLS working group was later formed to standardize the encapsulation formats and the label distribution protocols. Most recently several proposals have been put forward to extend the label distribution protocols to manage optical transport networks, making the MPLS signaling protocols the end-to-end and unified control mechanism.

In this chapter we present the architecture and protocols of MPLS. In Section 4.2 we first look at the motivation behind the development of label switching and the key benefits that MPLS brings to IP networks. In Section 4.3 we examine the evolution of MPLS and present an overview of four label switching proposals that led to the current

MPLS architecture. Section 4.4 describes the main concepts and the architecture of MPLS. In Section 4.5 we discuss and compare three label distribution protocols for MPLS, LDP, CR-LDP, and RSVP-TE.

4.2 Motivation

Although IP/ATM integration was the main driver in the development of label switching, it was not the only one. After the initial discussion at the IETF working group, the group recognized that label switching could potentially be the solution to a number of problems. For example, label switching can be used to simplify the packet-forwarding process or to make the forwarding process protocol independent, allowing multiple protocols to be implemented over the same forwarding path. The ability to support the explicit path in label switching is also useful since it provides an important capability that is currently missing in the Internet.

In this section we first examine the classical solutions for IP over ATM, its problems, and how label switching may simplify IP/ATM integration. We then look at some of benefits label switching brings to forwarding architecture and to Internet traffic engineering.

4.2.1 IP over ATM Integration

To understand how label switching can simplify IP/ATM integration, we must first illustrate the current approaches for running IP over ATM and the problems with those approaches.

The Overlay Model: Classical IP over ATM
The IETF standard for running IP over ATM, called *classical IP over ATM*, assumes that ATM networks are used very much like other subnet technologies, such as the Ethernet. However, an ATM network, when viewed as a subnet, is different from a point-to-point or shared media network in that multiple nodes can be accessed but there is no support for link-layer broadcast. In the classical IP over ATM model, an ATM network contains one or several *logical IP subnets* (LISs). The hosts and routers attached to an LIS share several logically imposed properties, such as the same subnet address, the same LLC/SNAP encapsulation of IP packets, and the same MTU between all LIS

members. This is also called the *Overlay Model* because an IP network is built as a logical network over the ATM network. In this scheme, the ATM network employs its own addressing and routing scheme completely independent of the IP network being "overlaid." Several LISs can be overlaid on top of a single ATM network. IP hosts and routers on an LIS form adjacencies by establishing a PVC or SVC connection to each member of the LIS, forming a mesh connectivity between the LIS members.

Address Resolution: ATM ARP

Since the IP address and the ATM address of the interface attached to the ATM network have no inherent relationship and ATM networks do not support link-layer broadcast, the classical IP approach uses the ATM address resolution protocol, or ATM ARP, for address resolution. Each member in an LIS registers its IP address and ATM address with LIS's ATM ARP server. Any device can then obtain the IP address of other members in the LIS from the server by requesting the server to resolve the ATM address for an IP address. Once the ATM address is obtained, an SVC connection can be established to that member. In the PVC case, an ATM ARP server is not needed because the IP address and PVC mapping can be configured when the PVCs are defined. Alternatively, the members can use the inverse ATM ARP mechanism to resolve the mapping between PVCs and IP addresses.

Next Hop Resolution Protocol (NHRP)

Packets between members of the same LIS are directly switched through the ATM infrastructure. However, when packets must be forwarded between hosts in two different LISs, they must be forwarded through a router that is a member in both LISs, even when both LISs are overlaid on the same ATM network. For example, in Figure 4.1 a host in LIS 1 must go through router *C* to communicate with another host in LIS 2. Typically a packet traverses several such routers before it reaches the destination host on the same ATM network.

To solve this problem, the IETF extended the standards to incorporate another mechanism called *Next Hop Resolution Protocol* (NHRP). NHRP is an extension of the ATM ARP mechanism, except that the address resolution is done across LISs. NHRP is based on a client/server model in which the NHRP client (NHC, a host, or a router) makes a request for address resolution for a destination IP address to

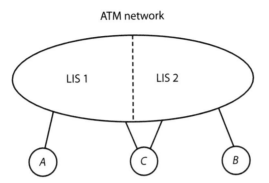

ATM network

Figure 4.1   Logical IP subnets in IP over ATM.

the nearest configured NHRP server (NHS). This request is forwarded along the normal hop-by-hop IP forwarding path toward the IP destination address whose ATM address resolution is requested. An NHS along the path that has the address resolution information responds to the requesting NHC with an ATM address. If the destination node is directly attached to the ATM network, then the resolved ATM address is that of the destination node. If the destination node is not directly attached to the ATM network, then the resolved ATM address is that of the egress router on the ATM network that is "nearest" the destination node. Once the NHC has the ATM address, it opens a direct SVC connection to the ATM address and forwards packets through the connection toward the destination IP address. NHRP specifications preclude both the NHC and the far-end node whose ATM address is supplied from routers. This is because the NHRP does not provide a mechanism to indicate to the NHC when a route change happens after the resolution is made, and in some situations this can lead to a stable routing loop.

LAN Emulation and MPOA

The ATM Forum standards are different from those of the IETF but are also based on the Overlay Model approach. The initial ATM Forum work is called *LAN Emulation* (LANE). Through the interaction between a set of servers, the host interface attached to the ATM network "appears" to the upper layers as a traditional shared media interface. To forward packets at a network layer between hosts in different emulated LANs but in the same ATM infrastructure, the ATM Forum extended the standard to include *Multiprotocol Over ATM* (MPOA), a combination of LANE and NHRP.

Problems with the Overlay Model

The IP over ATM approaches result in several scaling issues. First, these approaches require a complete or partial mesh of VCs to connect host members in a logical subnet. This implies that at a maximum $n \times (n-1)$ unidirectional connections are required to connect n members in a logical subnet. This can consume significant connections with large memberships, increasing the overhead to set up, maintain, and tear down these connections. Besides the resource factor, each member in a logical subnet has $n-1$ routing peers. This drastically increases the computational overhead for the routing protocols because it is directly proportional to the number of links (physical or virtual) in a network.

Second, in both classical IP and LANE the data must be forwarded at the IP layer between logical subnets, which does not fully exploit the switching infrastructure. Multicast is also based on logical subnet and must be forwarded at the IP layer between subnets. Although NHRP and MPOA provide mechanisms to shortcut the VC across multiple subnets for unicast data, the mechanism is traffic driven and so has the associated setup, maintenance, and tear-down overheads in addition to the cache latency issues.

Finally, although ATM switches support many QoS features, none of these approaches exploits that potential. The connections used in these schemes are equivalent to the best-effort model. The protocol and signaling mechanisms only increased the complexity of configuration, maintenance, and operations of an overlay network. When ATM is not end to end, translation between IP QoS classes and ATM service classes is required. Thus the benefits of ATM switching were available at a very high cost.

The difficulty in IP/ATM integration lies in the fact that IP and ATM have incompatible addressing and control protocols. Overlaying one over the other requires complex and expensive "gluing."

The Label-Switching Solution

The label-switching approach significantly simplifies IP/ATM integration by completely removing the overlaying of IP over the ATM network. Instead IP and ATM are tightly integrated. With label switching, IP routing and signaling protocols take over the control path, and the

ATM switches are used only for data transmission. Therefore ATM switches participate in full IP routing exchanges and become an integral part of the IP routing domain. From the perspective of the control path, all ATM switches are also IP routers. There is no need to use NHRP and on-demand cut-through SVCs for operation over ATM. Label switching also improves the scalability of routing as the *n*-squared mesh problem is eliminated. The IP protocols can exploit directly the QoS features and multicast capabilities of the ATM switches.

4.2.2 Simpler Forwarding Paradigm

Apart from improving the integration of IP over ATM, label switching is also seen by many people as a way to simplify IP packet forwarding. Forwarding IP packets is a rather complex operation; a concern is whether the speed of IP forwarding can keep up with the exponential increase in demand. Label switching offers a possible alternative approach that can significantly simplify IP packet forwarding and potentially reduce costs. Another attraction of label switching is that it makes forwarding independent of routing architectures, so that new and different schemes can be developed without changes in the forwarding path.

Simpler Packet Classification and IP Lookup

IP routers must perform several complex functions during packet forwarding, such as packet classification and route lookup (we discussed packet classification in Chapter 3). Packet classification involves finding matches for several fields in the packet header against a set of classification rules. IP lookup is based on longest-prefix match, which can be viewed as a special case of the classification problem. Both functions use complex algorithms that perform extensive preprocessing and require multiple memory accesses. With label switching, however, the problem becomes a simple exact match for a short label. Thus this simpler forwarding operation can scale to a very large number of classification rules and IP routers and to extremely high speeds.

But the simplification comes at a price: the label-switched paths must be set up by a signaling protocol or the label distribution protocol before packet forwarding. Therefore label switching in essence trades simple forwarding for extra overheads and complexity in signaling. It is not clear whether such simplification will actually result in significant cost reduction. The rapid development in silicon technologies has demonstrated that supporting packet classification and IP lookup at high speeds, such as OC48 speed (2.5 Gbits/sec) or even higher, is quite feasible, and chip sets for those functions are now commercially available. Thus the benefits of label switching in simplifying packet forwarding have somehow diminished over time.

Protocol-Independent Forwarding

Routing and forwarding are tightly coupled in current IP architecture. Any changes in routing architecture will affect the forwarding path. For example, IP forwarding used to be based on three classes with network prefixes 8, 16, and 24 bits long. The address exhaustion problem promoted the development of *Classless Inter Domain Routing* (CIDR). However, implementing CIDR requires a change in the forwarding algorithm of all IP routers to use longest-prefix lookup. The forwarding algorithm is implemented in hardware or fine-tuned software to ensure performance; making changes to it can be expensive.

Label switching decouples forwarding from routing. An LSP may be set up in a variety of ways, and once the LSP is established, packet forwarding is always the same. Thus new routing architectures can be implemented without any changes to the forwarding path. Take multicast as an example—unicast packet forwarding is typically based on the destination address. However, multicast forwarding may require a lookup based on both the source address and the destination address. Modifying the unicast forwarding engine to accommodate multicast requires substantial changes or a completely separate forwarding engine for multicast. With label switching, a label for a multicast stream will be associated with the source and destination addresses at the setup phase. The label lookup during multicast forwarding remains unchanged for multicast.

Forwarding Granularity

Forwarding granularity refers to the level of aggregation in the decision making of routing protocols. For example, forwarding granularity in current IP routing is destination based: all packets with the same network number are grouped and treated the same way. Although destination-based forwarding is highly scalable, different forwarding granularities are sometimes desirable. For example, an ISP may want specific customers to receive different forwarding treatment. Implementation of such a scheme requires routers to know from which customer a packet originates; this may in turn require packet filtering based on the source or destination address in routers throughout the network.

In many cases a customer can be identified by the ingress interface of the edge router to which the customer is connected. For example, company ABC connects to its ISP through a T3 link to interface X of the edge node in the ISP's point of presence (PoP); then all traffic coming into the ISP's network from interface X comes from company ABC. However, with the current IP architecture, it is difficult for a router in the middle of a network to know at which interface a packet enters the current network; this information is available only at the edge router.

Label switching allows multiple granularities to be supported in addition to the current destination-based one. Once an LSP is established, the mapping of packets onto this LSP depends only on the ingress router that starts the LSP. For example, an edge router may apply very sophisticated filer rules and put matching packets onto the LSP to receive a particular forwarding treatment. Information such as ingress interface can also be used to classify packets from a specific customer onto an LSP. We will discuss forwarding granularity again when we present the concept of forwarding equivalence class later in this chapter (Section 4.4.2).

4.2.3   Traffic Engineering

As we explained in Section 4.2.1, label switching was initially driven by the need for seamless IP/ATM integration and to simplify IP forwarding. However, rapidly changing technologies have made these considerations less important. Instead traffic engineering has emerged as the key application of label switching.

Traffic engineering refers to the process of optimizing the utilization of network resources through careful distribution of traffic across the network. In today's datagram routing, traffic engineering is difficult to achieve. IP routing is destination based, and traffic tends to distribute unevenly across the backbone. Although some links are heavily congested, others may see very little traffic. The result of such unbalanced traffic distribution is that resource utilization is typically poor. Some *m* of traffic engineering can be done by manipulating the link metrics. For example, when a link is congested, its cost metric can be increased in order to move traffic to other links. However, it is typically a trial-and-error process and becomes impractical for large networks.

Most Internet backbones today use ATM or FR to interconnect IP routers. The PVCs in ATM and FR allow engineers to manually configure multiple PVCs and adjust the routes to equalize the load of the traffic across the network. This is an important functionality currently missing in IP routing. Label switching uses similar connection-oriented approaches and can easily replace the PVC functionality in ATM and FR. With label switching, all traffic flows between an ingress node and an egress node can be individually identified and measured. LSPs can also be set up with explicitly specified routes, or explicit routes. The entire path can be computed based on sophisticated algorithms that optimize resource utilization. Traffic engineering will be discussed in depth in the next chapter.

4.3 Overview

In this section we introduce the basic concept of label switching and provide an overview of related label-switching proposals. The two basic approaches are then discussed in depth.

4.3.1 Routing vs. Switching

To understand label switching, let us first look at how packets are forwarded in IP routers (Figure 4.2). The operation of an IP router can be partitioned into two basic threads: a data path and a control path. The *data path* is the "executive branch," which performs the actual forwarding of packets from ingress ports to their appropriate egress ports. When a packet arrives at the router, the data path uses a forwarding table and the information contained in the packet header to determine where the packet should be forwarded.

The *control path,* on the other hand, is responsible for making forwarding decisions. In the control path, routing protocols exchange updates among routers and calculate the route to each network prefix based on the routing metrics. The forwarding table consists of the

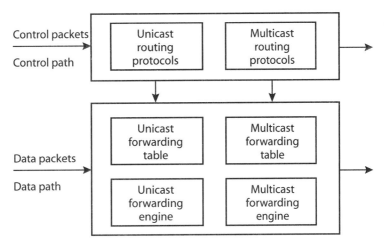

Figure 4.2 IP packet forwarding.

network prefix and the corresponding next-hop information produced by the routing protocols.

In typical layer-3 IP routers, unicast forwarding is done by taking the destination address of the incoming packet and performing a longest match against the entries in the forwarding table. Multicast forwarding is slightly more complicated since some multicast protocols such as DVMRP and PIM-SM use both the source address and the destination address (i.e., the group address) in the route lookup. The lookup involves a longest match on the source address and a fixed-length match with the destination address.

In contrast to layer-3 routers, layer-2 switches such as ATM, FR, or Ethernet switches all use a short, fixed-length label for route lookup. Typically a label does not encode any information from the packet headers and has local significance; it can be viewed simply as an index in the forwarding table. With this approach, the data path becomes very straightforward: it involves a direct lookup to find the outgoing interface and the label for the next hop. The simplification in the data path, however, comes at a price. The control path has to set up the labels across the path that packets traverse. This is done in ATM and FR by their own signaling protocols, which set up the connections.

These two different approaches are often referred to as *routing* versus *switching*. The main difference is that in the routing approach, the router has to look at the fields of the packet header in the data path and match the entries in the forwarding table; in the switching approach, the information in the packet header is examined in the control path and the result is associated with an index, which is used in the forwarding. Routing versus switching has once again become a focus of debate recently; it is a continuation of the two classic approaches to networking, datagram versus virtual circuit.

MPLS uses the switching approach. In many aspects it is very similar to ATM or FR. Let us look at the basic operations of MPLS. Figure 4.3 shows a simple MPLS backbone network connecting multiple customer sites. Two LSPs are established: one LSP connects customer 1 and customer 3 using labels 23 and 42 over path $A \rightarrow C \rightarrow E$, and the other connects customer 2 to customer 4 using labels 12, 96, and 24 through path $A \rightarrow B \rightarrow D \rightarrow E$. Suppose that customer 1 wants to send packets to customer 3. Node A attaches label 23 to the packets from customer 1. When node C receives the labeled packets from node A it looks them up in the label-forwarding table for the corresponding outgoing label, which is 42. Node C then replaces label 23 with 42 and sends the packet to node E. Node E realizes that it is the end of an LSP and removes the label, sending the packet on to customer 3.

In a broad sense MPLS is a general framework for the switching approach (Figure 4.4). There are two components: a signaling protocol, which can be IP, ATM, FR, and so on and sets up an LSP, and a data plane that forwards packets based on the labels in the packets. This framework can be mapped to a specific set of protocols in many different ways. For example, MPLS has been mapped to ATM by using IP control protocols to manage ATM switches. However, an alternative proposal could be to use ATM control protocols to manage label-switched routers.

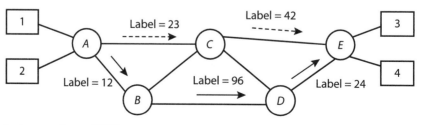

Figure 4.3   Basic operations of MPSL.

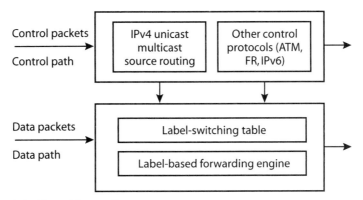

Figure 4.4 Label-based forwarding.

In practice, however, the control plane in MPLS is usually IP based. This is because IP control protocols, particularly routing protocols, have proved to be more mature and scalable than possible alternatives. An IP-based control plane in MPLS enables seamless integration between IP and MPLS, avoiding many of the problems in running IP over ATM.

MPLS, as standardized by the IETF, has an IP-based control plane that manages different types of label-based link layers. The MPLS signaling protocols may be used to set up LSPs for IP routers, ATM switches, and FR switches. MPLS has even been proposed to manage optical transport networks that do not perform label-based forwarding at all. The data plane may be ATM cells, FR frames, or IP packets with a shim header (described in Section 4.4.4).

A unified control plane tightly integrated with the IP control protocols that MPLS offers has considerable attraction. It brings simplicity to the management of large IP networks and provides the necessary mechanisms for performing traffic engineering and performance optimization, which the current IP network lacks.

4.3.2 Label-Switching Proposals

A number of vendors put forward several proposals for label switching before the IETF started the process of standardization. These proposals had a major influence on the development of MPLS, and in fact, the current MPLS standards derived much current architecture from them.

Although these proposals are all based on the same paradigm of label swapping, there are some fundamental differences in the details. The approaches can be broadly categorized into *control driven* and *data driven*. In the rest of this section we will look briefly at the five different proposals and discuss the two basic approaches.

Tag Switching

Tag Switching is based on the control-driven approach and is largely driven by IP routing protocols. In Tag Switching the setup of LSPs closely follows IP control messages such as routing updates and RSVP messages. For the unicast case the tag (label) bindings are carried by the tag distribution protocol (TDP). TDP peering between neighbors is established via a TCP connection between the peers. Tag bindings are distributed to the neighbors via TDP. Each tag switch router (TSR) distributes tag bindings to all its neighbors for all FECs (independent distribution). Higher-level tags for creating tag stacking may be done by remote TDP peering. However, in the case of BGP, the higher-level tags can be piggybacked in a BGP tag extension. For multicast, Tag Switching piggybacks binding information in a PIM control messages for supporting multicast in a PIM environment. Tag Switching also provides RSVP extension to piggyback tag binding information for RSVP flows. Support for explicit routing is achieved by extending RSVP to carry a new source route object.

Aggregate Route-Based IP Switching

Aggregate Route-based IP Switching (ARIS) from IBM is similar to Tag Switching in that it is also control driven. However, ARIS includes the concept of an *egress identifier* to express the granularity of an LSP. The LSP setup for an FEC starts at the "egress" node for the FEC. A node is considered an egress for an FEC if the next hop is a non-ARIS neighbor or the node is at a routing boundary. ARIS provides loop prevention and detection capability and also hop count on LSPs for TTL decrement at the ingress node. Multicast support is integral to ARIS and extends loop prevention and detection capabilities to multicast LSPs. Explicit routing support is also integral to the protocol. The only other distribution mechanism used is RSVP to support RSVP application flows. For ATM networks ARIS supports merging via VC merge and VP merge and can operate in nonmerge ATM networks. Label stacking or layer-2 tunneling is supported via piggybacking stack labels when lower-level LSPs are set up.

IP Navigator

IP Navigator is also a control-driven protocol. IP Navigator makes an ATM or Frame Relay cloud look like an IP network to the edge routers. Inside the cloud, a VC signaling protocol is employed to set up multi-point-to-point and point-to-multipoint VCs. When a packet arrives at the edge of the cloud, the ingress router performs a route lookup to determine the egress and then forwards the packet along the preestablished VC to the destination switch. Explicit source routing is used for setting up the VCs. It is assumed that OSPF is the internal routing protocol within a routing domain.

IP Switching

The Ipsilon Flow Management Protocol (IFMP) is a traffic-driven protocol that sets up shortcut paths on the fly for long-lasting flows. When a flow first starts to transmit data, IP packets are sent to the controller of the IP switch and are forwarded with normal destination-based IP forwarding. When the number of packets from a flow exceeds a predetermined threshold, the controller uses IFMP to set up an LSP for the particular flow. Once the LSP is established, the packets from the flow start to follow the shortcut LSPs rather than going through the controller. The LSPs are periodically refreshed to ensure that the LSPs are consistent with the underlying forwarding tables. If an LSP is idle for a period, it is automatically timed out and deleted.

Cell Switch Router (CSR)

The CSR proposal is similar to IP switching in many respects. CSR is primarily designed as a device for interconnecting ATM clouds. Within a logical IP subnet (LIS), ATM Forum standards are used to connect hosts and switches. Multiple LISs are then interconnected with CSRs that are capable of running both IP forwarding and cell forwarding. Based on the port number of the packets, CSRs may choose to set up LSPs for long-lasting flows. The set up of LSPs is data driven for best-effort traffic and RSVP driven for flows that require resource reservation. Once an LSP is set up, the packets will follow the shortcut paths and bypass IP-level forwarding in the CSRs.

4.3.3   Comparison of Approaches

One of the key issues in label switching is the way the LSPs are established. The many different approaches can be divided into two basic groups: data driven and control driven.

In a *control-driven* approach, the setup of LSPs is initiated by control messages such as routing updates and RSVP messages. This can be implemented in two ways. One way is to piggyback the label information in the control messages. For example, a label can be carried in the routing updates to pass on the label that a neighbor should use. This approach is simple but requires modifications to the existing protocols; for example, extensions to current routing protocols are needed in order to carry labels in routing updates. An alternative is to use a separate label distribution protocol for setting up LSPs. The label distribution protocol may be driven by the control protocols.

Label setup is decoupled from the data path in the sense that all LSPs are preestablished during the processing of control messages. Thus when the data packets arrive, the LSPs are already established. The control-driven approach allows flexible control over the way the LSPs are set up. For example, it is possible to set up an LSP for all traffic that exits from a specific egress router of a network or an explicitly specified route, as we will discuss later in this chapter (Section 4.4.1).

The control-driven approach has its downside too. LSPs may be confined to one control domain. For example, routing-based schemes, such as tag and ARIS, can establish LSPs only within a routing domain. Additional mechanisms such as label stacking are needed in order to cross the control domain borders. For a large network, preestablishing all LSPs may lead to scalability issues; the number of LSPs that have to be set up can easily run into the tens of thousands. The messaging overheads during routing changes may cause congestion and overloading in control processors.

The mechanisms used in a control-driven approach are inevitably specific to the control protocols on which the mechanisms are based. For example, both tag and ARIS use route-based mechanisms for setting up switched paths along the forwarding table produced by the routing protocol and use RSVP-based mechanisms for setting up switched paths for RSVP flows. Multicast may require another set of different mechanisms for label setup.

In the *data-driven* approach, the setup of an LSP is triggered by data packets. The LSPs are set up on the fly while the data packets are arriving. Obviously the first few packets must be processed at the IP level until the corresponding LSP is set up. In the Ipsilon scheme, for example, the setup of a switched path starts when a switch detects that a flow is long lasting (either by matching a well-known port number or by waiting for a threshold number of packets to be forwarded). Thus the data-driven approach is less deterministic since it depends on the traffic patterns in the network. When there are many short-lived connections, the performance of label switching tends to deteriorate since setting up LSPs for short-lived connections is much more costly in terms of overhead.

The data-driven approach is also less flexible than the control-driven approach. Note that in the data-driven approach, an LSP works like the "cache" of a path: it somewhat passively reflects the path that packets traverse. As such, it cannot be used to control the setup of the LSP. For example, it would be difficult to implement explicit routes with the data-driven approach.

4.4 MPLS Architecture

In this section we describe the basic concepts, architecture, and protocols in MPLS.

4.4.1 Key Concepts

Figure 4.5 shows a simple MPLS network with four LSRs and three LSPs ($A{\rightarrow}B{\rightarrow}C$, $A{\rightarrow}B{\rightarrow}D$, and $C{\rightarrow}B{\rightarrow}D$). The first and last LSRs over an LSP are called the ingress and egress, respectively. For LSP 1 in Figure 4.5, LSR A is the ingress and LSR C is the egress. The operation of ingress and egress LSRs is different from that of an intermediate LSR in many aspects. LSPs are directional. For any pair of LSRs, the LSR that transmits packets with respect to the direction of data flow is said to be upstream, whereas the LSR that receives packets is downstream. For example, for LSP 1 in Figure 4.5, LSR A is upstream of LSR B, and LSR B is downstream of LSR A.

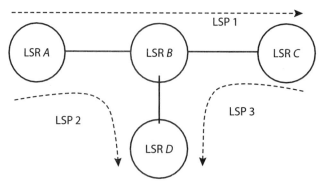

Figure 4.5   A simple MPLS network.

Label

As we described in Section 4.3, a label is a short, fixed-length, locally significant identifier that is used for label switching. A packet is called a labeled packet if a label has been encoded into the packet. The label may be encoded into a packet in many ways. In some cases the label may be mapped to some field in an existing data link or network layer protocol. For example, when we use ATM switches as LSRs, the VCI/ VPI fields are used as the MPLS label. However, this approach is not always feasible. A simple MPLS encapsulation has been standardized that will carry the label and some additional information. This adds another thin layer between the data link layer and the IP layer specifically for MPLS processing.

Because the label is the only identifier that is used for packet forwarding, an LSR must be able to associate the incoming label with an LSP. For LSRs that are connected by point-to-point connections, the label needs to be unique only to the point-to-point interface. In other words, the interface can use the entire label space, and the same label value may be used over different interfaces. When there are multiaccess interfaces, an LSR may not be able to determine, solely based on the label, which neighbor sent the packet. Thus the label must be allocated uniquely across all multiaccess interfaces. In actual implementations label space may be unique across the entire LSR. In this case label space is partitioned among all interfaces, so the usable space for each interface is much smaller.

Each label is associated with an FEC. An FEC defines a group of IP packets that are forwarded over the same LSP with the same treatment. It can be described as a set of classification rules that determine whether a packet belongs to a particular FEC or not. Different types of FEC will be discussed later in this section. It is important that the binding from a label to an FEC be one to one. If multiple FECs are associated with a label, a downstream LSR will not be able to distinguish packets of different FECs by simply looking at the label.

Hierarchical Label Stack

MPLS allows more than one label to be encoded in a packet. This is referred to as a *label stack* since the labels are organized as a last-in, first-out stack. A label stack is used to support nested tunnels. An LSP may have another nested LSP between an LSR and can push in a new label on top of the current label so that the packet will follow the tunnel pointed out by the new label on the top of the stack. When the packet reaches the end of the tunnel, the LSR at the end of the tunnel discards the top label and the one below pops up. Label stacking is discussed in depth in Section 4.4.3.

Label-Switching Table

The *label-switching table,* also called an *incoming label map* (ILM), maintains the mappings between an incoming label to the outgoing interface and the outgoing label (Figure 4.6). Its functions are similar to those of the packet-forwarding table in IP routers. The entry that the incoming label points to is called the *next-hop label-forwarding entry* (NHLFE). Each incoming label typically points to one NHLFE. However, in the case of load sharing, there may be multiple NHLFEs for an incoming label. The method for splitting traffic in the case of multiple NHLFEs is not specified in the standard.

Typically the NHLFE contains the next hop and the outgoing label for that next hop. If an LSR is the ingress or egress of an LSP, the NHLFE also specifies the actions for manipulating the label stack. NHLFEs may also contain additional state information related to the LSP; for example, hop count and data link encapsulation to use when transmitting the packet.

Figure 4.6   Label-forwarding table.

LSRs use the label-switching table for forwarding labeled packets. When a packet arrives, an LSR finds the corresponding NHLFE for the incoming label by performing a lookup in the label-switching table. The LSR then replaces the incoming label with the outgoing label and forwards the packet to the interface specified in the corresponding NHLFE.

Label Distribution Protocols

Before LSPs can be used, the label-switching table at each LSR must be populated with the mappings from any incoming label to the outgoing interface and the outgoing label. This process is called *LSP setup* or *label distribution.*

A *label distribution protocol* is a set of procedures by which two LSRs learn each other's MPLS capabilities and exchange label-mapping information. Label distribution protocols set up the state for LSPs in the network. Since protocols with similar functions are often called signaling protocols in ATM or circuit-based networks, the process of label distribution is sometimes called signaling, and label distribution protocols are called signaling protocols for the MPLS networks.

The MPLS architecture does not assume that there is only a single label distribution protocol. In fact, it specifically allows for multiple protocols for use in different scenarios. The IETF MPLS Working Group has specified LDP as a protocol for hop-by-hop label distribution based on IP routing information. For explicitly routed LSPs or LSPs that require QoS guarantees, CR-LDP and RSVP-TE are two protocols that support such functions. We will cover label distribution protocols in Section 4.5.

Label Assignment and Distribution

In MPLS the decision to bind a particular label to a particular FEC is always made by the downstream LSR with respect to the flow of the packets. The downstream LSR then informs the upstream LSR of the binding. Thus the data traffic and control traffic flow in opposite directions. For LSP 1 in Figure 4.5, packets flow from LSR *A* to LSR *B,* whereas label assignment between *A* and *B* is determined by LSR *B* and distributed to LSR *A.*

Although the upstream LSR can assign labels and inform the downstream LSR, downstream label distribution was chosen for good reasons. Consider LSR *A* and *B* in Figure 4.5. Suppose that the label for

LSP 1 between A and B is F. The upstream LSR A only has to put label F in a packet on LSP 1 before it sends to LSR B. When LSR B receives the packet from LSR A, it has to perform a lookup-based label F. Implementation is much easier when the downstream LSR, B, gets to choose the label so that the labels are assigned only from specific ranges and the lookup table can be made more compact. Label merging, which we will discuss next, also requires downstream label distribution.

There are two different modes of downstream label distribution: *downstream on demand* and *unsolicited downstream*. With the downstream-on-demand mode, an LSR explicitly requests a neighbor for a label binding for a particular FEC. The unsolicited downstream mode, on the other hand, allows an LSR to distribute label bindings to its neighbors that have not explicitly requested them. Depending on the characteristics of interfaces, actual implementations may provide only one of them or both. However, both of these label distribution techniques may be used in the same network at the same time. On any given label distribution adjacency, the upstream LSR and the downstream LSR must agree on which mode is to be used.

Label Merging

In MPLS, two or more LSPs may be merged into one. Take LSP 2 and LSP 3 in Figure 4.5 as an example again. Note that LSR B receives packets from LSR A for LSP 2 and packets from LSR C for LSP 3. However, all these packets go from LSR B to LSR D. Thus it is possible for LSR B to use the same label between LSR B and LSR D for all packets from LSP 2 and LSP 3. In essence the two LSPs are merged into one at LSR B and form a label-switched tree. In general, when an LSR has bound multiple incoming labels to a particular FEC, an LSR may have a single outgoing label to all packets in the same FEC. Once the packets are forwarded with the same outgoing label, the information that they arrived from different interfaces and/or with different incoming labels is lost.

Label merging may substantially reduce the requirement on label space. With label merging, the number of outgoing labels per FEC need only be one; without label merging, the number could be very large. Let us look at a practical example. Suppose that we would like to set up MPLS LSPs between all edge nodes of a network and there are N edge nodes. The worst-case label requirement without label merging, namely, the maximum number of labels required on a single link in one direction, is approximately $N^2/4$. However, if we merge labels of packets destined to the same destination node, the worst-case number is merely N.

Not all LSRs may be able to support label merging. For example, LSRs that are based on ATM cannot perform label merging because of cell interleaving. In such cases different labels should be used even though an LSR has packets from different interfaces with the same FEC. This issue will be discussed in Section 4.4.4.

Route Selection and Explicit Routing

During the label distribution process, an LSR needs to determine which is the next hop for the LSP that it tries to establish. There are two basic approaches to determine this: *hop-by-hop routing* and *explicit routing*.

The hop-by-hop approach relies on IP routing information to set up LSPs. The MPLS control module will, at each hop, call the routing module to get the next hop for a particular LSP. The routing module at each LSR independently chooses the next hop based on IP routing or other routing methods. The other approach is explicit routing. In this mode a single LSR, generally the ingress or the egress of the LSP, specifies the entire route for the LSP. The routes for the LSPs can be computed by routing algorithms designed to achieve certain prespecified objectives. Such routing algorithms are often referred to as *constraint-based routing*.

If the entire route for the LSP is specified, the LSP is "strictly" explicitly routed. If only part of the route for an LSP is specified, the LSP is "loosely" explicitly routed. This is very similar to the concept of strict source routing and loose source routing in IP. Once a loosely explicitly routed LSP is established, it may change or it can be pinned so that it always uses the same route.

The explicitly routed LSP, or explicit route, has emerged as one of the most important features in MPLS. It provides a mechanism for overriding the routes established by IP routing. This can be used to route traffic around congested hot spots and optimize resource utilization across the network. Without the explicit route mechanism, such features cannot be easily implemented in current IP networks.

4.4.2 Forwarding Equivalency Classes

IP routers currently use a small number of fields in a packet header to make forwarding decisions. In destination-based routing, only the network number part of the destination address is used to select the next hop. All packets that have the same destination network number follow the same path and receive the same treatment. Thus the forwarding process can be viewed as one that partitions packets into a finite number of sets. Within the same set, all packets are treated the same way. We call a set of packets that are treated identically in the forwarding process an FEC.

An FEC can be expressed as a set of classification rules that determine if a packet belongs to the FEC. For example, a set of packets with the same destination network number is an FEC for destination-based IP routing—these packets receive identical treatment in the forwarding process.

IP-based networks currently do not support many different types of FECs since this would require classification of packets during packet processing to match the packets to FECs. As we discussed in Chapter 3, multidimensional classification is a difficult problem that is still under active research. MPLS can, however, easily support many different types of FECs. In MPLS the classification of packets is moved from the data plane to the control plane. Once an LSP is set up, only the ingress LSR needs to classify packets to FECs.

FEC is closely related to the concept of forwarding granularity discussed early in Section 4.2.2. The types of FECs supported by a network in fact determine the forwarding granularity. For example, suppose that a network supports an FEC that classifies packets based on their source and destination addresses. This will result in a finer forwarding granularity than current destination-based forwarding. A coarse forwarding granularity is essential to scale to large networks, whereas a fine granularity allows maximal control over the forwarding of packets inside the network.

MPLS allows multiple types of granularity to coexist over the same forwarding path. The common types of FECs that MPLS supports include

- ○ **IP prefix.** Packets that match an IP destination prefix in the routing table are considered as one FEC. This is a direct mapping from the routing table to the label-switching table, enabling MPLS to support the destination-based forwarding in current IP routing. One advantage of such FECs is that the label distribution may be closely coupled with IP routing and driven by the events in routing protocols. It is also feasible to piggyback on the routing protocols so that the message overheads for label distribution are minimized.

○ **Egress router.** In most backbone networks, packets come in from the ingress node and go out from the egress node. A useful FEC includes all the packets that go out on the same egress node. Such granularity is very hard to support in a datagram model. With MPLS, however, one can set up LSPs to a particular egress LSR based on the information from the BGP Next Hop in a BGP update message, from the OSPF Router ID in the OSPF advertisement, or directly via MPLS label distribution. This represents the coarsest granularity currently available and can scale to large networks. The ability to identify streams between ingress and egress node pairs is also useful when it comes to supporting traffic engineering within a backbone network.

○ **Application flow.** This type of FEC results in the finest granularity since each application flow is one FEC. It is the least scalable of all granularity types. The advantage of application flow is, however, that it provides end-to-end switching and allows maximum control of the traffic flows in the network. Application flow is best suited for handling special purposes.

There is a clear trade-off between scalability and controllability. The ability of MPLS to support multiple FECs with different types of forwarding granularity gives a lot of flexibility in accommodating different requirements and combining different forwarding granularities in the same network.

4.4.3 Hierarchy and Label Stacking

MPLS allows multiple labels to be encoded into a packet to form a label stack. Label stacking is used to construct nested LSPs, similar to the capability of IP-in-IP tunneling or loose source routing in IP routing. Such nested LSPs can create a multilevel hierarchy where multiple LSPs can be aggregated into one LSP tunnel.

Consider the backbone network shown in Figure 4.7, which connects many networks. Suppose that LSR *A* and *B* want to set up two LSPs to LSR *C* and *D*, respectively. We can set up two LSPs as

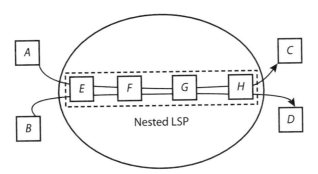

Figure 4.7   Nested LSP.

$A{\rightarrow}E{\rightarrow}F{\rightarrow}G{\rightarrow}H{\rightarrow}C$ and $B{\rightarrow}E{\rightarrow}F{\rightarrow}G{\rightarrow}H{\rightarrow}D$. With label stacking, we can first set up an LSP tunnel as $E{\rightarrow}F{\rightarrow}G{\rightarrow}H$ and LSPs from A to C and B to D through this tunnel: $A{\rightarrow}E{\rightarrow}H{\rightarrow}C$, $B{\rightarrow}E{\rightarrow}H{\rightarrow}D$. Note that only LSR E and H, the ingress and egress of the LSP tunnel, appear in the LSPs from A to C and B to D.

The benefit of label stacking is that we can aggregate multiple LSPs into a single LSP tunnel. For example, thousands of LSPs may go through $E{\rightarrow}F{\rightarrow}G{\rightarrow}H$. Without the hierarchy, all backbone nodes (E, F, G, H) have to be involved in the setup of these LSPs. By creating an LSP tunnel, the information about these LSPs becomes invisible to the interior nodes of the backbone (nodes F and G). The interior nodes of the backbone are not affected by any changes of the LSPs going through the tunnel.

Let us look at processing when a packet travels from A to C via the LSR tunnel $E{\rightarrow}F{\rightarrow}G{\rightarrow}H$. When the packet P travels from A to E, it has a label stack of depth 1. Based on the incoming label, node E determines that the packet must enter the tunnel. Node E first replaces the incoming label with a label that it has agreed on with H, the egress of the tunnel, and then pushes a new label onto the label stack. This level-2 label is used for label switching within the LSP tunnel. Nodes F and G switch the packet using only the level-2 label. When node H receives the packet, it realizes that it is the end of the tunnel. So node H pops up the top-level label and switches the packet with the level-1 label to C.

MPLS also supports a mode called *penultimate hop popping,* where the top-level label may pop up at the penultimate LSR of the LSP rather than the egress of the LSP. Note that in normal operation, the egress of an LSP tunnel must perform two lookups. For example, node H must determine that it is the egress of the tunnel. It then pops the top-level label and switches the packet to node C with the next-level label.

When penultimate hop popping is used, the penultimate node G looks up the top-level label and decides that it is the penultimate node of the tunnel and node H is the egress node of the LSP. The penultimate node then pops up the top-level label and forwards to the egress node H. When H receives the packet, the label used for the LSP tunnel is already gone. Thus node H can simply forward the packet based on the current label to C. Penultimate hop popping can also be used when there is only a single label. In this case the penultimate node removes the label header and sends an unlabeled packet to the egress. To illustrate this, let us examine how node H processes the packet from G. When node H receives the packet from G, the packet has only one label left in the stack. Node H performs a lookup with the label and finds that it is the penultimate node of LSP from A to C and the next hop is C. If node H operates in the penultimate hop-popping mode, it removes the label header and sends the unlabeled packet to node C. In this example there are two labels in the stack, and both are popped out by the penultimate nodes of their respective LSPs.

MPLS supports two types of peering for exchanging stack labels: explicit and implicit. Explicit peering is similar to MPLS neighbor peering for LDP; the only difference is that the peering is between remote LSRs. In explicit peering, LDP connections are set up between remote LDP peers, exactly like the local LDP peers. This is most useful when the number of remote LDP peers is small or the number of higher-level label mappings is large.

Implicit peering does not have an LDP connection to a remote LDP peer. Instead the stack labels are piggybacked onto the LDP messages when the lower-level LSP is set up between the implicit-peering LSRs. The intermediate LDP peers of the lower-level LSP propagate the stack labels as attributes of the lower-level labels. This way the ingress nodes of the lower-level LSP receive the stack label from the egress LSR. The advantage of this peering scheme is that it does not require the n-square peering mesh, as in explicit peering, especially when the number of remote peers is very large. However, this requires that the intermediate LSR maintain the label stack information even when it is not in use.

4.4.4 Label Stack Encoding

MPLS works over many different link-layer technologies. The exact encoding of an MPLS label stack depends on the type of link-layer technologies. For packet-based technologies such as Packet over SONET (POS) and Ethernet, the MPLS header is inserted between the link-layer and the IP layer and is used for label switching. Figure 4.8 shows MPLS encoding over POS links. The MPLS frame consists of the original IP packet and the MPLS header.

For ATM and FR, which are inherently label switching, the top entry of the MPLS label stack is mapped to certain fields in the ATM cell header or FR frame header. Thus label switching is actually performed with the native header of the link-layer protocols. For example, when MPLS is used over ATM, the top-level label may be mapped to the VPI/VCI space in the cell header. The MPLS stack, however, is still carried in the payload. Figure 4.9 shows the MPLS label stack encoding for ATM links. The complete MPLS stack in the AAL5 PUD makes it easier for LSRs to switch from an ATM interface to packet-based interfaces, such as POS interfaces, by simply adding the outgoing label in the existing top-level entry. For FR the top label of the MPLS stack is copied into the data link connection identifier (DLCI) in the FR header.

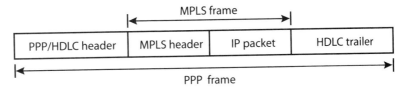

Figure 4.8   MPLS encoding over POS links.

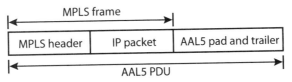

Figure 4.9   MPLS encoding over ATM links.

Label Stack Header

The MPLS label stack header is also called the MPLS shim header. The top of the label stack appears first in the packet, and the bottom appears last. The network layer packet (e.g., IP packet) follows the last entry of the label stack.

The label stack header consists of a sequence of label stack entries. Each entry is 32 bits long and has the format shown in Figure 4.10.

Each label stack entry has the following fields:

○ **Label value.** The label field is 20 bits long. When a labeled packet is received, an LSR uses the label at the top of the stack to find the information associated with the label, including the next hop to which the packet is to be forwarded; the operation to be performed on the label stack, such as label swapping or stack pop-up; and other information such as network layer encapsulation and bandwidth allocation.

○ **Experimental use.** The 3-bit field is reserved for experimental use. One possible use is to set drop priorities for packets in a way similar to that in Differentiated Services.

○ **Bottom of stack (S).** The S bit is used to indicate the bottom of the label stack. The bit is set to 1 for the last entry in the label stack and to 0 for all other entries.

○ **Time to live (TTL).** The 8-bit field is used to encode a time-to-live value for detecting loops in LSPs.

Several reserved label values have special meanings:

○ **Label value 0.** This value represents the *IPv4 Explicit NULL label*. This label value is legal only when it is the sole label stack entry. It indicates that the label stack must be popped and the resulting packet should be forwarded based on the IPv4 header.

○ **Label value 1.** This value is used to indicate *Router Alert*, similar to the Router Alert option in IP packets. This Router Alert label can

Figure 4.10 Label stack entry format.

appear anywhere in the stack except at the bottom. When a packet is received with this label on the top of the stack, the packet should be delivered to the local controller for processing. The forwarding of the packet is determined by the label beneath the Router Alert label. The Router Alert label should be pushed in if the packet is to be forwarded further. The Router Alert label can be used to indicate that a packet contains control information that needs to be processed at each hop by the local control processor.

○ **Label value 2.** This value represents the *IPv6 Explicit NULL label*. This label value is similar to label value 0 except that it is reserved for IPv6.

○ **Label value 3.** This label value represents the *Implicit NULL label*. Label value 3 may be assigned and distributed but should never appear in the label stack. When an LSR would otherwise replace the label at the top of the stack with a new label but the new label is the Implicit NULL label, the LSR will pop the stack instead of doing the replacement.

○ **Label values 4 to 15.** These values are reserved.

Determining the Network Layer Protocol

The label stack header does not have a field that explicitly identifies the network layer protocol for processing the packet at the bottom of the label stack. This information should be associated with the label at the bottom of the stack during the label distribution process. Thus when an LSR pops the last label off a packet, it can determine which network layer protocol should be used to process the packet.

With this approach labeled packets from multiple network layer protocols can coexist. Under normal conditions only egress routers pop off the last label and process the packet inside. However, when there are errors, for example, undeliverable packets, it becomes necessary for an intermediate LSR to generate error messages specifically to the network layer protocol. Therefore the information about the network layer protocol should be associated with the entire LSP rather than just the egress node.

4.4.5 Loop Detection

Loops in LSPs can cause severe damage to an MPLS network; traffic in a loop remains in that loop for as long as the LSP exists. IP routing protocols routinely form transient routing loops while routing convergence is taking place. Since MPLS may use IP routing information for setting up LSPs, loops could be formed as a result of IP routing inconsistency. Configuration errors and software bugs may also create loops in LSPs.

In IP routing, the damage from routing loops is mitigated by the use of a TTL field within the packet header. This field decrements by 1 at each forwarding hop. If the value decrements to zero, the packet is discarded. The label stack header also has a TTL field for this purpose. When an IP packet is labeled at the ingress node, the TTL field in the label stack header is set to the TTL value of the IP header. When the last label is popped off the stack, the TTL value of the label stack is copied back to the TTL field of the IP header.

MPLS packets forwarded on ATM labels, however, have no such mechanism since the ATM header does not have a TTL field. The solution to this problem requires loop detection during the setup phase of LSPs.

Loop detection is achieved by the use of a path vector field within the label distribution messages. This path vector contains a list of the LSRs that the message has traversed. When an LSR propagates a message containing a path vector, it adds its LSR ID to the path vector list. An LSR that receives a message with a path vector that contains its LSR ID detects that the message has traversed a loop. In addition, a hop count is used to record the number of LSRs that the message has traversed. When an LSR propagates a message, it increments the count. When an LSR detects that a hop count has reached a configured maximum value, it considers the LSP to have a loop. The hop count limits the maximum number of hops that an LSP can traverse.

4.5 Label Distribution Protocols

The IETF MPLS working group initially considered only one label distribution protocol (LDP). LDP was largely based on Tag Switching and ARIS proposals, which were designed to support hop-by-hop routing. The support for explicit routing became critical after it became apparent that traffic engineering is a key application of MPLS. Two different proposals were put forward. One proposal, *"Constraint-based LSP Setup using LDP,"* adds a set of extensions to LDP to support explicit routing.

The other proposal, *"Extensions to RSVP for LSP Tunnels,"* extends RSVP protocols to perform label distribution.

The two competing proposals have caused some heated debates in the MPLS working group, but a consensus could not be reached to pick one of them. In the end the working group decided that both proposals would be standardized. The two protocols are often referred to as CR-LDP (constraint routing label distribution protocol) and RSVP-TE (RSVP with traffic-engineering extension). CR-LDP and RSVP-TE can also perform hop-by-hop LSP setup.

In this section we first describe LDP and then compare the similarities of and differences between CR-LDP and RSVP-TE.

4.5.1   LDP

LDP is the first label distribution protocol standardized by the MPLS working group. The protocol is designed to support hop-by-hop routing. Two LSRs that use LDP to exchange label/FEC mapping information are known as *LDP peers*.

LDP Messages

LDP peers exchange four categories of messages with each other:

○ Discovery messages for announcing and maintaining the presence of an LSR in a network
○ Session messages for establishing, maintaining, or terminating sessions between LDP peers
○ Advertisement messages for creating, changing, or deleting label mappings for FECs
○ Notification messages for distributing advisory information and error information

Discovery messages allow LSRs to indicate their presence in a network by sending the Hello message periodically. This message is transmitted as a UDP packet to the LDP port at the all-routers-on-this-subnet group multicast address. Once a session is established between two peers, all subsequent messages are exchanged over TCP.

Mapping FEC to LSP

When to request a label or advertise a label mapping to a peer is largely a local decision made by an LSR. In general, the LSR requests a label mapping from a neighboring LSR when it needs one and advertises a label mapping to a neighboring LSR when it wants the neighbor to use a label.

LDP specifies the FEC that is mapped to an LSP. Currently only two types of FECs are defined: *address prefix* and *host address*. In order to avoid loops, the following set of rules is used by an ingress LSR to map a particular packet to a particular LSP:

○ If the destination address of the packet matches the host address FEC of at one LSP, the packet is mapped to the LSP. If multiple LSPs have the same matched FECs, the packet may be mapped to any one of these LSPs.

○ If the destination of the packet matches the prefix FEC of one LSP, the packet is mapped to that LSP. If there are multiple matched LSPs, the packet is mapped to the one with the longest prefix match.

○ If a packet must traverse a particular egress router (e.g., from the BGP routing information) and an LSP has an address prefix FEC element that is an address of that router, the packet is mapped to that LSP.

LDP Identifiers

Since each interface of an LSR may use the entire label space, it is important that an LSR identify each label space within the LSR in any message exchanges with its peers. The LDP identifier is used to identify an LSR label space. An LDP identifier is 6 bytes long. The first 4 bytes encode an IP address assigned to the LSR, and the last two octets identify a specific label space within the LSR. The last two octets of LDP identifiers for platform-wide label spaces are always set to zero.

LDP Discovery

LDP allows an LSR to automatically detect its LDP peers. There are two mechanisms, one for discovering LSR neighbors that are directly connected and the other for detecting LSR neighbors that are remotely connected. The basic discovery mechanism sends out LDP Link Hello messages on each interface. The messages are sent as UDP packets addressed to the LDP discovery port with the *all-routers-on-this-subnet* group multicast address. To detect LDP neighbors that are remotely connected, an LSR can send Targeted Hello messages to a specific IP address at the LDP discovery port. An LSR that receives

Hello messages may choose to reply with Hello messages if it wants to establish a peer relationship. The exchanges of Hello messages establish the adjacency.

LDP Session Management

The exchange of Hello messages between any two LSRs establishes the communication channel between them and the label space that the LSRs will use in their peer relationship. After that the two LSRs can establish a session for the specified label space by setting up transport connections and starting the initialization process. Initialization includes negotiation of protocol version, label distribution method, timer values, VPI/VCI ranges for label-controlled ATM, and DLCI ranges for label-controlled Frame Relay. An LSR can accept only initialization messages from LSRs that it has exchanged a Hello message with.

LSRs maintain their peer and session relationship by sending Hello and Keepalive messages periodically to each other. Timers are set when these messages are received. An LSR considers the peer or the session down if the corresponding timer expires before new messages are received.

Label Distribution and Management

LDP supports both *downstream on demand* and *downstream unsolicited* label distribution. Both of these label distribution techniques may be used in the same network at the same time. However, for any given LDP session, only one should be used.

LSPs may be set up independently between all LSRs along the path or in order from egress to ingress. An LSR may support both types of control as a configurable option. When using an independent approach, each LSR may advertise label mappings to its neighbors at any time it desires. Note that in this case an upstream label can be advertised before a downstream label is received. When setting up LSP with the orderly approach, an LSR may send a label mapping only for a FEC for which it has a label mapping for the FEC next hop or for which the LSR is the egress. For each FEC for which the LSR is not the egress and no mapping exists, the LSR must wait until a label from a downstream LSR is received before mapping the FEC and passing corresponding labels to upstream LSRs.

4.5.2   CR-LDP

CR-LDP is a label distribution protocol specifically designed to support traffic engineering. It is largely based on the LDP specification with a set of extensions for carrying explicit routes and resource reservations. The new features introduced in CR-LDP include

- ○ Explicit routing
- ○ Resource reservation and classes
- ○ Route pinning
- ○ Path preemption
- ○ Handling failures
- ○ LSP ID

Setup of Explicit Routes

In CR-LDP an explicit route is also referred to as a *constraint-based route* or CR-LSP. CR-LDP supports both the strict and loose modes of explicit routes. An explicit route is represented in a Label Request message as a list of nodes or groups of nodes along the explicit route. Each CR-LSP is identified by an LSP ID, a unique identifier within an MPLS network. An LSP ID is composed of the ingress LSR Router ID and a locally unique CR-LSP ID to that LSR. An LSP ID is used when the parameters of an existing LSP need to be modified.

In the strict mode each hop of the explicit route is uniquely identified by an IP address. In the loose mode there is more flexibility in the construction of the route. A loose explicit route may contain some so-called abstract nodes. An abstract node represents a set of nodes. The following types of abstract nodes are defined in CR-LDP: IPv4 prefix, IPv6 prefix, autonomous system (AS) number, and LSP ID. With an abstract node the exact path within the set of nodes represented by the abstract node is determined locally rather than by the explicit route itself. For example, a loose explicit path may specify a list of AS numbers that the explicit routes must follow. The exact route within each AS is not specified and is decided based on routing information and policies within the AS. This adds a different level of abstraction and allows LSPs to be specified in such a way that the effect of changes in individual links may be isolated within the AS.

The basic flow for an LSP setup with CR-LDP is shown in Figure 4.11. The ingress node, LSR *A*, initiates the setup of LSP from LSR *A* to LSR *C*. LSR *A* determines that the LSP should follow an explicit route

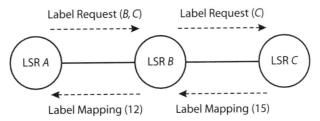

Figure 4.11   CR-LDP LSP setup.

from LSR *B*. It then sends a Label Request message to LSR *B* with an explicit route (*B, C*). LSR *B* receives the message and forwards it to LSR *C* after modifying the explicit route. LSR *C* determines that it is the egress of the LSP. It sends a Label Mapping message backward to LSR *B* with allocated label 15 for the LSP. LSR *B* uses the LSP ID in the Label Mapping message to match the original Label Request message. It then sends a Label Mapping message to LSR *A* with label 12. LSR *B* also populates the label-switching table with incoming label 12 pointing to outgoing label 15.

Resource Reservation and Class

CR-LDP allows sources to be reserved for explicit routes. The characteristics of a path can be described in terms of peak data rate (PDR), committed data rate (CDR), peak burst size (PBS), committed burst size (CBS), weight, and service granularity. The peak and committed rates describe the bandwidth constraints of a path, and the service granularity specifies the granularity at which the data rates are calculated. The weight determines the relative share of excess bandwidth about the committed rate. These parameters are very similar to those used for traffic policing in Differentiated Services. An option also exists to indicate that the resource requirement can be negotiable: an LSR may specify a smaller value for a particular parameter if it cannot be satisfied with existing resources. Network resources can also be classified into resource classes or colors so that NSPs can specify which class an explicit route must draw resources from.

Path Preemption and Priorities

If an LSP requires a certain resource reservation and sufficient resources are not available, the LSP may preempt existing LSPs. Two parameters are associated with an LSP for this purpose: *setup priority* and *holding priority*. The setup priority and holding priority reflect the preference for adding a new LSP and holding an existing LSP. A new LSP can preempt an existing LSP if the setup priority of the new LSP is higher than the holding priority of the existing LSP. The setup and holding priority values range from 0 to 7, where 0 is the priority assigned to the most important path, or the highest priority.

Path Reoptimization and Route Pinning

For a loose explicit route the exact route within an abstract node is not specified. Thus the segment of the route with an abstract node may adapt when traffic patterns change. CR-LDP can reoptimize an LSP, and an LSP ID can be used to avoid double booking during optimization. Under some circumstances route changes may not be desirable. CR-LDP has a route pinning option. When the route pinning option is used, an LSP cannot change its route once it is set up.

4.5.3   RSVP-TE

As we know, RSVP was initially designed as a protocol for setting up resource reservation in IP networks. The RSVP-TE protocol extends the original RSVP protocol to perform label distribution and support explicit routing. The new features added to the original RSVP include

○ Label distribution
○ Explicit routing
○ Bandwidth reservation for LSPs
○ Rerouting of LSPs after failures
○ Tracking of the actual route of an LSP
○ The concept of nodal abstraction
○ Preemption options

RSVP-TE introduces five new objects, defined in this section (Table 4.1).

LSP Tunnel

Although the original RSVP protocol was designed to set up reserved paths across IP networks, there is an important difference between a reserved path set up by the original RSVP protocol and an LSP. In original RSVP a reserved path is always associated with a particular destination and transport-layer protocol, and the intermediate nodes

Table 4.1	New objects in RSVP-TE
Object name	Applicable RSVP messages
LABEL_REQUEST	PATH
LABEL	RESV
EXPLICIT_ROUTE	PATH
RECORD_ROUTE	PATH, RESV
SESSION_ATTRIBUTE	PATH

forward packets based on the IP header. In contrast, with an LSP set up by RSVP-TE, the ingress node of the LSP can determine which packets can be sent over the LSP and the packets are opaque to the intermediate nodes along the LSP. To reflect this difference, an LSP in the RSVP-TE specification is referred to as an *LSP tunnel*.

Figure 4.12 shows the flow in setting up an explicit route with RSVP-TE. To create an LSP tunnel, the ingress node LSR *A* first creates a PATH message with a session type LSP_TUNNEL. The PATH message includes a LABEL_REQUEST object, which indicates that a label binding for this path is requested and also provides an indication of the network layer protocol that is to be carried over this path.

To set up an explicit route, LSR *A* needs to specify the route in an EXPLICIT_ROUTE object and adds it to the PATH message. LSR *A* may add a RECORD_ROUTE object to the PATH message so that the actual route is recorded and returns to the sender. The RECORD_ROUTE object may also be used to request notification from the network about changes of the actual route or to detect loops in the route.

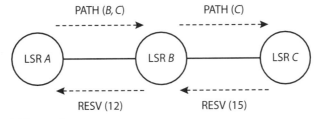

Figure 4.12   LSP tunnel setup.

Additional control information such as preemption, priority, local protection, and diagnostics may be included by adding a SESSION_ ATTRIBUTE object to the PATH message.

Once the PATH message is constructed, LSR *A* sends it to the next hop as indicated by the EXPLICIT_ROUTE object. If no EXPLICIT_ ROUTE object is present, the next hop is provided by the hop-by-hop routing.

Intermediate node LSR *B* modifies the EXPLICIT_ROUTE object and forwards to the egress node LSR *C*. LSR *C* allocates a new label, includes it in a LABEL object, and inserts into the RESV message. LSR *C* then sends the RESV message backward to the sender, following the path state created by the PATH message, in reverse order.

When the intermediate node LSR *B* receives an RESV message, it retrieves the label in the LABEL object and uses it as the outgoing label for the LSP. It also allocates a new label and places that label in the corresponding LABEL object of the RESV message, which it sends upstream to the previous hop (PHOP). LSR *B* then adds this new pair of labels to the label switching table. When the RESV message propagates upstream to the ingress node LSR *A*, an LSP is established.

Reservation Styles

For each RSVP session, the egress node has to select a reservation style. The original RSVP protocol has three styles: fixed filter (FF), wild filter (WF), and shared explici (SE). In RSVP-TE only FF and SE reservation styles are supported.

The *fixed filter* reservation style creates a distinct reservation for traffic from each sender that is not shared by other senders. With RSVP-TE this will create a point-to-point LSP for each ingress and egress pair. Most LSPs are expected to be set up using this filter.

The *shared explicit* style allows a receiver to specify explicitly the senders to be included in a reservation. There is a single reservation on a link for all the senders listed. This in essence creates a multi-point-to-point tree to the egress. With RSVP-TE, because each sender is explicitly listed in the RESV message, different labels may be assigned to different senders, thereby creating separate LSPs. The SE style is particularly useful for backup LSPs, which are used only if their corresponding active LSPs have failed. Thus these backup LSPs can share bandwidth among themselves and with active LSPs during normal operation.

Rerouting LSP Tunnels

Under many circumstances it may be desirable to reroute existing LSPs. For example, an LSP tunnel may be rerouted in order to optimize the resource utilization in the network or to restore connectivity after network failures.

RSVP-TE uses a technique called *make before break* to minimize the disruption of traffic flows during such rerouting. To reroute an existing LSP tunnel, a replacement LSP tunnel is first set up, then the traffic switches over, and finally the old LSP tunnel tears down.

During the transition period the old and new LSP tunnels may coexist and so compete with each other for resources on network segments that they have in common. This may lead to a racing condition where the new LSP tunnel cannot be established because the old LSP tunnel has not released resources, yet the old LSP tunnel cannot release the resources before the new LSP tunnel is established. To resolve this problem, it is necessary to make sure that the resource reservation is not counted twice for both the old and new LSP tunnels. This can be achieved in RSVP-TE by using SE reservation style. The basic idea is that the old and new LSP tunnels share resources along links that they have in common.

To make this scheme work, the LSP_TUNNEL object is used to narrow the scope of the RSVP session to the particular tunnel in question. The combination of the tunnel egress IP address, a tunnel ID, and the tunnel ingress IP address is used as a unique identifier for an LSP tunnel. During the reroute operation the tunnel ingress needs to appear as two different senders to the RSVP session. A new LSP ID is used in the SENDER_TEMPLATE and FILTER_SPEC objects for the new LSP tunnel.

The ingress node of the LSP tunnel initiates rerouting by sending a new PATH message using the original SESSION object with a new SENDER_TEMPLATE, a new EXPLICIT_ROUTE object, and a new LSP ID. This new PATH message is treated as a conventional new LSP tunnel setup. However, on links that are common to the old and new LSP tunnels, the SE reservation style ensures that the old and new tunnel share the same reservation. Once the ingress receives an RESV message for the new LSP, it can switch traffic to the new LSP tunnel and tear down the old LSP tunnel.

4.5.4   Comparison

As we mentioned at the beginning of Section 4.5, the fact that we have two competing label distribution protocols was more a result of the compromise by the MPLS working group than a conscious technical decision. It is not clear whether the two protocols will both be supported in the long run or whether one of them will emerge as the winner in the marketplace. Although CR-LDP and RSVP-TE share many similarities (Table 4.2), there are also some key differences. We will discuss these differences and their implications in the rest of this section.

Transport Protocol
CR-LDP and RSVP-TE are based on different transport mechanisms for communicating between peers. CR-LDP uses TCP and UDP, whereas RSVP-TE uses raw IP and requires Router Alert option support. This difference has a number of implications that must be considered in selecting one or the other:

Table 4.2	Comparison of CR-LDP and RSVP-TE	
Feature	CR-LDP	RSVP-TE
Transport	TCP and UDP	Raw IP
Security	IPSEC	RSVP Authentication
Multipoint to point	Yes	Yes
LSP merging	Yes	Yes
LSP state	Hard	Soft
LSP refresh	Not needed	Periodic, hop by hop
Redundancy	Hard	Easy
Rerouting	Yes	Yes
Explicit routing	Strict and loose	Strict and loose
Route pinning	Yes	By recording path
LSP preemption	Priority based	Priority based
LSP protection	Yes	Yes
Shared reservations	No	Yes
Traffic control	Forward Path	Reverse path
Policy control	Implicit	Explicit
Layer-3 protocol ID	No	Yes

○ Although most operating systems support full TCP/IP stack, TCP may not be available in some embedded systems. On some platforms raw IP and the Router Alter option may not be supported.

○ Since raw IP does not provide any reliable transport, RSVP-TE must implement mechanisms for detecting and retranslating lost packets within its own protocol. CR-LDP can assume orderly and reliable delivery of packets provided by TCP.

○ CR-LDP may use the standard security mechanisms available to TCP/IP such as IPSEC or TCP MD5 authentication. Because the messages in RSVP-TE are addressed to the egress of the LSP rather than the next-hop intermediate node, RSVP-TE must use its own security mechanisms.

○ The need for high availability often necessitates the implementation of redundant network controllers. When the active controller fails, the backup one can take over and continue the operations. Because RSVP-TE is running over connectionless raw IP and handles packet losses within its protocol, it is easier to implement a smooth failover to the backup system. For TCP, a smooth failover is not impossible, but it is known to be a difficult problem because of the connection-oriented nature of and complex internal state keeping in this system.

State Keeping

In network protocol design, the issue of soft state versus hard state often causes much debate. With the soft-state approach, each state has an associated time-out value. Once the time-out period expires, the state is automatically deleted. To keep the state alive, it is necessary to refresh it before it expires. In contrast, in a hard-state system, once a state is installed, it remains there until it is explicitly removed.

RSVP-TE is based on the soft-state approach. Thus it is necessary for RSVP-TE to periodically refresh the state for each LSP in order to keep it alive. In a large network with a substantial number of LSPs, the refreshing may pose significant messaging and processing overheads. Because of this, concerns have arisen about the scalability of RSVP-TE to large networks. To address this issue, the IETF has adopted a proposal to add the refresh reduction extensions to the RSVP-TE protocols.

CR-LDP uses the hard-state approach, so it has fewer messaging and CUP overheads compared with RSVP-TE. However, as a hard-state-based system, all error scenarios must be examined and handled properly. Since any state will remain in the system in a hard-state system unless explicitly removed, some LSPs may be left in limbo as a result of unforeseeable errors in the system. In a soft-state system this will not happen because the state for the LSPs is removed after the time-out period expires.

4.6 Summary

MPLS uses a technique called label switching. With label switching, packets are forwarded based on a short, fixed-length label. The connection-oriented nature of label switching offers IP-based networks a number of important capabilities that are currently unavailable. MPLS has been used to ease the integration of IP over ATM and simplify packet forwarding, and its support for explicit routing provides a critical mechanism for implementing traffic engineering in Internet backbones.

Before packets can be transmitted in an MPLS network, an LSP must be set up. There are two basic approaches: control driven and data driven. In the control-driven approach the setup of LSPs is initiated by control messages such as routing updates. In the data-driven approach the LSPs are triggered by data packets and set up on the fly while the data packets are arriving. The MPLS standards use the control-driven approach, in which the LSPs are set up by label distribution protocols that are driven by IP routing or explicit routes from the network management systems.

MPLS supports variable forwarding granularity through multiple types of FECs. Edge LSRs have the responsibility for mapping packets onto FECs. MPLS allows multiple labels to be encoded into a packet to form a label stack. An MPLS label stack consists of 32-bit entries, and each entry contains a 20-bit field for the label value. The MPLS label stack header is inserted between the IP packet and the link-layer header. In ATM and FR the top-level label is mapped to fields in the ATM cell header or FR header.

Three label distribution protocols, LDP, CR-LDP, and RSVP-TE, have been standardized. LDP is primarily used for supporting hop-by-hop routing, whereas CR-LDP and RSVP-TE are designed to provide explicit routing support for traffic engineering. Although CR-LDP and RSVP-TE share many similarities, some important differences also exist in the use of transport mechanisms and state keeping.

Further Reading

The following two Internet drafts describe the overall architecture and framework of MPLS:

Callon, R., A. Viswanathan, and E. Rosen. "Multiprotocol Label Switching Architecture." Internet draft (work in progress), Internet Engineering Task Force, August 1999.

Andersson, L., A. Fredette, B. Jamoussi, R. Callon, P. Doolan, N. Feldman, E. Gray, J. Halpern, J. Heinanen, T. Kilty, A. Malis, M. Girish, K. Sundell, P. Vaananen, T. Worster, L. Wu, and R. Dantu. "Constraint-Based LSP Setup Using LDP." Internet draft (work in progress), Internet Engineering Task Force, September 1999.

The following article and book give a comprehensive overview of MPLS:

Viswanathan, A., N. Feldman, Z. Wang, and R. Callon. "Evolution of Multiprotocol Label Switching." *IEEE Communications* 36, no. 5 (May 1998).

Davie, B., and Y. Rekhter. *MPLS—Technology and Applications.* San Francisco: Morgan Kaufmann, 2000.

For a general discussion on IP over ATM and full references for the label-switching proposals we described in Section 4.3.2, we recommend:

Ahmed, H., R. Callon, A. Malis, and J. Moy. "IP Switching for Scalable IP Services." *Proc. of the IEEE* 85, no. 12 (December 1997).

Anderson, L., P. Doolan, N. Feldman, A. Fredette, and B. Thomas. "LDP Specification." Internet draft (work in progress), October 1999.

Awduche, D., L. Berger, D. Gan, T. Li, G. Swallow, and V. Srinivasan. "Extensions to RSVP for LSP Tunnels." Internet draft (work in progress), February 2000.

Berger, L., D. Gan, G. Swallow, P. Pan, F. Tommasi, and S. Molendini. "RSVP Refresh Overhead Reduction Extensions." Internet draft (work in progress), April 2000.

Cole, R., D. Shur, and C. Villamizar. "IP over ATM: A Framework Document." RFC 1932, April 1996.

Conta, A., P. Doolan, and A. Malis. "Use of Label Switching on Frame Relay Networks." Internet draft (work in progress), May 2000.

Davie, B., P. Doolan, J. Lawrence, K. McGloghrie, Y. Rekhter, E. Rosen, and G. Swallow. "MPLS Using LDP and ATM VC Switching." Internet draft (work in progress), May 2000.

Jamoussi, B. "Constraint-Based LSP Setup Using LDP." Internet draft (work in progress), September 1999.

Katsube, Y., K. Nagami, S. Matsuzawa, and H. Esaki. "Internetworking Based on Cell Switch Router—Architecture and Protocol Overview." *Proc. of the IEEE* 85, no. 12 (December 1997).

Newman, P., T. Lyon, and G. Minshall. "Flow Labeled IP: A Connectionless Approach to ATM." Proc. of IEEE Infocom, March 1996.

Rekhter, Y., B. Davie, E. Rosen, G. Swallow, D. Farinacci, and D. Katz. "Tag Switching Architecture Overview." *Proc. of the IEEE* 85, no. 12 (December 1997).

Rosen, E., Y. Rekhter, D. Tappan, D. Farinacci, G. Fedorkow, T. Li, and A. Conta. "MPLS Label Stack Encoding." Internet draft (work in progress), September 1999.

Viswanathan, A., N. Feldman, R. Boivie, and R. Woundy. "ARIS: Aggregate Route-Based IP Switching." IBM Technical Report TR 29.2353, February 1998.

5

Internet Traffic Engineering

5.1 Introduction

n Chapters 2 and 3, we looked at the architectures and mechanisms for supporting resource assurance to application flows and end users. We now move to a different issue: how service providers can efficiently provision and manage their network resources to accommodate their resource commitments. In this very competitive business, service providers must balance two conflicting goals. On the one hand, they must meet the customer's expectation of guaranteed and differentiated services. On the other, they must manage network resources well to reduce the cost of provisioning the services.

Many of these important issues are addressed by techniques collectively called *traffic engineering*. Traffic engineering is concerned with the performance optimization of operational networks. Its main objective is to reduce congestion hot spots and improve resource utilization across the network through carefully managing the traffic distribution inside a network. Over the past few years traffic engineering has become an indispensable tool in the performance management of large Internet backbones.

In this chapter we describe the architectures and mechanisms for Internet traffic engineering, beginning with a simple example in Section 5.2 to illustrate why current IP routing is not sufficient from the traffic-engineering perspective. We then present an overview of traffic-engineering solutions to these problems in Section 5.3 and discuss traffic-engineering objectives in Section 5.4. In Section 5.5 we describe the five key building blocks in a traffic-engineering system. Section 5.6 discusses topology and state discovery, and Section 5.7 explores the algorithms for constraint-based routing for both the Overlay Model and the Peer Model. In Section 5.8 we present several hashing-based schemes for multipath load sharing for supporting efficient traffic engineering.

Traffic engineering uses many mathematical techniques, so some sections may seem a bit heavy to read. Readers who do not have the necessary mathematical background may skip them. In addition there are many different approaches for achieving optimization goals in traffic engineering; it is not possible to cover all of them in this chapter. The solutions presented here are intended as examples to illustrate the general principles and approaches for solving traffic-engineering problems.

5.2 The Fish Problem

In today's Internet, IP routing is generally based on destination address and uses simple metrics such as hop count or delay for routing decisions. Although the simplicity of this approach allows IP routing to scale to very large networks, the utilization of network resources within backbones is typically not optimized.

The poor utilization of network resources can be illustrated with the so-called "fish problem." The topology in Figure 5.1 bears some resemblance to a fish, where G is the head and A and B are the tail.

Although there are two paths from the tail to the head (path $C{\rightarrow}D{\rightarrow}F$ or $C{\rightarrow}E{\rightarrow}F$), all traffic from A and B to G will be routed over one of the two paths. This can lead to extremely unbalanced traffic distribution—one path may be heavily loaded while the other is idle.

The fish problem is primarily caused by two properties of current Internet routing protocols.

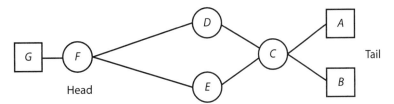

Figure 5.1   The "fish" problem.

First, IP routing is destination based: all packets whose destination addresses share the same prefix have the same next hop. Thus for each destination network there is typically only one path in the routing table, except in the case where there are multiple equal-cost paths. With destination-based routing it is often difficult to take advantage of the diverse connections available in the network. The traffic distribution in the network tends to be unbalanced, causing unnecessary congestion hot spots. Routing protocols may also alternate between the multiple paths, causing permanent route oscillation.

Second, the decision making in current routing is based on local optimization—any node simply selects a path that is best from its own perspective. The assumption here is that one node's decision has no or little impact on the overall system. However, this is generally not true. In shortest-path routing, for example, if all nodes use the shortest path, it may well become congested, and a non–shortest path may be a better choice. To optimize overall network resources, the routing decision making must take into account the overall system objective and have a global view of the network.

Let us use the topology in Figure 5.1 again as an example. Suppose at one point in time the routing protocol selects $C{\rightarrow}D{\rightarrow}F$ as the shortest path from C to F. Since all traffic is routed over this path, it becomes heavily congested while the other path, $C{\rightarrow}E{\rightarrow}F$, is idle. At the next routing update the routing protocol decides that path $C{\rightarrow}E{\rightarrow}F$ is a better choice and selects it as the current shortest path from C to F. However, all traffic is now moved from path $C{\rightarrow}D{\rightarrow}F$ to $C{\rightarrow}E{\rightarrow}F$, so path $C{\rightarrow}E{\rightarrow}F$ becomes congested; at the same time path $C{\rightarrow}D{\rightarrow}F$ becomes idle. The path selection will be reversed in the next routing update, and the process goes on forever.

5.3   Traffic-Engineering Solutions

Fundamentally, the fish problem can be solved only by going beyond current destination-based routing and by providing mechanisms to explicitly manage the traffic inside the network.

The problems with IP routing are well understood. In fact, few of the current Internet backbones are built with native IP routing. Large service providers typically use ATM VCs to construct a virtual network between edge nodes and then run IP routing on top of this virtual network. The traffic distribution is managed by carefully mapping VCs to the physical network topology. As we discussed in Chapter 4, the traffic-engineering extensions to the MPLS signaling protocols provide an ideal IP-based mechanism for managing and autoprovisioning such virtual networks.

This approach is often referred to as the *Overlay Model*. It allows service providers to build arbitrary virtual topologies over the network's physical topology. Service providers usually build a virtual network that comprises a full mesh of logical connections between all edge nodes. These logical connections can be set up as MPLS explicit routes with signaling protocols. Traffic-engineering objectives can be achieved by routing these explicit routes over the physical network in such a way that the traffic distribution is balanced across all traffic trunks.

The overlay approach works well with the BGP routing protocol. In a typical Internet backbone the edge nodes are BGP routers connecting to other routing domains. To exchange routing information of other routing domains, the BGP routers must establish a routing peer relationship with each other. These logical peer connections between BGP routers can simply use the LSPs established by the overlay approach between all pairs of edge routers. In another words, the LSPs can be used to replace the routes between BGP routes normally provided by Interior Gateway Protocols (IGPs) such as OSPF. The MPLS LSPs can be viewed as the shortcuts between the BGP routers.

Each route from external routing domains has a parameter called BGP NEXT HOP associated with it; the BGP NEXT HOP indicates the egress BGP router in the backbone that leads to the destination. In the overlay approach this information can be used to determine which LSP a packet should be mapped to. The prefixes associated with a route are the FECs for the LSP to the router indicated by the BGP

NEXT HOP. Thus a packet whose destination address matches a route should be put on the LSP leading to the corresponding BGP NEXT HOP of that route.

Take the backbone network in Figure 5.2. Nodes A, B, C, D, and E are the BGP edge routers that connect to external routing domains. The solid lines are physical links. The dotted lines are logical connections between BGP routers, which in reality are mapped onto the physical links. To exchange routing information, each pair of BGP routes establishes a peer relationship. Thus the dotted lines represent the logical BGP peer connections among the BGP routers. With the overlay approach these dotted lines are also LSPs between edge nodes, and so the BGP peer connections and the LSPs established by the Overlay Model match perfectly.

Let us now look at how packets are forwarded from node A. Node A has four LSPs to nodes B, C, D, and E, respectively. When node A receives a packet, it performs a lookup in the forwarding table. The BGP NEXT HOP of the route that matches the packet's destination address is the egress node from which the packet leaves the backbone network. Suppose that node C is the BGP NEXT HOP. Node A can simply put this packet on the LSP A→C. The packet will go all the way to node C. The difference between the overlay approach and the one without overlaying lies in the way the connections between the BGP

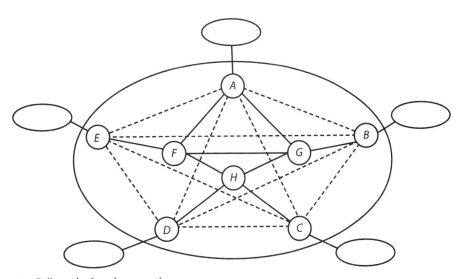

Figure 5.2   Full-mesh virtual connections.

nodes are set up. There are four feasible paths between A and C: $A{\rightarrow}G{\rightarrow}H{\rightarrow}C$, $A{\rightarrow}F{\rightarrow}H{\rightarrow}C$, $A{\rightarrow}G{\rightarrow}F{\rightarrow}H{\rightarrow}C$, and $A{\rightarrow}F{\rightarrow}G{\rightarrow}H{\rightarrow}C$. Without overlaying, the path from A to C is determined by an IGP such as OSPF. Suppose that the shortest path from A to C is $A{\rightarrow}G{\rightarrow}H{\rightarrow}C$, so the traffic from A to C will use $A{\rightarrow}G{\rightarrow}H{\rightarrow}C$. With the overlaying approach, there is much more flexibility. Any of the four feasible paths can be used, and the decision can be made based on the traffic between other BGP nodes. For example, if there is substantial traffic between nodes A to B, we can set up an explicit route for A to C via $A{\rightarrow}F{\rightarrow}H{\rightarrow}C$, leaving all bandwidth on link $A{\rightarrow}G$ for traffic between A and B.

Although the Overlay Model is simple and has been widely implemented in current Internet backbones, it does have some scalability issues. First, it suffers from the so-called the N-square problem. The problem is that to establish full-meshed logical connections between N edge nodes, each node must set up an explicit LSP to $(N - 1)$ other nodes. Thus $N \times (N - 1)$ explicit LSPs are required for the virtual network. As the size of the backbone network increases, the number of explicit routes to be established rises drastically, adding considerable management complexity and messaging overheads.

Let us look at the simple network shown in Figure 5.2, which has five edge nodes and one interior node. Each node needs to set up an LSP to four other nodes; therefore in total there are 20 explicit routes (each dotted line represents two unidirectional LSPs). Now, suppose we have a backbone network with 20 PoPs and each PoP has 10 edge nodes—we need to set up 39,800 explicit routes. The number of LSPs can go up very quickly as the network grows large.

The fully meshed virtual topology can substantially increase the loads on IP routing protocols. Note that multiple LSPs may go over the same physical trunk. The breakdown of a single physical trunk may cause multiple LSPs to fail, exaggerating the amount of routing updates and processing that routers have to deal with.

An alternative approach, which we refer to as the *Peer Model*, achieves balanced traffic distribution by manipulating link weights in the OSPF routing protocol. This approach can accomplish similar traffic-engineering objectives to the overlay approach but in a much more scalable way. It does not require any changes to the basic IP routing architecture and can be readily implemented in networks. With this approach the link weights are calculated to ensure balanced traffic distribution. Once the link weights are set, the network can operate as it does today: the OSPF routing protocol calculates the forwarding paths using the shortest-path-first computation, and packets are forwarded based on longest-prefix match. This eliminates the N-square problem altogether and reduces messaging overheads in setting up explicit routes.

5.4 Optimization Objectives

Traffic engineering aims to improve network performance through optimization of resource utilization in the network. One important issue that we need to address before we go further is the objective of the optimization. The optimization objective tends to vary depending on the specific problem that service providers try to solve. However, common objectives include

○ Minimizing congestion and packet losses in the network
○ Improving link utilization
○ Minimizing the total delay experienced by packets
○ Increasing the number of customers with the current assets

Congestion is one of the most difficult problems that service providers face in their networks. When a network is congested, the perceived performance suffers as queuing delay and packet losses increase. Therefore one useful objective would be to minimize congestion.

Two main factors have caused network congestion. Inadequate network resources are often the reason for congestion in many networks. The traffic demands simply far exceed what networks can accommodate. In this case all network resources are highly utilized. Congestion, however, can also be caused by unbalanced traffic distribution. When the traffic is distributed unevenly across the network, some links in the network are overloaded while other links are underutilized.

Although the problem of inadequate network resources must be solved with new capacity or by reducing and controlling the demands, unbalanced traffic distribution can be addressed through better management of the resources in the network. With carefully arranged traffic trunks, service providers can spread traffic across the network to avoid hot spots in parts of the network. When we translate this into a mathematical formulation, the objective is in essence to minimize the maximum of link utilization in a network. Intuitively the hot spots are the points with the highest link utilization. Reducing the link utilization at these points balances the traffic distribution across the network.

It turns out that when all links are utilized to the same level, the network tends to perform at an optimal level in terms of packet losses, total delay, or bandwidth efficiency. Intuitively this is rather obvious. The queuing delay increases nonlinearly and indeed much faster as link utilization becomes higher. Thus the maximum queuing delay that packets experience will increase when traffic distribution is unbalanced. Take the simple network in Figure 5.3 to illustrate this. Let us assume that all links have the same capacity and node A can split traffic so that all traffic demands from nodes A to C are evenly distributed over the two paths $A{\rightarrow}D{\rightarrow}C$ and $A{\rightarrow}B{\rightarrow}C$. Therefore the two paths should have the same the link utilization. Now suppose that we move some traffic from path $A{\rightarrow}B{\rightarrow}C$ to path $A{\rightarrow}D{\rightarrow}C$. Consequently the utilization on path $A{\rightarrow}B{\rightarrow}C$ is reduced while the utilization on path $A{\rightarrow}D{\rightarrow}C$ is increased. The queuing delay on $A{\rightarrow}B{\rightarrow}C$ will drop while the queuing delay on $A{\rightarrow}D{\rightarrow}C$ will rise. The interesting question is whether the total delay experienced by all packets is increased or decreased. Because the queuing delay increases more rapidly as the utilization increases, for the same amount of change in traffic, the increase of the delay on path $A{\rightarrow}D{\rightarrow}C$ is always larger than the decrease of the delay on path $A{\rightarrow}B{\rightarrow}C$. This shows that when the maximum of link utilization is minimized, the total delay the packets experience is also minimized.

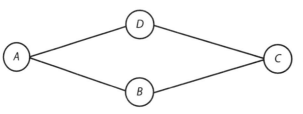

Figure 5.3   A simple network.

This optimization objective of minimizing the maximum of link utilization has a number of desirable features. First, as we have shown minimizing the maximum of link utilization can at the same time reduce the total delay experienced by the packets. Similarly it can also be shown that the total losses are minimized. Second, this optimization objective moves traffic away from congested hot spots to less utilized parts of the network, so that the distribution of traffic tends to be balanced. Finally, it also leaves more space for future traffic growth. When the maximum of link utilization is minimized, the percentage of the residual bandwidth on links (unused bandwidth) is also maximized. The growth in traffic therefore is more likely to be accommodated and can be accepted without requiring the rearrangement of connections. If we assume that traffic grows in proportion to the current traffic pattern (i.e., scale up), this objective will ensure that the extra traffic causes minimum congestion.

5.5 Building Blocks

Figure 5.4 shows a block diagram of a traffic-engineering system. It consists of six main components: topology and state discovery, traffic demand estimation, route computation, graphical user interface, network interface, and data repository. We give an overview for each of the components here and discuss the details in the next few sections.

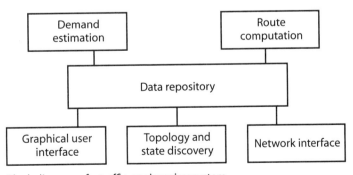

Figure 5.4   Block diagram of a traffic-engineering system.

5.5.1   Data Repository

The data repository module provides a central database and persistent storage for all shared data objects, such as the network topology, link state, traffic demands, routes, and policies. Other modules in the system can store, access, and exchange information through the database. Each object also has an associated state machine where each transition is linked to the originating module, the input event, the ending module, and the output event.

5.5.2   Topology and State Discovery

In a traffic-engineering system, any changes in the network topology and link state must be monitored. There are a number of possible approaches for performing topology and state discovery. For example, some information is available as part of the network configuration, although this applies mostly to static information. Dynamic information such as residual bandwidth or link utilization may be collected through network management systems such as SNMP traps and polling. Another approach is to extend routing protocols such as OSPF to broadcast link state periodically. This approach is likely to be widely supported by equipment vendors and service providers: it makes possible quick deployment through incremental changes to existing standard routing protocols and maintains multivendor interoperability.

5.5.3   Traffic Demand Estimation

A traffic-engineering system relies on reasonably accurate information about the traffic demands of users. In some scenarios, for example, a VPN service, the traffic demands may be specified explicitly as part of the service agreement between the service providers and the customers. In other cases the demands may have to be estimated based on traffic measurement. Many types of statistics are available from the networks, such as traffic loads on links and breakdown of traffic types. However, traffic engineering typically uses aggregated traffic statistics. For route optimization, for example, it is necessary to know the traffic load between any pair of ingress and egress nodes.

5.5.4   Route Computation

Central to a traffic-engineering system is the route computation engine, which calculates routes based on traffic demands. In current IP routing, the shortest-path computation is used to select routes based on the weights assigned to links. For traffic engineering, however, the route selection must be subject to multiple complex constraints; for example, resource optimization objectives and policy constraints such as restoration and preemptive constraints. For this reason, routing for traffic engineering is often referred to as *constraint-based routing.*

Constraint-based routing can be performed in two different modes: off-line or on-line. In the off-line mode, route computation is performed for all routes periodically with current information, and the network cuts over to the new routes during maintenance periods. This approach tends to yield optimal results since all routes are systematically reoptimized after changes. However, frequent and large-scale rerouting of existing connections will cause disruption to traffic flows; thus it may be undesirable from the operational point of view. In addition, extra delays result from adding new traffic demands to the network as route computation is performed periodically.

In the on-line mode, route computation is performed in an incremental fashion as each new traffic demand arrives. When a new demand is requested, the route computation module calculates the optimal route for the new demand only, without changing the routes for existing demands. Therefore rerouting to existing traffic flows is minimized, although the resource utilization may not be as efficient as that in the off-line mode. The benefits of on-demand route computation and minimum impacts on existing traffic, however, often outweigh the loss in efficiency.

The two modes may be combined at different time scales. For example, the routes for new demands can be placed incrementally, and after some time interval complete reoptimization is performed for all demands during less busy periods.

5.5.5   Network Interface

Once the traffic-engineering system has worked out the optimal routes for the demands, it has to configure the network elements in the network accordingly. A traffic-engineering system can interface a number of options with the network elements. Embedded Web servers have been gaining popularity among vendors. When a Web server is embedded in the controller of the network elements, a traffic-engineering system can configure network elements via a Web-based user interface; thus this approach is highly flexible. However, such an interface is vendor-specific, and so it will not work between different vendors. An alternative, standard-based approach is to use SNMP for configuration of network elements. More recently COPS has been proposed as a standard for a traffic-engineering system to instruct an edge node to set up MPLS explicit routes. COPS was originally designed to pass resource reservation information to a server and allow the server to pass policy decisions back. The same mechanism can also be used to communicate the result of route computation from a traffic-engineering server to the network nodes. When the explicit routes are computed, they are passed to the egress nodes of the explicit routes, and the label distribution protocols are then used to set these routes.

5.6 Topology and State Discovery

Topology and state discovery and constraint-based routing are two critical components in a traffic-engineering system. We will cover topology and state discovery in this section and discuss constraint-based routing in the next section.

In Section 5.5 we discussed a number of approaches to topology and state discovery. In this section we focus on the OSPF-based scheme, which provides most of the features for automatic topology and state discovery. The OSPF-based approach has the advantage that OSPF is widely deployed and already has the necessary mechanisms for distributing link status and constructing a topology database. By extending OSPF for topology and state discovery in traffic engineering, we eliminate the need for an additional protocol. This should help in the rapid deployment of traffic-engineering systems in operational networks.

In the OSPF-based approach, all nodes first try to establish and maintain a peer relationship with their neighbors. A node's neighbors (sometimes called peers) are the nodes with which that node directly exchanges control information. Each node keeps track of its local link state, and the information is communicated to all other nodes in the network or to the network management station. A traffic-engineering system can build a topology database with link state information from the OSPF routing exchanges.

The following is an overview of how OSPF maintains peer relationships and distributes link state information.

In OSPF a node discovers and maintains its peer relationship by periodically sending out OSPF Hello packets to all its interfaces. Normally a neighbor will reply with a Hello packet. If a neighbor fails to reply within a configurable interval (called RouterDeadInterval, whose default value is 40 seconds), the neighbor is considered dead. Link failure can usually be detected by data link layer protocols much earlier than through the Hello packets. Once the node detects that its connection with a neighbor has failed, it will start to inform all other nodes by sending out a link state advertisement throughout the routing domain.

To ensure that the new link state information is distributed reliably to all nodes even in the event of failures, OSPF uses a reliable-flooding mechanism for link state updates. A node will send new link state information to all its neighbors and keep retransmitting to them until an acknowledgment is received. Because of the flooding mechanism, a node may receive multiple identical updates from its neighbors. Sequence numbers are used to detect duplicated copies, which are discarded. In addition, OSPF mandates that a node refresh any link state information originated from it every 30 minutes to ensure that any inconsistency in the topology database due to software errors is corrected.

Since traffic engineering requires additional parameters in the link state advertisement other than what OSPF has now, an extension has been proposed to add the following traffic-engineering link state advertisements to OSPF:

○ **Local and remote interface IP addresses.** Specify the IP address of the interface corresponding to the link and the IP address of the neighbor's interface corresponding to this link. The pair of addresses can be used to discern multiple parallel links between two systems.

○ **Traffic-engineering metric.** Specifies the link metric for traffic-engineering purposes. This metric may be different from the OSPF link metric and will be used by constraint-based routing for route computation.

○ **Maximum bandwidth.** Specifies the maximum bandwidth that can be used on this link in this direction. Note that the bandwidth available to the IP layer is typically smaller than that of the physical layer.

○ **Maximum reservable bandwidth.** Specifies the maximum bandwidth that may be reserved on this link in this direction. Some links may internally consist of multiple channels; thus the maximum reservable bandwidth is limited to the maximum channel size.

○ **Unreserved bandwidth.** Specifies the amount of bandwidth that has not been reserved. This information is used during signaling to check if a particular connection can be accepted or not.

○ **Resource class.** Specifies the administrative group membership of this link in terms of bit mask. A link that is a member of a group has the corresponding bit set. This allows administrative policies such as priorities and customer classes to be implemented.

Once the topology database and link state information are available, the constraint-based routing can compute routes for demands that meet our traffic-engineering objective.

5.7 Constraint-Based Routing

Constraint-based routing has two basic elements: route optimization and route placement. *Route optimization* is responsible for selecting routes for traffic demands subject to a given set of constraints. Once the routes are decided, *route placement* implements these routes in the network so that the traffic flows will follow them. In this section we look at the design of a constraint-based routing scheme that accomplishes the optimization objective we described in Section 5.4; that is, minimizing the maximum of link utilization.

This optimization problem is related to some of the classic mathematical problems that have been extensively examined in the past in the context of network design. The topology design and link capacity assignment are often considered together to optimize the utilization of network resources. The conventional approach is to choose the average packet delay as the minimization objective, which results in a nonlinear objective function under some queuing assumptions. The optimization problem is then formulated as a nonlinear multicommodity network flow problem. Because of the nonlinear objective function, the optimization problem is difficult to solve. Many heuristic algorithms have been proposed, such as the flow deviation method and the proximal decomposition method.

Although closely related, route optimization in traffic engineering and network design are different in many respects. The key difference is that in traffic engineering, the traffic flows are moved around in order to improve the resource utilization in an existing network, whereas in network design the network is dimensioned to fit a given traffic pattern.

A topic related to constraint-based routing is QoS routing. Several schemes have been proposed for finding a path under multiple constraints; for example, bandwidth and delay. These algorithms, however, are typically "greedy" in the sense that they try to find a path that meets a particular request without considering the networkwide impacts. In contrast, the objective of traffic engineering is the optimization of overall network performance.

5.7.1 Mathematical Formulation

We now describe a mathematical formulation of the route optimization problem and basic solutions to the problem.

We model the backbone IP network as a set of nodes connected by links with fixed capacities. The network is represented as a directed graph. The links in the network and their capacities are directional; that is, link (i,j) is considered different from link (j,i), each with its own capacity. Edge nodes are nodes that connect to customers' networks and other backbones. The average traffic demand from one edge node to another is assumed to be is known, either by measurement or as configuration parameters. The traffic demand between two edge nodes is also directional; that is, the demand from node s to node t is different from that from node t to node s. The objective of route optimization is to route the demands between edge nodes over the physical network topology such that all the traffic demands are fulfilled and the maximum of link utilization is minimized.

This route optimization can be formulated as a linear-programming problem. Let diagram $G = (V, E)$ represent the physical network, where V is the set of nodes and E is the set of links. For each link $(i,j) \in E$, let c_{ij} be the capacity of the link. Let K be the set of traffic demands between a pair of edge nodes. For each $k \in K$, let d_k, s_k, t_k be the bandwidth demand, the source node, and the destination node, respectively. Note that a demand may be split over multiple paths, with each path satisfying a fraction of the demand. For each link $(i,j) \in E$ and for each demand $k \in K$, let X_{ij}^k represent the percentage of k's bandwidth demand satisfied by link (i,j). Let α represent the maximum of link utilization among all the links. We can derive the following linear-programming formulation (LPF)

$$\min \alpha \tag{1}$$

$$\sum_{j:(i,j) \in E} X_{ij}^k - \sum_{j:(j,i) \in E} X_{ji}^k = 0 \qquad k \in K, i \neq s_k, i \neq t_k \tag{2}$$

$$\sum_{j:(i,j) \in E} X_{ij}^k - \sum_{j:(j,i) \in E} X_{ji}^k = 1 \qquad k \in K, i \neq s_k \quad i = s_k \tag{3}$$

$$\sum d_k X_{ij}^k \leq c_{ij}\alpha \qquad (i,j) \in E \tag{4}$$

$$0 \leq X_{ij}^k \leq 1 \qquad \alpha \geq 0 \tag{5}$$

The objective function (1) says the variable to be minimized is the maximum of link utilization. Constraints (2) and (3) are flow conservation constraints. Equation (2) says that the traffic flowing into a node must equal the traffic flowing out of the node for any node other than the source node and the destination node for each demand. Equation (3) says that the net flow out of the source node is 1, which is the total required bandwidth after scaling by d_k. Constraint (4) is the link capacity utilization constraint. It says that the total amount of bandwidth consumed by all logical connections on a link should not exceed the maximum utilization rate times the total capacity of the link. The last constraint restricts all the variables to nonnegative real numbers and the X_{ij}^k variables to be no more than 1.

The solution to the LPF equations will produce the best routes for traffic demands between all edge nodes. Although these routes are optimal, the problem is that the demand between two edge nodes may be split over multiple routes. For example, in Figure 5.1, suppose that the demand between nodes A and G is d_{ag}. The optimal routing solution by LPF may require two routes, $A{\rightarrow}C{\rightarrow}E{\rightarrow}F{\rightarrow}G$ and $A{\rightarrow}C{\rightarrow}D{\rightarrow}F{\rightarrow}G$, to be set up for the demands. The demand d_{ag} must be split between these two routes with the defined ratio (e.g., 2:3).

To split demands over multiple routes, the edge nodes must perform load sharing over multiple LSPs. Node C in Figure 5.1, for example, must divide the traffic into two streams and send over the two routes to G. Although many commercial products do support load sharing over multiple paths to some degree, only a small number of equal-cost paths are normally supported. Traffic splitting must also be done carefully so that the packets from the same flow are not sent over different routes. Otherwise different delay may cause misordering of packets in TCP flows and hence the degradation of performance. We will discuss the load sharing issue in detail in Section 5.8.

From the operational perspective, it is certainly more desirable to have each demand routed over a single path, even with less optimal performance. The mathematical formulation for the case where each demand must be routed over a single path is quite straightforward. We can use the same formulation as in LPF but with the additional restriction that the X_{ij}^k variables must be either 0 or 1 so that no fraction of a demand can be put on a route. This optimization problem then becomes an integer-programming one. It can be shown that the problem is NP hard, so no efficient algorithms exist that can provide exact solutions. Nevertheless, heuristic solutions do exist that provide sufficiently good results to the problem. In the next section we will examine several heuristic algorithms and compare their performance against the optimal solution by LPF.

5.7.2 Overlay Model

In this section we examine several constraint-based routing schemes for the Overlay Model. As we described in Section 5.3, the Overlay Model builds a full-mesh virtual network between all edge nodes. This approach involves three basic steps. First, the traffic-engineering system collects the information about the network topology and the traffic demands between all edge nodes. The constraint-based routing then calculates a set of optimal routes for these demands. These routes between edge nodes are set up as MPLS explicit routes.

As we discussed in the previous section, LPF produces the best routes for traffic demands but may require a demand to be split over multiple LSPs. Although load sharing over multiple LSPs is certainly feasible, most current routers do not support such features yet. Most service providers would also prefer an incremental approach for setting up LSPs that minimizes the disruption to the traffic to established LSPs.

The heuristic schemes we describe below are similar to current IP routing except different cost metrics are used for route computation. Implementation of these schemes is therefore quite straightforward. These schemes require no split of demands and allow incremental setup of LSPs. Performance analysis shows that they perform exceptionally well when compared with the optimal routes produced by LPF.

Shortest Path (SP) and Minimum Hop (MH)

The first scheme that we will consider here is simply to use the *shortest-path* (SP) algorithm. When there is a demand, we use the shortest path to the destination to set up an LSP for the new demand. This approach requires few changes to the existing routing infrastructure. The cost metric for link *i,j* is calculated as a value inversely proportional to the bandwidth.

A simple variation to shortest-path routing is *minimum-hop* (MH) routing. In this case the link metric is set to 1 uniformly for each hop and the shortest-path algorithm always chooses the route that has minimum hops.

Shortest-Widest Path (SWP)

Shortest-widest-path algorithms have been proposed to support per-flow bandwidth reservation. The shortest-widest-path routing uses bandwidth as a metric, and it always selects the paths that have the largest bottleneck bandwidth. The bottleneck bandwidth of a path is defined as the minimum unused capacity of all the links on the path. If there are multiple paths with the same amount of bottleneck bandwidth, the one with minimum hops or the shortest distance is chosen. For constraint-based routing we consider each demand as a request to add a new traffic demand and choose the path with the largest bottleneck to set up the explicit path for the demand. If multiple such paths are available, the one with minimum hops is used.

Hybrid Algorithm

Shortest-path algorithms minimize the total resource consumption per route. The optimization is local in the sense that it does not consider other and future demands. For example, taking a longer path to avoid a bottleneck may consume more bandwidth because of the extra hops, but it would leave more bandwidth at critical bottleneck links for future demands.

The shortest-widest-path algorithm is the other extreme. It tries to avoid overloading any bottleneck links by maximizing the residual capacity across the network. This approach may, however, result in taking unnecessarily longer paths to avoid a bottleneck.

There is a basic trade-off between avoiding the bottleneck links and taking a longer path. The hybrid approach tries to balance the two objectives by assigning appropriate weights for them. In addition we use link utilization instead of link residual capacity since our optimization objective is to minimize the maximum of link utilization.

The hybrid scheme uses a metric combining both the cost of a path and the contribution to the maximum of link utilization. For each link let f_{ij} be its current load (used capacity) and c_{ij} be its total capacity. Let α be the current maximal link utilization. We initially set f_{ij} and α to be zero (or the appropriate numbers if the network is already loaded with existing traffic) and update them every time a demand is routed.

Now let's define the following link cost metric:

$$\alpha_{ij} = \frac{f_{ij} + d_k}{c_{ij}} + T \times \text{MAX}\left[0, \frac{f_{ij} + d_k}{c_{ij}} - \alpha\right]$$

where T is a tunable parameter.

The routes are selected as the least-cost paths based on the above link cost metric. In the link cost metric the first term is the link utilization after the new demand is added and the second term is the increase of the maximum link utilization α caused by the route selection. This second term will produce optimal routes in terms of minimizing maximum utilization. If this is used as the only criterion, cases may arise where the route optimization algorithm selects a very long route in order to meet the optimization objective, which is often undesirable from the operational perspective. The first term is added to take into account the increase in link utilization of the link. The parameter T allows us to give different weights to the two terms.

For example, if T is 5, then each unit increase in the maximum utilization is equivalent to five times the increase in the utilization of the current link.

The maximum of link utilization α should not normally be larger than 1 if all the demands are routable. However, if the computation indicates that α is larger than 1, this means that the network does not have sufficient bandwidth to meet all demands. In fact, α represents precisely the level of overbooking at the bottlenecks. To bring down the maximum of link utilization to 1, either the bottleneck link capacities must be scaled up by a factor of α or the bottleneck demands must be scaled down by a factor of α.

To examine the performance of the schemes, we will now show some testing results based on a network topology similar to one of the largest Internet backbones in the United States. These results illustrate the performance of these simple schemes against the optimal result produced by the LPF.

The test network has 54 nodes and 174 directional links. The link capacities are generated as random numbers with a uniform integer distribution in [800, 1200]. We construct 10 test sets, with the number of demands varying from 300 to 1200 in increments of 100. The size of each individual demand is generated by a random variable with a uniform integer distribution in [1, 10]. The source and destination pairs are also selected randomly among all edge nodes, although all duplicate pairs are removed.

All the quantities here are specified in a common bandwidth unit (such as DS1). The exact value of the bandwidth unit and the overall sizes of the total link capacities versus total bandwidth demand do not affect the results; our problem formulation uses link utilization as the objective, which works like a scalor.

The number of demands, the total of all demands, and the total of all link capacities in the network are summarized in Table 5.1.

The computation was performed in the following way. The optimal LPF solutions were obtained for all 10 test sets by solving the centralized linear-programming problems. These solutions have two meanings: first, they are the optimal solutions for the static routing problems, and second, they provide lower bounds for the dynamic-routing problems. The computation for the four dynamic-routing algorithms is then simulated with the same configuration. Random

Table 5.1		Characteristics of traffic demands	
Test set	Number of demands	Total demands	Total capacity
1	300	1801	172,632
2	400	2410	172,632
3	500	2996	172,632
4	600	3659	172,632
5	700	4126	172,632
6	800	4965	172,632
7	900	5466	172,632
8	1000	5940	172,632
9	1100	6617	172,632
10	1200	7211	172,632

numbers are used to determine the order of demands to be routed. The network is assumed idle at the beginning of the computation.

Table 5.2 shows the maximum link utilization as results of the four dynamic-routing algorithms. Among the four algorithms presented, two of them are from the shortest-path category: one is the shortest path using inverse link bandwidth as cost and the other is the minimum hop path.

We can make a number of observations from the limited test results. Among the four algorithms the hybrid has the best performance. Its maximum link utilization matches very closely to the LPF solution. Note that α_{lpf} is the exact optimal value only for the case where demands can be split.

The optimal value for the nonsplitting case may in fact be higher than the LPF number. Thus α_{lpf} is merely a lower bound for the dynamic-routing problem. Its optimal value lies somewhere between α_{lpf} and α_{hybrid}. We also observe that performance does not degrade as the number of demands grows.

As we expected, the shortest-path algorithm does not perform very well—its maximum link utilization is about twice that for the hybrid. The result for the minimum hop algorithm is even worse. In fact, the maximum utilization exceeds 1 when there are 1,100 demands or

Table 5.2	**Maximum of link utilization**				
Number of demands	α_{lpf}	α_{hybrid}	α_{sp}	α_{mh}	α_{swp}
300	0.1149	0.1193	0.2606	0.3251	0.5030
400	0.1286	0.1343	0.3005	0.4214	0.5030
500	0.1660	0.1684	0.3630	0.4938	0.5169
600	0.2200	0.2252	0.6053	0.6705	0.6019
700	0.2461	0.2514	0.5794	0.7157	0.6192
800	0.2587	0.2658	0.6466	0.7955	0.6435
900	0.2787	0.2838	0.6184	0.8105	0.6574
1000	0.3531	0.3606	0.8604	0.9426	0.7204
1100	0.3645	0.3690	0.9384	1.1122	0.7456
1200	0.3850	0.3921	0.8968	1.1396	0.7470

more, indicating that the network cannot satisfy all demands unless the bottleneck capacities increase by a factor of α_{mh}.

The high utilization value is a result of the unbalanced traffic distribution in the network, causing unnecessary hot spots in the network. Without adding any extra network bandwidth, using the hybrid scheme to set up the explicit routes will reduce the maximum link utilization below 40%.

The shortest-widest-path algorithm produces the worst results when the traffic load is light. However, the maximum link utilization increases much more slowly than that in any other schemes as the number of demands rises. The average performance is close to that of the shortest-path algorithm.

5.7.3 Peer Model

We now turn to a constraint-based routing scheme for the Peer Model. The basic idea behind the Peer Model is remarkably simple. The current IP routing protocols select the shortest paths based on the link weights. Intuitively we can change the route selection by increasing or decreasing link weights. For example, when the weight for a link is increased, traffic tends to move away from the link. In fact, service providers have been using such techniques in dealing with unbalanced traffic distribution in backbone networks. The question is whether a systematic approach exists that can achieve a similar optimization objective by manipulating the link weights and then simply forward traffic along the shortest path. This is still an area of active research. Some initial results show that when the traffic-engineering problem can be formulated as a linear-programming optimization problem, it can always be converted to a shortest-path routing with respect to some set of link weights. In other words, the peer model can achieve the same result as the overlay model.

Before we describe the theoretic results, let us first give an example of how this approach may work in an OSPF-based network. The network topology, link capacity, and traffic demands are shown in Figure 5.5. Each link has five units of capacity, and each demand represents four units of bandwidth.

For simplicity, we assume that link capacity, weight, and traffic demands are unidirectional. For a network of that size, it is easy to figure out manually that the optimal routes (see Table 5.3) are as follows:

Demand A to B takes the hop path $A{\rightarrow}B$, and demand A to F takes $A{\rightarrow}F$. Demand B to F is split over two paths. Half of the demand goes $B{\rightarrow}C{\rightarrow}D{\rightarrow}G{\rightarrow}F$, and the other half goes $B{\rightarrow}C{\rightarrow}E{\rightarrow}G{\rightarrow}F$. Demand A to E also uses two routes: $A{\rightarrow}D{\rightarrow}C{\rightarrow}E$ and $A{\rightarrow}D{\rightarrow}G{\rightarrow}E$.

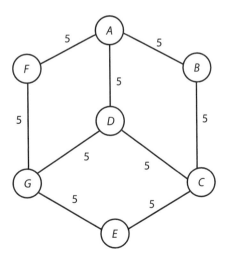

Traffic demands: $A{\rightarrow}B$: 4, $A{\rightarrow}F$: 4, $B{\rightarrow}F$: 4, $A{\rightarrow}E$:4

Figure 5.5   Link capacity and traffic demands.

Table 5.3	Optimal routes for traffic demands	
Traffic demand	Bandwidth	Route
$A \rightarrow B$	4	A-B
$A \rightarrow F$	4	A-F
$B \rightarrow F$	2	B-C-D-G-F
$B \rightarrow F$	2	B-C-E-G-F
$A \rightarrow E$	2	A-D-G-E
$A \rightarrow E$	2	A-D-C-E

This arrangement places four units of demand on each link; the traffic distribution is balanced, and the link utilization is 80% uniformly for the entire network. With the Overlay Model this arrangement of traffic flows can be implemented through setting up MPLS explicit routes between the edge nodes and putting traffic demands on these routes.

With carefully chosen link weights, however, we can achieve the same result with the Peer Model. Figure 5.6 shows a set of link weights with which the OSPF shortest-path computation produces the same optimal traffic distribution. The only assumption here is that the OSPF supports multiple-path load sharing. For example, for demand B to F and demand A to E, there are two optimal paths for each, with both demands equally split between the two equal-cost paths. Although this is an example with only a small network, the result holds in general.

The formal mathematical solution to the above example involves solving two linear-programming problems. First, we obtain the optimal routes by solving the LPF and then work out the link weights by solving a so-called *dual problem* of the LPF. We will now give a brief overview of *linear-programming duality theory*. The duality theory says that each linear-programming problem (P) is associated with another linear-programming problem (D). (D) is called the dual problem of (P), and (P) is called the primal problem. (P) is in turn the dual of (D). (P) and (D) are mathematically equivalent in the sense that they have the same optimal objective value, and the optimal solution of (D) can be derived from the optimal solution of (P) and vice versa by the rela-

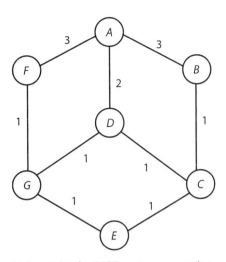

Figure 5.6   Link weights for OSPF route computation.

tionship of complementary slackness. The variables in (D) can be interpreted as the shadow for the constraints in (P).

Intuitively the two linear-programming problems (D) and (P) with different parameters are simply two different ways of describing the same problem and can be shown to be equivalent. Thus for the given LPF, we can construct the dual problem of LPF with link weights. We then solve the dual problem to get the optimal link weight set. Note that there may be multiple equal-cost shortest paths between the same edge node pair. In this case we need to solve the primal problem (LPF) to determine exactly how traffic is split over multiple paths.

The details of the computation of the two linear-programming problems are beyond the scope of this book. Interested readers may find further information on the subject in the references at the end of this chapter.

5.8 Multipath Load Sharing

Load sharing can substantially improve the performance of a traffic-engineering scheme. When traffic demands are large, any movement of a traffic demand may cause substantial shifting of the traffic between different links. When traffic demands can be split into smaller sizes, there is more flexibility in managing them. The use of load sharing in the Internet may increase substantially as Dense Wavelength Division Multiplexing (DWDM) gets more widely deployed. In this section we briefly describe some hashing-based traffic-splitting schemes that may be used to implement the traffic-engineering approaches covered in this chapter.

Figure 5.7 shows a load-balancing system. The traffic splitter takes incoming packets and dispatches them to multiple outgoing links. The traffic may be split equally among all outgoing links or in some specified proportion. The traffic-splitting schemes must take into consideration a number of basic requirements. First, traffic splitting is in the packet-forwarding path and must be executed for every packet. The per-packet overhead therefore has to be small, and to reduce implementation complexity, the system should preferably keep no or little state information. Second, the traffic-splitting schemes produce stable traffic distribution across multiple outgoing links with minimum fluctuation. Last but not least, the traffic-splitting algorithms must maintain per-flow packet ordering. Packet misordering within a TCP flow can produce a false congestion signal and cause unnecessary throughput degradation.

Simple schemes for traffic splitting based on packet-by-packet round robin result in low overheads and good performance. They may, however, cause per-flow ordering. Sequence numbers or state may be added to reordering, but these additional mechanisms increase complexities drastically and in many cases work only over point-to-point links.

Hashing-based traffic-splitting algorithms are stateless and easy to implement, particularly with hardware assistance. For hash functions that use any combination of the five-tuple as input, per-flow ordering can be preserved; all packets within the same TCP flow have the same

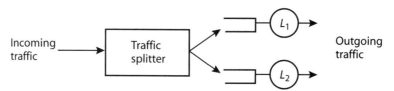

Figure 5.7   Traffic splitting for load sharing.

five-tuple, and so the output of the hash function with the five-tuple as input should always be the same.

We will now describe several hashing-based schemes for supporting traffic engineering.

5.8.1 Direct Hashing

There are two types of hashing-based schemes: direct hashing and table-based hashing. *Direct hashing* is a simple form of traffic splitting. With direct hashing the traffic splitter applies a hash function with a set of fields of the five-tuple and uses the hash value to select the outgoing link. It is very simple to implement and requires no extra state to be maintained.

Hashing of Destination Address
The simplest scheme is to hash the IP destination address modulo by the number of outgoing links, N. It can be expressed as

$$H(\bullet) = \text{DestIP MOD } N$$

In this scheme, if $N = 2^k$, we effectively use the last k bits of the destination address as an index of the outgoing link.

Hashing Using XOR Folding of Source/Destination Addresses
XOR folding has been used in many hash functions and has been shown to provide good performance in related applications. For traffic splitting, a hash function with XOR folding of the source and destination IP addresses can be expressed as

$$H(\bullet) = (S_1 \otimes S_2 \otimes S_3 \otimes S_4 \otimes D_1 \otimes D_2 \otimes D_3 \otimes D_4) \text{ MOD } N$$

where S_i and D_i are the ith octet of the source and destination IP addresses, respectively.

CRC16
The 16-bit CRC (cyclic redundant checksum) algorithm has many interesting properties as a candidate for load balancing. Although it is more complex compared with the other hash functions, CRC16 has been successfully implemented in high-speed systems. In the CRC16 scheme the traffic splitter takes the five-tuple, applies CRC16, and

takes the modulo by N to obtain the outgoing link. The hash function can be expressed as

$$H(\bullet) = CRC16(\text{5-tuple}) \text{ MOD } N$$

5.8.2 Table-Based Hashing

Direct hashing is simple but has some limitations. Direct hashing can split a load only into equal amounts to multiple outgoing paths. Distributing the traffic load evenly, however, is not always desirable. For example, an organization may have two links to Internet backbones, with one link twice the speed of the other. The organization may wish to distribute the traffic with a 2:1 ratio. With direct hashing it is almost impossible to tune the load distribution. The table-based hashing approach we discuss below addresses both issues by separating traffic splitting and load allocation.

A table-based hashing scheme first splits a traffic stream into M bins. The M bins are then mapped to N outgoing links based on an allocation table. By changing the allocation of the bins to the outgoing links, we can distribute traffic in a predefined ratio.

A simple way of implementing this is to associate an outgoing link with each of the M bins (see Figure 5.8). When a packet arrives, we first compute the hash value, then use the hash value as an index to find the outgoing port number. The allocation of bandwidth can be

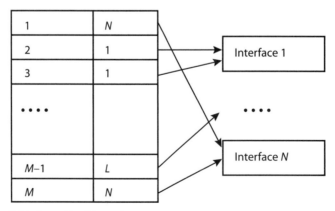

Figure 5.8   Table-based hashing scheme.

done by changing the number of hash values assigned to a particular outgoing port.

5.9 Summary

Traffic engineering is concerned with performance optimization of operational networks. It provides a set of tools for efficiently provisioning and managing backbone networks and making the best use of the resources. Service providers can use traffic engineering to avoid congestion hot spots, improve the overall utilization of networks, and reduce the cost for meeting resource commitments to their customers.

Topology and state discovery and constraint-based routing are two key components in a traffic-engineering system. Topology and state discovery is responsible for collecting information about the current network topology and link state. This information is then used for route computation. Constraint-based routing differs from conventional IP routing in that it uses advanced optimization techniques to select routes that meet traffic-engineering objectives, such as minimizing congestion hot spots and balanced traffic distribution.

There are two basic approaches to traffic engineering. In the Overlay Model constraint-based routing calculates the routes for traffic demands between the edge nodes. Service providers then set up MPLS explicit routes between edge nodes and match traffic demands over them, creating a full-mesh virtual network. In the Peer Model constraint-based routing produces a link weight for each link in the network. The link weight is calculated in such a way that the resulting shortest-path computation will generate a set of routes that meet the traffic-engineering objectives.

Further Reading

An excellent overview of the requirements for traffic engineering over MPLS can be found in

Awduche, D., J. Malcolm, J. Agogbua, M. O'Dell, and J. McManus. "Requirements for Traffic Engineering over MPLS." RFC 2702, September 1999.

The following two special issues on Internet traffic engineering and MPLS include a number of papers on traffic engineering:

Kuo, G., ed. "Multiprotocol Label Switching." *IEEE Communications* 37, no. 12 (December 1999).

Wang, Z., ed. "Internet Traffic Engineering." *IEEE Networks* 14, no. 2 (March/April 2000).

For information on BGP and OSPF routing protocols, we recommend:

Stewart, J. BGP4: Inter-Domain Routing in the Internet. New York: Addison-Wesley, 1999.

Moy, J. OSPF: Anatomy of an Internet Routing Protocol. New York: Addison-Wesley, 1998.

The following papers give further details on QoS routing, network design, and the linear-programming duality theory:

Guerin, R., and A. Orda. "QoS Based Routing in Networks with Inaccurate Information: Theory and Algorithms." Proc. of INFOCOM'97, 1997.

Wang, Z., and J. Crowcroft. "Quality of Service Routing for Supporting Multimedia Communications." IEEE JSAC, September 1996.

Ma, Q., and P. Steenkiste. "Routing Traffic with Quality-of-Service Guarantees in Integrated Service Networks." Proc. of NOSSDAV'98, 1998.

Wang, Y., and Z. Wang. "Explicit Routing Algorithms for Internet Traffic Engineering." Proc. of ICCCN'99, September 1999.

Fratta, L., M. Gerla, and L. Kleinrock. "The Flow Deviation Method: An Approach to Store-and-Forward Communication Network Design." *Networks* 3, (1973):97–133.

Chifflet, J., P. Mahey, and V. Reynier. "Proximal Decomposition for Multicommodity Flow Problems with Convex Cost." *Telecommunication Systems* 3 (1994):1–10.

Chvatel, V. *Linear Programming*. San Francisco: Freeman 1983.

Closing Remarks

A t this point readers should have a good grasp of the core technologies for supporting QoS in the Internet. Some key questions remain, however, as to how QoS may actually play out in the Internet and what new services may be developed using the new capabilities. All these are complex issues, and since things are changing at Internet speed, nobody can really predict what is going to happen in the next year or so. I will nevertheless try to offer some of my personal perspectives on QoS deployment and the changing Internet landscape.

Although a strong consensus on the need for QoS and demands for new services made possible by QoS exists, we have not yet seen a rapid, widespread deployment of QoS in the Internet. There is no simple explanation for that. As I said at the beginning of the book, deploying QoS is really about creating new services, which is driven more by business and operational considerations than technological advances. We must look at key issues and understand business perspectives in the development of a QoS-enabled Internet.

An important question is, What are the killer applications for QoS, or for what new services are users willing to pay a premium? Video conferencing or multiuser gaming were a few past predictors, but so far, none of them have taken off significantly. This is a chicken-and-egg problem. Without performance assurance, many new applications cannot work well over the Internet. On the other hand, the deployment of QoS capabilities can be driven only by wide use of such applications. The sheer size of the Internet and the large number of service providers also pose a dilemma. QoS capabilities become really useful only when they are deployed in a large part of the Internet, but this can be a slow process and may take years. But without immediate short-term benefits, service providers are reluctant to invest for the necessary upgrade.

The problem is compounded by the fact that Internet traffic is growing so fast, service providers can barely keep up. The rise of broadband Internet access, such as DSL, cable, and fixed wireless, has increased the access bandwidth hundred of times in one shot. Service providers have to deal with immediate problems of bandwidth shortage and keep adding more bandwidth to meet the demands. The shortage of skilled professionals and the rapidly changing Internet landscape also make deploying QoS a daunting task.

On the positive side, the short life cycle of network equipment and the continuous upgrade of the network infrastructure will help QoS deployment in the long run. Since more new equipment incorporates QoS in the systems, QoS capabilities are being added to networks, although these capabilities may not be immediately used. Nevertheless, this will make it much easier for service providers to experiment and create new services with QoS features when the time comes.

The initial deployment of QoS is likely to happen for some specific applications. A number of new applications and services have started to gain momentum in the marketplace, and a sound business case can be made to deploy QoS in them. One such service is virtual private networks (VPNs). Currently most enterprises connect different locations with private leased lines or Frame Relay connections. As the cost for Internet access continues to decrease drastically, Internet-based VPN becomes an attractive option. With Internet-based VPN, enterprises can substantially reduce costs and simplify management. However, to make the transition happen, it is essential that Internet connections offer bandwidth guarantees and performance assurance comparable to that of private leased lines.

Another application of QoS is enterprise access to data centers. Because of the high cost in maintaining Information Technology (IT) services and a shortage of skilled workers, enterprises increasingly outsource their business applications, such as human resources, accounting, and data storage, to application service providers (ASPs). ASPs host business applications in their data centers and link servers to enterprise networks. The mission-critical nature of these applications requires that access to servers in the data centers be secure and reliable. QoS-enabled Internet connections with bandwidth and delay guarantees or virtual leased lines are ideal for such applications.

VPNs and virtual leased lines are most likely to be the first set of applications to which QoS is applied. There is a sound business case for this since they offer substantial cost reductions for customers and business users are more willing to pay a premium for enhanced services. Deployment is simpler in these scenarios since traffic patterns and topologies are relatively stable and the geographic scope is limited. Voice over IP (VoIP) can also be a major driver for QoS deployment. VoIP has the potential to radically alter patterns of Internet traffic. The majority of current Internet traffic is information access, which can tolerate large delay variation. Voice traffic, however, is much more demanding in terms of delay and packet losses. To ensure high-quality telephony over the Internet, QoS capabilities must be deployed throughout the networks.

QoS capabilities are likely to roll out first in the backbone networks for improving traffic control and resource utilization. MPLS in particular will play a central role in this evolution. Service providers have in the past relied on ATM as the backbone technology, partly because ATM vendors always had the lead in interface speeds and ATM has better bandwidth management and traffic-engineering capabilities. But this has started to change. ATM has lagged behind in the race for OC192 speed, and MPLS has emerged as a mature alternative. MPLS has bandwidth management and traffic-engineering capabilities similar to those of ATM. In addition, MPLS supports variable packet size and smaller overhead. More important, MPLS can be tightly integrated with the rest of the IP networks since it uses IP-based control protocols.

The use of MPLS in backbone networks will facilitate the development of premium services such as VPNs and secure virtual leased lines. As the competition intensifies and basic Internet access becomes a commodity, these new services will become an important part of the revenue sources for service providers. The recent proposal to use MPLS as the signaling protocol in an optical transport network, called multiprotocol lambda switching (MPLambdaS), will further consolidate MPLS as the unified control and provisioning protocol for backbone networks. The tight integration of IP and transport networks simplifies the provisioning of services and creates bandwidth on demand, where a user could dynamically create a guaranteed pipe over the networks when needed.

QoS support for the mass consumer market and global Internet remains a difficult problem. Since the traffic can go anywhere, a blanket QoS guarantee cannot be provided across the entire Internet. It is, however, conceivable that some forms of simple priorities, such as drop priorities in Differentiated Services, may be used for some destinations. The packets are colored based on users' profiles. During congestion premium-class packets get preferential treatment. The rapid rise of data centers may also help solve the problem. Most content providers and e-businesses use data centers to host their servers. Although users may access a large number of servers on the Internet, most packets in fact go to one of the large data centers. This makes the problem more manageable, and data centers can provide packet-marking services on behalf of their customers.

A fully QoS-enabled Internet remains the Holy Grail of the Internet world. The Internet community has made tremendous progress in the past decade, but we are still far from our goal, which will take some time to reach. But in this Internet era, no one can really predict exactly how things will turn out in the future.

Glossary

BA (behavior aggregator)   A collection of packets with the same DS codepoint crossing a link in a particular direction.

BA classifier   A classifier that selects packets based on the contents of the DS field only.

Boundary link   A link connecting the edge nodes of two domains.

Classifier   An entity that selects packets based on the content of packet headers according to defined rules.

Constraint-based routing   The process of selecting routes based on a variety of constraints such as minimum bandwidth.

Delay jitter   The difference between the largest and smallest delay.

Downstream DS domain   The DS domain downstream of traffic flow on a boundary link.

DS (Differentiated Services)   A QoS architecture for service differentiation using a small number of forwarding classes.

DS boundary node   A DS node that connects one DS domain to a node either in another DS domain or in a domain that is not DS capable.

DS-capable   Capable of supporting Differentiated Services.

DSCP (DS codepoint)   A specific value of the DSCP part of the DS field, used to select a PHB.

DS domain   A DS-capable domain; a contiguous set of nodes that operate with a common set of service provisioning policies and PHB definitions.

DS egress node   A DS boundary node in its role in handling traffic as it leaves a DS domain.

DS field   The IPv4 header TOS octet or the IPv6 traffic class octet when interpreted in confirmation with the definition in RFC 2472.

DS ingress node   A DS boundary node in its role in handling traffic as it enters a DS domain.

DS interior node   A DS node that is not a DS boundary node.

DS region   A set of contiguous DS domains that can offer Differentiated Services over paths across those DS domains.

Flow   A single instance of an application-to-application flow of data. In IP networks a flow is uniquely identified by the source address, destination address, source port, destination port, and protocol ID.

Flow identification   The process of identifying packets that belong to reserved RSVP flows.

Flow specification   The description of traffic characteristics and service requirements.

Forwarding equivalence class (FEC)   A group of packets that are forwarded in the same manner (e.g., over the same path, with the same forwarding treatment).

Intolerant application   Application that requires strictly faithful playback because the application cannot deal with lost packets or distortion of timing.

Label   A short, fixed-length, physically contiguous, locally significant identifier that is used to identify a stream label information base; the database of information containing label bindings.

Label stack   An ordered set of labels.

Label swap   The basic forwarding operation of packets, consisting of looking up an incoming label to determine the outgoing label, encapsulation, port, and other data-handling information.

Label-switched path (LSP)   The path created by the concatenation of one or more label-switched hops, allowing a packet to be forwarded by swapping labels from an MPLS node to another MPLS node.

Label-switched router (LSR)   Any node that supports label switching.

Label switching   A forwarding paradigm allowing streamlined forwarding of data by using labels to identify streams of data to be forwarded.

Label switching router (LSR)   An MPLS node that is capable of forwarding native L3 packets.

Layer 2   The protocol layer under layer 3 or the link layer.

Layer 3   The protocol layer at which IP and its associated routing protocols operate.

Leaky bucket   A class of traffic regulators that use token rate and bucket depth to characterize traffic flows.

Link layer   Synonymous with layer 2.

Loop detection   A method of detecting and breaking loops in networks.

Loop prevention   A method of preventing loops from forming.

Marking   The process of setting the DS codepoint in a packet based on defined rules.

Metering   The process of measuring the temporal properties (e.g., rate) of a traffic stream selected by a classifier.

MF classifier   A multifield (MF) classifier that selects packets based on the content of some arbitrary number of header fields.

Microflow   A single instance of an application-to-application flow of packets that is identified by source address, source port, destination address, destination port, and protocol ID.

MPLS (Multiprotocol Label Switching)   A set of Internet standards for label switching defined by the IETF MPLS working group and the effort associated with the working group.

MPLS domain   A contiguous set of nodes that operate MPLS routing and forwarding and are also in one routing or administrative domain.

MPLS edge node   An MPLS node that connects an MPLS domain with a node that is in a different domain or does not support MPLS.

MPLS egress node   An MPLS edge node in its role in handling traffic as it leaves an MPLS domain.

MPLS ingress node   An MPLS edge node in its role in handling traffic as it enters an MPLS domain.

MPLS label   A label placed in a short MPLS shim header used to identify streams.

MPLS node   A node that supports MPLS control protocols, operates one or more L3 routing protocols, and is capable of forwarding packets based on labels.

Network layer   Synonymous with layer 3.

Overlay Model   An approach in which nodes communicate via logical connections built over physical links.

Packet scheduling   The process of selecting a packet to transmit when the outgoing link becomes ready.

Peer model   An approach in which nodes communicate through physical connections.

PHB (per-hop behavior)   The externally observable forwarding behavior applied at a DS node to a DS behavior aggregate.

PHB group   A set of one or more PHBs that can only be meaningfully specified and implemented simultaneously due to a common constraint applying to all PHBs in the set, such as a queue servicing or queue management policy. A PHB group provides a service building block that allows a set of related forwarding behaviors to be specified together (e.g., four dropping priorities). A single PHB is a special case of a PHB group.

Policing   The process of discarding packets within a traffic stream to enforce a traffic profile.

Premark   To set the DS codepoint of a packet prior to entry into a downstream DS domain.

RED (random early detection)   A congestion avoidance scheme that drops a fraction of packets when queue length exceeds a threshold.

Remark   To change the DS codepoint of a packet, usually performed by a marker in accordance with a TCA.

Route selection The process of selecting routes based on defined objectives.

Service The overall treatment of a defined subset of a customer's traffic within a DS domain or end to end.

Service level agreement (SLA) A service contract between a customer and a service provider that specifies the forwarding service a customer should receive.

Shaping The process of delaying packets within a traffic stream to make it conform to some defined traffic profile.

Soft state State that will go away when the associated timer expires unless it is refreshed.

Switched path Synonymous with label-switched path.

Traffic conditioner An entity that performs traffic-conditioning functions and that may contain meters, markers, droppers, and shapers.

Traffic conditioning Control functions performed to enforce rules specified in a TCA, including metering, marking, shaping, and policing.

Traffic conditioning agreement (TCA) An agreement specifying classifier rules and any corresponding traffic profiles and metering, marking, discarding, and/or shaping rules that are to apply to the traffic streams selected by the classifier.

Traffic profile A description of the temporal properties of a traffic stream, such as rate and burst size.

Upstream DS domain The DS domain upstream of traffic flow on a boundary link.

VC merge Merging multiple VCs into one single VC.

Virtual circuit (VC) Circuit used by a connection-oriented layer 2 technology such as MPLS, ATM, or frame relay, requiring the maintenance of state information in layer 2 switches.

VPI/VCI A label used in ATM networks to identify ATM virtual circuits.

Bibliography

[AHMED97] Ahmed, H., R. Callon, A. Malis, and J. Moy, "IP Switching for Scalable IP Services." Proc. of the IEEE 85, no. 12 (December 1997).

[ANDER99a] Anderson, L., P. Doolan, N. Feldman, A. Fredette, and B. Thomas. "LDP Specification." Internet draft (work in progress), October 1999.

[ANDER99b] Anderson, L., A. Fredette, B. Jamoussi, R. Callon, P. Doolan, N. Feldman, E. Gray, J. Halpern, J. Heinanen, T. Kilty, A. Malis, M. Girish, K. Sundell, P. Vaananen, T. Worster, L. Wu, and R. Dantu. "Constraint-Based LSP Setup using LDP." Internet draft (work in progress), Internet Engineering Task Force, September 1999.

[AWDUC00] Awduche, D., L. Berger, D. Gan, T. Li, G. Swallow, and V. Srinivasan. "Extensions to RSVP for LSP Tunnels." Internet draft (work in progress), February 2000.

[AWDUC99] Awduche, D., J. Malcolm, J. Agogbua, M. O'Dell, and J. McManus. "Requirements for Traffic Engineering over MPLS." RFC 2702, September 1999.

[BASU99] Basu, A., and Z. Wang. "Fair Bandwidth Allocation of Differentiated Service." Proc. of Protocols for High-Speed Networks (PfHSN99), August 1999.

[BENNE96] Bennett, J. C. R., and H. Zhang. "WF2Q: Worst-Case Fair Weighted Fair Queueing." Proc. of IEEE INFOCOM'96, March 1996.

[BERGER00] Berger, L., D. Gan, G. Swallow, P. Pan, F. Tommasi, and S. Molendini. "RSVP Refresh Overhead Reduction Extensions." Internet draft (work in progress), April 2000.

[BRADE94] Braden, R., D. Clark, and S. Shenker. "Integrated Services in the Internet Architecture: An Overview." RFC 1633, Internet Engineering Task Force, June 1994.

[CALLO99] Callon, R., A. Viswanathan, and E. Rosen. "Multiprotocol Label Switching Architecture." Internet draft (work in progress), Internet Engineering Task Force, August 1999.

[CAO00] Cao, Z., Z. Wang, and E. Zegura. "Performance of Hashing-Based Schemes for Internet Load Balancing." Proc. of INFOCOM'2000, March 2000.

[CARLS98] Carlson, M., W. Weiss, S. Blake, Z. Wang, D. Black, and E. Davies. "An Architecture for Differentiated Services." RFC 2475, December 1998.

[CHIFF94] Chifflet, J., P. Mahey, and V. Reynier. "Proximal Decomposition for Multicommodity Flow Problems with Convex Cost." *Telecommunication Systems* 3, (1994):1–10.

[CHVAT83] Chvatel, V. *Linear Programming.* San Francisco: Freeman, 1983.

[CLARK98] Clark, D., and W. Fang. "Explicit Allocation of Best Effort Packet Delivery Service." *IEEE/ACM Trans. on Networking* 6, no. 4 (1998).

[CLARK92] Clark, D., S. Shenker, and L. Zhang. "Supporting Real-Time Applications in an Integrated Services Packet Network: Architecture and Mechanism." Proc. of ACM SIGCOMM'92, August 1992.

[COLE96] Cole, R., D. Shur, and C. Villamizar. "IP over ATM: A Framework Document." RFC 1932, April 1996.

[CONTA00] Conta, A., P. Doolan, and A. Malis. "Use of Label Switching on Frame Relay Networks." Internet draft (work in progress), May 2000.

[DAVIE00] Davie, B., P. Doolan, J. Lawrence, K. McGloghrie, Y. Rekhter, E. Rosen, and G. Swallow. "MPLS Using LDP and ATM VC Switching." Internet draft (work in progress), May 2000.

[FLOYD93] Floyd, S., and V. Jacobson. "Random Early Detection Gateways for Congestion Avoidance." IEEE/ACM Transactions on Networking, August 1993.

[FRATT73] Fratta, L., M. Gerla, and L. Kleinrock. "The Flow Deviation Method: An Approach to Store-and-Forward Communication Network Design." *Networks* 3 (1973):97–133.

[GOLES94] Golestani, S. J. "A Self-Clocked Fair Queueing Scheme for Broadband Applications." Proc. of IEEE INFOCOM'94, June 1994.

[GUERI97] Guerin, R., and A. Orda. "QoS Based Routing in Networks with Inaccurate Information: Theory and Algorithms." Proc. of INFOCOM'97, 1997.

[HEINA99a] Heinanen, J., and R. Guerin. "A Single Rate Three Color Marker." RFC 2697, September 1999.

[HEINA99b] Heinanen, J., and R. Guerin. "A Two Rate Three Color Marker." RFC 2698, September 1999.

[JAMOU99] Jamoussi, B. "Constraint-Based LSP Setup Using LDP." Internet draft (work in progress), September 1999.

[KALMA90] Kalmanek, C. R., H. Kanakia, and S. Keshav. "Rate Controlled Servers for Very High Speed Networks." Proc. of IEEE Globecom'90, December 1990.

[KATSU97] Katsube, Y., K. Nagami, S. Matsuzawa, and H. Esaki. "Internetworking Based on Cell Switch Router—Architecture and Protocol Overview." Proc. of the IEEE 85, no. 12 (December 1997).

[KODIA00] Kodialam, M., and T. V. Lakshman. "Minimum Interference Routing with Applications to MPLS Traffic Engineering." Proc. of INFOCOM'2000, March 2000.

[KUMAR98] Kumar, V. P., T. V. Lakshman, and D. Stiliadis. "Beyond Best Effort: Router Architectures for the Differentiated Services of Tomorrow's Internet." *IEEE Communications* 36, no. 5 (May 1998).

[KUO99] Kuo, G., ed. "Multiprotocol Label Switching." *IEEE Communications* 37, no. 12 (December 1999).

[LAKSH98] Lakshman, T. V., and D. Stiliadis. "High Speed Policy-based Packet Forwarding Using Efficient Multi-Dimensional

Range Matching." Proc. of ACM SIGCOMM'98, September 1998.

[MA98] Ma, Q., and P. Steenkiste. "Routing Traffic with Quality-of-Service Guarantees in Integrated Service Networks." Proc. of NOSSDAV'98, 1998.

[MOY98] Moy, J. OSPF: *Anatomy of an Internet Routing Protocol*. New York: Addison-Wesley, 1998.

[NEWMA96] Newman, P., T. Lyon, and G. Minshall. "Flow Labeled IP: A Connectionless Approach to ATM." Proc. of IEEE INFOCOM, March 1996.

[NICHO97] Nichols, K., V. Jacobson, and L. Zhang. "A Two-Bit Differentiated Services Architecture for the Internet." Internet draft, November 1997.

[PAREK92a] Parekh, A. K. "A Generalized Processor Sharing Approach to Flow Control in Integrated Services Networks." Ph.D. diss., Massachusetts Institute of Technology, 1992.

[PAREK92b] Parekh, A. K., and G. R. Gallager. "A Generalized Processor Sharing Approach to Flow Control—The Single Node Case." Proc. of IEEE INFOCOM'92, April 1992.

[PETES99] Peterson, L., and B. Davie. *Computer Networks: A Systems Approach*. San Francisco: Morgan Kaufmann, 1999.

[REKHT97] Rekhter, Y., B. Davie, E. Rosen, G. Swallow, D. Farinacci, and D. Katz. "Tag Switching Architecture Overview." Proc. of the IEEE 85, no. 12 (December 1997).

[ROSEN99] Rosen, E., Y. Rekhter, D. Tappan, D. Farinacci, G. Fedorkow, T. Li, and A. Conta. "MPLS Label Stack Encoding." Internet draft (work in progress), September 1999.

[SHRED95] Shreedhar, M., and G. Varghese. "Efficient Fair Queueing Using Deficit Round Robin." Proc. of ACM SIGCOMM'95, September 1995.

[SRINI98] Srinivasan, V., and G. Varghese. "Fast IP Lookups Using Controlled Prefix Expansion." Proc. of ACM SIGCOMM'98, September 1998.

[STEWA99] Stewart, J. BGP4: *Inter-Domain Routing in the Internet*. New York: Addison-Wesley, 1999.

[STILI96] Stiliadis, D. "Traffic Scheduling in Packet Switched Networks: Analysis, Design and Implementation." Ph.D. diss. UC Santa Cruz, 1996.

[VISWA98a] Viswanathan, A., N. Feldman, R. Boivie, and R. Woundy. "ARIS: Aggregate Route-Based IP Switching." IBM Technical Report TR 29.2353, February 1998.

[VISWA98b] Viswanathan, A., N. Feldman, Z. Wang, and R. Callon. "Evolution of Multiprotocol Label Switching." *IEEE Communications* 36, no. 5 (May 1998).

[WANG98] Wang, Z. "USD: Scalable Bandwidth Allocation for the Internet." Proc. of High Performance Networking '98, September 1998.

[WANG00] Wang, Z., ed. *Internet Traffic Engineering. IEEE Networks* 14, no. 2 (March/April 2000).

[WANG96] Wang, Z., and J. Crowcroft. "Quality of Service Routing for Supporting Multimedia Communications." IEEE JSAC, September 1996.

[WANG99] Wang, Y., and Z. Wang. "Explicit Routing Algorithms for Internet Traffic Engineering." Proc. of ICCCN'99, September 1999.

[ZHANG93] Zhang, L., S. Deering, D. Estrin, S. Shenker, and D. Zappala. "RSVP: A New Resource Reservation Protocol." *IEEE Network* 7 (September 1993).

Index

About the Author

Zheng Wang has been involved in Internet-related research and development for the last 14 years. He is currently with Bell Labs, Lucent Technologies, working on high-speed routers and optical transport systems. He received his Ph.D. in computer science from University College London (UCL), England, in 1992. Prior to joining Bell Labs, he worked at Cambridge University and UCL in England. He has numerous publications and patents in IP routing, QoS mechanisms, Differentiated Services, MPLS, traffic engineering, and optical networking. He is an active member of the IETF and the author of several RFCs and Internet drafts.